IN MY OPINION

Jonbenet Ramsey
THE TRAVESTY OF
INNOCENCE REVISITED

by

John H. Walker

RoseDog🐾Books

PITTSBURGH, PENNSYLVANIA 15222

ISBN: 978-1-4349-9904-7
Printed in the United States of America

First Printing

For more information or to order additional books, please contact:
RoseDog Books
701 Smithfield Street
Pittsburgh, Pennsylvania 15222
U.S.A.
1-800-834-1803
www.rosedogbookstore.com

Table of Contents

(1) Introduction...1

(2) The First Concourse. A Supposition 83
  1. A Theory of Relevance 83
  2. A Perfect Town 83
  3. Motive For Her Death 88
  4. Point of No Return..91
  5. Patsy's World 107
  6. JonBenet's Death Premeditated....................111
  7. Maternal and Paternal Affinity 113
  8. She Was Not Kidnaped 114
  9. Don't Call the Police 117
  10. Police Compromization of the Crime Scene......118
  11. The Ingenuity of Automation Technology 123
  12. Guilty or Not Guilty 129

(3) The Second Concourse-A Supposition 131
  1. Hate and Jealousy Killed JonBenet Ramsey........131
  2. No Trace of Blood..133
  3. Killed In Her Sleep 134
  4. Time of Death Crucial....................................139
  5. The Murder of JonBenet Was Premeditated........145
  6. The Ransom Note Dissected and
    Psycho-analyzed 151

7. The Guilt Complex 159
8. The Motive Revealed...161
9. Pedophile Incest...170
10. The True Motive Redefined...............................172
11. Mother-Daughter Violent Confrontation 172
12. Death Threat Wish Carried Out.......................178
13. John Ramsey-A Victim of His Own
    Circumstance 179
14. Concluding Arguments and Closing Remarks ...223
15. The Ramseys Are Guilty Based On At Least
    three Reasons...226
16. Some Facts in the Case....................................228
17. About the Author...235

FOREPAGE

"JonBenet Ramsey, The Travesty of Innocence Revisited, Now Hear the Truth" puts together factual information extracted for the most part from the ransom note that for the first time proves that the true culprits of her death were indeed her parents, John and Patsy Ramsey.

Other information is crucial to the investigation of this young child's death, but it is the ransom note that holds the convicting clues to this hideous murder investigation and the ransom note also hold the convicting clues as to who the real culprits are, her mother and her father. One of the primary intent/purposes of this book is to prove via the ransom note that those persons guilty of this six year old's death came from within the Ramsey's immediate household, and that the entire incident in and of itself had nothing to do with intruders, kidnappers, or the ransom note. The premeditated death of JonBenet Ramsey was an event preplanned by the Ramseys, staged and meticulously put together by them.

The ovarian cancer and the thought of death set to motion the most intriguing murder incident to come to pass since the Orange Juice episode. How in the world could anyone suspect that the infestation of ovarian cancer would set off such a chain reaction in human behavior that would rival many a murder mystery to this point in time. On June 24, 2006. death made good its promise to once again visit the Ramsey household. Patsy Ramsey met up with her destiny, death came and took her away to an eternal place on the dark side of existence.

The intent of the author is to take the reader (s) on a mind bending experience into murder and mayhem that rivals the imagination and set the heart to pulsating almost out of rhythm. For the first time since the death of little JonBenet Ramsey, hear the truth, the whole truth, and nothing but the truth, so help me God. Before your very eyes in plain sight, the author will destroy any and all contents of the ransom note along with the intruder theory, the false kidnapping and cast them into a virtual world of make believe. Which is also to say, these three fictitious elements of deception only existed on paper and in the minds of the persons who conceive them.

The writer cautions the reader to fasten all seat beats and get ready for a ride into a dark and benighted world of mystery and mayhem. Not since this child's death, know and understand why people are creatures given to murder more than given to be creatures of habit. Learn the truth about what went on in the Ramsey home the night death took JonBenet away. Understand more clearly the reasons this little child had to die in light of her participation in nationwide beauty pageants.

This Book (in graphic depiction of and the harsh reality of immoral human behavior) also paints a clear and concise picture regarding the motive (the coin has many faces) that lead to JonBenet's death which the author extracted from the fictitious ransom note written by the mother of the deceased. And quite possibly written in left-hand penmanship.

The Book also is intended to paint a vivid picture of an act of murder in the first degree and to show that no one else except the immediate family namely, John and Patsy Ramsey, are the sole respondents involved in the murder of their little daughter.

Fact: the latter statement is given in the proof positive because it has not been proven beyond reasonable suspicion and doubt by either law enforcement, or the Ramseys themselves that there was anyone else in the home of the Ramseys, the night JonBenet was killed. The local authorities (the Boulder Police Dept.) cannot prove that there were other people in the home the night JonBenet's life was so tragically taken. And, her parents cannot prove beyond reasonable suspicion and doubt that there were other people in their home the night their daughter died.

The Author's Comments/Disclaimer

In the first printing of the author's book entitled, "JonBenet Ramsey, The Travesty of Innocence," several errors were made relative to the writer's response to latent parental incest. Two comments by readers of the first edition, labeled the author as one who is guilty of being a latent pedophile, which is highly refuted and disclaimed. In the writer's effort to accentuate the temptation of the sexual impulse situated with close relatives, and the irreparable harm that may result from such an encounter, the wrong impression of the writer was inappropriately and falsely conveyed, and given to ridicule. The latter statement is also a total misrepresentation of the writer's sentiments.

Because the first edition of "JonBenet Ramsey The Travesty of Innocence," in regards to the author, the entire text of the book was unedited by the writer and the publishing company. Had this been done, it is highly unlikely that the word pedophile would have been used to describe the author's attempt to use himself as a statement of expression to accentuate the temptation of parental incest.

In light of and in view of all that has been said and done, the author makes this statement of a disclaimer to refute the statement in the first edition. The latter is simply not true and does not convey the intent of purpose associated with the author at all, not in the least.

Let it be known to anyone of whom it may concern, though misquotes/errors were made in the first printing of "The Travesty of Innocence," the author's personal testimony of latent or potential parental incest is congruent to the truth, but the author is not guilty of being a latent pedophile. Furthermore to make such an accusation based on a misquote and the fallacy of misuse of words, the author considers it to be an expression of shallow and narrow mindedness. To make such false and unwarranted statements based solely on those two individuals concerted efforts to take the blame of JonBenet's death and child molestation away from John Ramsey, does not justify the writer's true purpose of intent.

And, whoever else after reading my book considers the author to be of a pedophile nature, are also wrong and shallow in their thinking, needless to say narrow minded. And, the only reason this negative statement was made by those two respondents was nothing more than a vain effort to try and assuage or deny the truth as to what really happened in the Ramsey home the night JonBenet Ramsey died. These negative statements about the author were also a covert incentive to take away the attention of other aspects of my book that made a great deal of sense, relating to the Ramseys themselves, and the undeniable umbrella of suspicion, in association with the author's point of view. John and Patsy Ramsey being the primary and true culprits of little JonBenet's death.

No matter how one might respond to the issues of significance contained in this book does not in any way change the truth. Someone in the home of the Ramseys is responsible for this child's death, and the liability for such lies directly in the pathway of John and Patsy Ramsey. Everything else is nothing but lies and false innuendoes congruent to a massive cover-up of the truth.

To those two personalities on Amazon.com who made several negative comments about the author in regards to latent pedophilia, and whoever else it may concern, I, the creator and the author of "The Travesty of Innocence," am truly sorry you misunderstood my intent of purpose. The author also apologizes to those of you who feel the same way, please accept this apology in all honesty and sincerity.

May Her Memory Live Forever

THE COIN HAS MANY FACES

When considering The Travesty of Innocence and the truth of the issues concerning the death of innocence is like unto a coin with many faces; meaning more or less, that finding out who killed little JonBenet Ramsey (JBR) will go in many directions. The same involves any number of subject matters to get at the truth and the various reasons why this crown jewel of a beautiful little child had to die, and the horrible manner in which she died.

The author/writer clearly understands that there are many issues associated with the facts of life and life's injustices. But the bottom line of inference relative the murder of JonBenet is this, the truth about who killed JBR, the reasons why her life was cut so drastically short, will be confronted in such a way the reader will be able to comprehend with relative ease the travesty of innocence. But the author will have to deal with or be concerned with many subject matters to arrive at the truth about who killed JonBenet.

And, the intent of purpose associated with the coin has many faces, is to prove beyond any reasonable doubt that John and Patsy Ramsey are the soul respondents/participants in the death of innocence. One of the main objectives of the writer is to prove also that the ransom note, the intruder theory, and the kidnap theory are all part of a carefully planned but failed attempt by the

Ramseys to avoid the responsibility for the death of this young beauty queen. And, to show how careful and how meticulously they planned and carried the ungodly destruction of young innocence. In order to do this, the reader must have an open mind void of any self prejudices relative to getting to the truth.

In the human realm of life and its related circumstances, the reader should be cognizance of the fact that mankind is capable of anything imaginable, which is also to say, it's a naive state of mind to think that people of high social status are not capable of committing the unthinkable. For some people, it is just as easy to kill as it is to refrain from killing, no matter what the social status.

For anyone to think that a man or a woman are not capable of molesting their own children, their own flesh and blood, are the respondents of a very naive state of mind, in bad need of a mental, social, and moral upgrade. There is nothing beyond human comprehension that does not fall within the psychic impulse of man's capabilities associated with his intent to do evil. That is to say, the Ramseys, because of their social status in conjunction with their wealth and financial standing in the community, are not beyond the impulse of and their intent to commit murder.

Most readers today are not accustomed to the harsh rhetoric and what it takes to get to the heart of situations like the death of innocence conjunctive to the tragic circumstances centered around the horrible death of this six year old star of beauty. In the harsh manner and the harsh way this child was murdered, it also takes harsh standards of logic and harsh rhetoric to get to the truth to reveal those who were responsible for her death.

Sometimes, when the coin has many faces, getting to the truth of the matter may appear to be harsh and very painful, every face on the coin must be dealt with. There will be issues and subject matters that may curl the stomach. But it is highly necessary to venture into avenues of rhetoric not easily digested, but the author/writer promises the reader that the truth in its entirety will come to pass. But only if the individual can comprehend the capabilities of the human response to do the unthinkable, so endowed in human nature and the human recourse into tragic situations.

Now in short response what the author is trying to say is, don't be upset when the rhetoric is not so soothing to your thought perception, its going to take all of this and more to get to the bottom of this murder mystery. As the author said before, the truth behind the murder, the killing of JonBenet Ramsey, will soon spread across the front pages of every major newspaper in the world. This you can take to the bank, because divine intervention will play a major role in the truth coming to pass. Then, finally at last, the spirit of JonBenet Ramsey will be put to rest in peace, and the book can be closed.

Let it be known to all who are concerned about the death of innocence understand that this child's death was and is not remotely given to a happenstance or for that matter an accident by any remote degree. Please also understand that behind every action there is an opposite if not greater reaction, which is simply to say, something happened in the Ramsey household that invoked the tragic circumstances which eventually lead to the unwarranted death of JonBenet Ramsey.

Time and chance had nothing to do with this little child's death, her being born at the wrong time and given to the wrong household or family had nothing to do with it, and the fact that she was only six years old had nothing to do with it, but evil in and of itself, (via her parents) planned and plotted its way into her life through no fault of her own. It was not this child's decision to be paraded around in various provocative costumes capturing the air of an adult demeanor, especially those who were given to have the nature of a pedophile disposition.

Her untimely death was the culmination of a preplanned pre-orchestrated attempt on her life, again, by those of whom she trusted the most, her mother and her father. When one really considers the circumstances surrounding the situational conditions of the parents concerted effort to make a child prodigy out of their daughter, they apparently had no remote idea what they were getting themselves into, long before push came to shove.

The author has said it once, and the author will say it again, and a thousand times more if necessary, the orchestration of the murder of JonBenet Ramsey cannot be attributed to anyone else other than her mother and her father. They are the ones who had the greatest motive to see this child dead.

If only it were possible to go back and change the hands of time, perhaps the beauty pageants and if possible to cancel out the ovarian cyst that started the whole shebang in the first place, then, maybe just then, none of these frightening moments of death and mayhem would have happened at all. But the sad part of it all is, who has the knowledge of awareness to predict the future? Perhaps John Ramsey would not be silently saying to himself, "Oh, if I could turn back the hands of time!" And again, if only time and chance could have been a foreseeable godfather; "their daughter would be alive today."

Introduction

Common Sense Logic and the Burden of Proof: The JonBenet murder mystery has baffled the media and the public for many years, with no apparent conclusion to those person (s) responsible for the homicide of JBR. It is highly suggested that logic and common sense ethics are the only remaining avenues contingent upon the successful outcome of this horrendous crime that took the life of this innocence child.

Truth and Logic: These in combination with *common sense,* will undoubtedly, and beyond the reproach of reasonable fallacy, bring about a more positive conclusion to convict those who are responsible for this travesty of innocence. The line between truth, logic and common sense is very thin which also suggest that careful exegesis of the evidence made readily available at the crime scene (especially the ransom note) can greatly assist the inquisitive mind and the authorities in arriving at a conclusion strong enough to expose the real culprits.

Common Sense Logic given to the burden of proof is necessary in this instance for several reasons:

1. No Confession
2. No Eyewitnesses
3. No Concrete Criminal Evidence

The author feels that these three criteria are important in arriving at any remote degree of truth leading to the capture and the criminal prosecution of that entity responsible for the death of JonBenet Ramsey. And because all other means to bring about an indictment or conviction appertaining to those who are responsible is all but exhausted, the only other recourse is to consider logic and common sense ethics based on truth analysis and the present evidence to expose the guilty party (s).

The Way to the Truth by Supposition: It is apparent that so far the truth and those who are responsible for the killing of innocence have not been given to criminal prosecution to date, and neither have there been an indictment brought against those who are under the umbrella of suspicion, primarily the child's parents. It is felt for this reason the way to the truth is contingent upon five areas of significant indulgence and positive contentions:

1. Disprove or refute the Intruder Theory
2. Disprove or refute the Ransom Note
3. Disprove or refute the Kidnap Theory
4. Authenticate the Writer of the Ransom Note
5. Expose the Motive for JBR's Death

This document/book is intended to prove beyond reasonable doubt, beyond reasonable suspicion the fallacy of the intruder theory, the fallacy of the ransom note, the fallacy of the kidnaped theory, and finally computer analysis of the ransom note to authenticate its writer. Theoretically, when these suppositions are proven to a positive degree of fallacy and none participatory existence, then the only other alternative is to place the first three of the five suppositions into a category of non-existent criminal intent. Which would ultimately mean that only the writer of the ransom note and the extraction of a motive for the death of JonBenet Ramsey are given to be proven statements of facts. What does all this mean? It means:

(1) There were never any intruders in the home of the Ramseys, which will ultimately place them (the Ramseys minus Burke) into the cate-

gory of being the primary suspects in the death of JBR. And the dis-proved intruder theory becomes an apparition of sorts, or a visible but false appearance of something not present, especially of a dead person in regards to the ransom note. Or, in other words, the latter is to say, the intruder theory was a made up excuse to hide the criminal intent of the real culprits-the killers themselves.

(2) The fallacy of the ransom note was never written by intruders, be-cause intruders into the home of the Ramseys never existed. And a statement of fact is this: It has not been proven by either party, the Ramseys or law enforcement significant to the District Attorneys office, that there were actually other persons in the home of the Ramseys the night JonBenet's life was so brutally taken. This again ultimately places the burden of guilt in the front yard of John and Patsy Ramsey.

(3) The kidnaped theory also never existed, here again, it has not been proven at any time during the night JonBenet died that her body was taken outside of the home. Neither the Ramseys nor the District Attorneys office have not proven beyond reasonable suspicion that the child was actually kidnaped or at any time was she taken from her home. So, if she wasn't taken from her home, she was not kidnaped, which means the writer of the ransom note was either brain storming, (letting go with false insinuations) or he or she did not know what they were talking about. Or, they did not fully understand the meaning of the word...Kidnaped.

Fact: The night little JonBenet Ramsey was brutalized and murdered, she never left the confines of her home. Again, this too has not been proven beyond reasonable suspicion by the office of the District Attorney to warrant any truthfulness that JonBenet was actually kidnaped and taken by blunt force from the confines of her home. And there is not any remote evidence that she was outside of her home during the time her life was taken; therefore, the kidnaped theory is nothing more than a lie, false, and totally untrue, which means that the writer of the ransom note stands accused of murder in the first degree. And it means that the person who found the ransom note given to the kidnaped theory was obviously the person who took the life of this young child.

No One Is Above the Law: To live in a nation so great and so strong as the United States of America, it is very ironic that the death of a little child has become an almost unsolvable mystery, baffling the minds of some of the most trained and experienced criminologist, known the world over. An innocent child is murdered in her own home, and it appears that no one has the slightest clue given to the guilty party or parties, saving the Ramsey Family.

The death of JonBenet Ramsey has become one of the greatest unsolved mysteries of this decade and the new millennium, and second only to the Orange Juice Story, and Michael Jackson fiasco. The great question posed on the mind set of society as an exponential mark of great inquisition is, will this murder case ever be solved and those responsible for the death of innocence be given to the just recompense of the law? Or, will the travesty of innocence take to the corridors of a by gone era situated in the historical archives of mysteries deemed unsolvable? God forbid that such should be the final case scenario.

Question: Are there people in this nation and society who are above the law, who have the controlling voice of power through financial empowerment to bend the justice system and those who are chosen to enforce the laws against criminal intent to bow to the requiem of the so-called almighty dollar? The author would hate to think so!

Question: Has society and those given to law enforcement gone to the cesspool of sordid indifference so great and so profound that it has become a covert degree of demagoguery likened to Show Me The Money? Or, is the same a blatant scenario of stereotypical behavior weighed heavily against righteous judgment? Again, the author would hate to think so. For example, when a family hires an investigator to investigate a certain criminal act, especially when the family themselves are under the umbrella of suspicion, no detective in his right mind is going to come upon evidence that would remotely incriminate the people who are paying him. And by the same token no family is going to hire someone in criminology to investigate a situation contrary to their well being that might place them at the center of controversy with the possibility of criminal intent, not so one would think and remain in their right mind. And it would be ludicrous to think that an attorney representing those who are under the umbrella of suspicion to hire someone who would condescend the credibility of the very people he is called to represent. If anything, the attorney representing his clients who are under the umbrella of suspicion, 99% of the time, would call in someone who was partial to his clients as oppose to someone who was impartial.

Even so, the final analysis of the private detective's investigation into the Ramsey murder incident, found that the Ramseys themselves had nothing to do with the murder of their young daughter, JBR. The investigating detective hired by the Ramsey attorney had no other recourse but to come to the conclusion that the parents of JonBenet were innocent of any involvement in the death of their daughter. And the sad part of it all, the investigating private detective was able to convince the public to some degree that the parents had no involvement in the travesty of innocence, how ironic.

Food for thought: Apparently, there are some people in society who are able to rise above the law, and needless to say, the author is caught up in bewilderment to remotely think that the law itself only applies to those whose insignia ($$$) represented by the dollar sign are vindicated in their wealth. Are we all so stupid and given to so gullible insensitivity of the attorney-client psychic deeanor that we cannot see the logic behind hiring one's own private investigator?

Justice Will Come: When an event or a circumstance so publicized into media awareness as the horrific murder of a young beauty queen, sooner or later the truth will surface. All together provided the continuous mind set of those who want to see this mystery solved does not allow those persons responsible to sit back on a flowery bed of ease and think that the whole situation is over with, not even when the Boulder Colorado prosecutor's office says that her death is unsolvable by closing the door to any further investigation. Believe it or not, justice will come for JonBenet Ramsey, whether it be by divine intervention, or by the investigative arm of law enforcement's long tentacles of criminal salvation, justice will come to the forefront of this whole unsolved mystery.

Should law enforcement fail in its efforts to bring to justice to those persons responsible for the life of JBR, then society and the public will intercede on behalf of justice to see that the guilty parties are brought to the full extent of the law. Because of the prolonged negative result of the investigation, there are those who feel the sensitivity of this young child's death is extremely vulnerable to situations that could possibly take place in their own households, are not so willing to let this murder, this travesty of innocence, go away so easily. And, God forbid that such should be the case.

Perhaps, just perhaps, the salvation of JonBenet Ramsey will come to pass as a result of this manuscript. Also, as a direct result of a multiplicity of incriminating evidence overlooked by others investigating the murder incident, the author's dissection of the ransom note will undoubtedly add a breath of fresh air to the motive centered around this family and the uneventful loss of one six-year-old child modeling prodigy. With this latter statement taken in seriousness of concern, the conclusion to one of the most talked about murder mysteries of the new millennium will not be long in coming.

Voice of Reason: People can talk, (word of mouth) because talking is a powerful tool. Word of mouth has withstood the test of time, time and time again. And when the cumulative voice of the people and or a society congealed in the truth synthesis begin to speak....Justice listens! The same is referred to in today's vernacular as *the voice of reason.* Justice and the voice of reason says that truth is always an inevitable outcome to any situation thought unsolvable. And, when *the voice of reason and justice* come together on the same plain of existence, the same will intercede into the affairs of society and rise above that all too familiar insignia ($$$, some say the almighty dollar) to reward society with *the truth, the whole truth, and nothing but the truth.* People deserve to hear the truth or an alternative viewpoint not yet brought to their attention or awareness. Good common sense also enters the picture to take side with the voice of reason as justice begins to evaluate certain situations and circumstances that warrants a justifiable conclusion. A conclusion conductive to the probability of satisfying the inquisitive mind of people who seek answers to any perplexing concourse in human behavior. And certainly, the criminal element in society is by no means....an exception to the rule.

Getting away with murder
"It was the savage killing that gripped America-the six-year-old beauty queen found strangled in her parents' basement, a bizarre ransom note left on the stairs and an extraordinary cast of suspects. But 10 years after the death of JonBenet Ramsey, her killer remains at large. Gaby Wood travels to Colorado to meet the investigators still trying to solve one of the most notorious murders of the 20th century."

Sunday June 25, 2006 The Observer "The house on 15th Street isn't quite the house it used to be. Indeed, some effort has been made to claim that it no longer exists at all. Five years ago, the number was officially changed from 755 15th Street to 749. There is no 755 any more.

The owners are anxious to sell it,' says the estate agent in charge of the empty mansion. 'It's been on the market for a while.' The house has five bedrooms and seven bathrooms. It's in a wealthy part of what is often referred to as a 'perfect town', just by the university campus and near the foot of the Rocky Mountains. The views are breathtaking. Nevertheless, I suggest, perhaps at $1.5m it's too expensive. 'Oh, it's worth the money by far,' says the estate agent. 'It's worth $2m. It's just that there's some history that has to be sorted out by whoever buys it ...' He tapers off, then adds: 'But I mean, it's been sold three times since the event.

Article continues

At 1:05pm on Boxing Day 1996, the body of six-year-old beauty queen JonBenet Ramsey was found by her father in the basement of this house in Boulder, Colorado. Her arms had been pulled up over her head and tied together at the wrists. A broken paint-brush had been used to tighten a garrote around her neck. Her skull was severely fractured, but there was no blood. Her mouth was covered with duct tape. Her body showed signs of sexual abuse. She was blue, rigid, half-wrapped in a blanket, and stuck to the blanket was a pink Barbie doll nightie. John Ramsey pulled off the duct tape, untied some of the cord, picked up his daughter and ran, screaming, up the stairs. He put her down in the front hallway, at the base of the Christmas tree. His wife, Patsy, threw herself over the child's body and cried: 'Jesus, you raised Lazarus from the dead, please raise my baby!

The police had arrived early that morning. They had been called at 5:52am, 20 minutes after Patsy had woken up and found a three-page handwritten ransom note at the foot of the stairs (the Ramseys were up early; they were due to leave for Michigan in their private plane at 7am). Strange as the ransom note was-long, literate, over-familiar, written with a pen and paper found in the kitchen and demanding a ransom that was the exact amount of John Ramsey's Christmas bonus - it was taken at face value. The case was treated as a kidnaping. Police searched the house and found nothing. At 10am, John went down to the basement: he found a window open and broken. Beneath it stood a suitcase on the floor. He closed the window and went back upstairs."

People were anxiously milling about, waiting for the kidnappers to call. Along with police officers, John and Patsy Ramsey had been joined by two sets of friends-the Whites and the Fernies-and Reverend Hoverstock, the Ramseys' pastor. Their nine-year-old son, Burke, was taken to a friend's house. Priscilla White started cleaning the kitchen, not thinking she might be destroying evidence. Just before one o'clock Detective Linda Arndt dispatched John Ramsey and his friend Fleet White to search the house again. And that was when, in the labyrinthine basement, behind a door that had been bolted shut, John found his daughter. White, who was a few feet behind him and claimed to have searched that room earlier, felt sure Ramsey had shouted, 'Oh my God!' before turning on the light.

Linda Arndt called headquarters and revised the initial report. It was not a kidnaping. It was a homicide. And the evidence had been smeared and left lying all over the place.

JonBenet Ramsey's was the only murder in Boulder that year. None of the Boulder police detectives who went on to investigate the case had ever dealt with a murder before, and this was the day after Christmas. The coroner didn't get there until after 8pm, and by the time he performed the autopsy the following morning, he was unable to determine the time of death. Within days, this was to become one of the most infamous murders of the 20th century. Pandemonium descended on the house, and on Boulder. One TV channel alone sent 20 people. Money started flying around-supermarket tabloids were offering to hire informants for vast sums and trying to buy copies of the ransom note for tens of thousands of dollars. A photo-lab technician stole autopsy photographs and sold them to The Globe newspaper. In 1996, 804 children were murdered in America. But the country didn't care about any of them as much as it cared about JonBenet.

"A high metal fence now cuts across the front lawn of 749 15th Street, and fortifies the entire property. Recently planted trees shade the mock-tudor building from potential voyeurs. At the back of the house is a public alleyway that runs the length of the block. Local kids used to ride their bikes here, and if you look up you'll see a sign, a little obscured by overgrown branches: 'Children At Play.' Ten years ago, you used to be able to walk right into the Ramseys' back yard. Now, where the fence has been erected, a large, indelible letter has been carved deep into the bark of a big old tree. A capital letter for the capital crime that refuses to be forgotten: M'."

'**I'll always remember that day.** Shortly after dinner I got a call from my office saying that there was this kidnaping situation at a home in Boulder, nearby, and could I get over there.'

Charlie Brennan is a reporter for the Rocky Mountain News. He was the first journalist to arrive at the Ramsey home on 26 December, and he is perhaps the only one who has followed the story consistently for the past 10 years. In 1997, Brennan teamed up with Lawrence Schiller, who had written a bestseller about O.J. Simpson, and conducted almost 600 interviews for a book that was to become the most authoritative on the Ramsey case, "Perfect Murder, Perfect Town." Over breakfast in downtown Denver, he recalls those first days.

'Before I left home I called one source I had at the DA's office, and I was told that yes, it's a kidnaping, and the child is inside the home. And I thought, these facts do not belong in the same sentence. It sounded like the craziest kidnaping I'd ever heard of, and my source agreed, and said it did not add up.'

Statistically speaking, in cases where a child's body is found in the family home, the culprit is almost always a 'family member perpetrator. Early on the morning of the 26th, when the Ramsey case was thought to be a kidnaping in a wealthy neighbourhood, the Ramseys were treated as victims. As soon as the body was found, they became prime suspects. Except that they were never exactly declared to be suspects-the foggy phrase 'under the umbrella of suspicion' was used. Police, however, appeared to have made up their minds. They thought, in the words of one ex-officer, that 'it was a slam-dunk case, and they would question people with the opening line: The Ramseys say you did it. You don't say that to someone who could possibly be a suspect! When you focus on the Ramseys, you taint whatever you're going to get from other people.

But the press went with them. It wasn't long before the police leaked the following: there were no footprints in the snow, and no signs of forced entry. The garrotte was an unusual method of strangulation, though one which was common in the Philippines, where John Ramsey had once been stationed at a naval base. The geography of the house was so complicated you'd have to be extremely familiar with it to know which was JonBenet's room and how to get to the basement. Both John and Patsy Ramsey told police that Burke was not awake when they called 911, but when the tape was analyzed a third voice was heard in the background, and it sounded like Burke. Midway through the afternoon, John Ramsey insisted that he had to catch a plane. The ransom note, with its mysteriously precise sum and in-joke about John Ramsey's 'good southern common sense' (Ramsey was not from the south, Patsy was; that he had a more 'southern' character than she had was a family joke), was so long it was referred to by one FBI profiler as the War and Peace of ransom notes. Clearly, whoever had written it on the Ramsey's notepaper had no fear of being caught in the act.

Charlie Brennan arrived to find a macabre scene. Patsy Ramsey's over-the-top Christmas decorations were still in place-red and white striped candy canes dotted along the walkway, white lights around the doorframe, an illuminated Santa in a sled on the snow-strewn front lawn. And all around the house, crime scene investigation tape, investigators' vans, police cars. There was only one other reporter there that night and Brennan thought: Where is everyone? When the body was brought out, he remembers thinking, that's the most bizarre name. And I thought: this is going to be an unusual case.

Eventually, other details emerged which competed with the original picture. Though there was no sign of forced entry, there was that small broken window into the basement that had been left open. Though there were no footprints in the snow, there was no snow on the part of the lawn that would need to be crossed to get in through the window. There was a footprint near the body left by a Hi-Tec boot. There was a latent hand print on the doorframe that didn't match any of the Ramseys. If you looked closely, there were marks on the child's back and neck that were consistent with the use of a stun gun. The garrotte was viciously tightened: would a parent kill their child that way?

When I had just come to Boulder, says Brennan, 'my editors explained to me that it's an unusual community-it's described as 27 square miles surrounded by reality. They said, "We want you to look into the only in Boulder story. The kind of story that couldn't happen anywhere else." Well, this is the "only in Boulder" murder. We're talking about a murder that occurred on Christmas night in which Santa Claus is actually a suspect. You can't make that up.

For those committed to the intruder theory, there was no shortage of strange characters, though none was ever charged. Bill McReynolds had played Santa at the Ramseys' Christmas party three days earlier, for the third year in a row. He had been given a tour of the house, so he would have been familiar with its complicated geography, and he had written JonBenet a Christmas card saying that Santa would be giving her a 'special present' after Christmas. It was found in her rubbish bin after her death. On the very same day in 1974-Boxing Day-McReynolds's nine-year-old daughter had been abducted with a friend, and had witnessed the sexual molestation of her friend. No suspects were ever found. In 1976, McReynolds's wife Janet had written a play in which a young girl is molested, tortured, murdered and left in a basement. Bill McReynolds died in 2002.

Other suspects cropped up: there was Gary Oliva, a convicted sex offender who had been seen hanging around the alleyway at the back of the house. He had spent time in prison for raping a seven-year-old girl in Oregon, and talked about making bacon out of a little girl's skin. In March 1997, a tip came in about Oliva: he had called a friend on 26 December and sobbed hysterically, saying he had done something terrible to a little girl. A year later, he attended JonBenet's memorial service. Four years later, two weeks before Christmas, he was arrested on the Colorado University campus for trespassing. The policeman who made the arrest searched his backpack and found a stun gun, a photo of JonBenet and an ode to her.

Chris Wolf, a freelance journalist, became a suspect when his girlfriend called the police and said he had stormed out of the house on Christmas night and came back the following morning, with muddy clothes. He became furious when he saw news reports of JonBenet's death on TV. The ransom note was signed 'S.B.T.C; Wolf had a sweatshirt bearing those initials-they stood for Santa Barbara Tennis Club. He had written an article about John Ramsey's company, Access Graphics, and may have had access to information about his bonus. He was a friend of Bill McReynolds. The theory that there was more than one intruder had been seriously considered.

But the suspect who looked most likely was dead within two months of the murder. Michael Helgoth seemed to have shot himself the day after District Attorney Alex Hunter announced they were closing in on the killer. But this, too, began to look like murder. Helgoth was right-handed, but the trajectory of the fatal bullet went from left to right. In Helgoth's apartment were found a pair of Hi-Tec boots, a stun gun, a baseball cap with the letters 'SBTC' on it, and a videotape of a news story about the unsolved kidnap and murder of a six-year-old girl. If there were two assailants, could the other have silenced this one?

On New Year's Day 1997, Patsy Ramsey went on CNN. "Hold your babies close, she said. There's a killer out there." Ten years on, the case is still open.

Judith Phillips had known the Ramseys since before they moved to Boulder. They had lived in Atlanta together, Patsy had been a colleague of Judith's then-husband, the two women had been pregnant at the same time. Burke Ramsey and Lindsey Phillips were born a month apart.

Judith, a photographer, now lives in Denver with Tom 'Doc' Miller, a wild-eyed, electric-haired lawyer, private investigator and handwriting expert who she met through the Ramsey case. Miller is trying to find a publisher for his book about JonBenet's death. By way of introductory warning, he tells me that everyone who has written about JonBenet has profited from her death. 'Every drop of her blood has been sold! There's not enough blood in that girl's body to pay for all the ink that's been spent on her.'

Judith brings down a black and white photo she took of Patsy, Burke and JonBenet in the year before the murder. 'It haunts a lot of people,' she says. 'A lot of people have said they see a lot of evil in Patsy's eyes.' She pauses and fiddles with that opinion for a second. 'I'm too close to it, I don't know.'

In the photograph, Patsy is wearing a dramatically ruffled cream blouse; Burke is seated on her right; JonBenet is draped over her left shoulder, looking at the camera with hooded, seductive, melancholic eyes. It is the pose of a much older woman, a worn-out temptress, and she is heavily made-up with great sweeps of powder and shadow and dark, fifties eyeliner. Later, when pictures of JonBenet as a miniature prom queen began to circulate in the supermarket tabloids, John Ramsey would say that they had been retouched. Yet here was the black and white truth of how Patsy wanted her children to be seen."

"In the year of her death, JonBenet Ramsey had been crowned Little Miss Colorado. She had also been America's Royale Little Miss, National Tiny Miss Beauty, and Colorado State All-Star Kids Cover Girl, among others. In her youth, Patsy had been crowned Miss West Virginia, and so had her sister Pam. A special display case was made to house JonBenet's pageant trophies. Once, when Judith's daughter Lindsey Phillips asked JonBenet about these, she said: 'They're not really mine. They're more my mom's trophies.' JonBenet was dressed in outfits reminiscent of a Vegas showgirl; she wore tiaras and lipstick; her hair was lightened and curled; she was taught to dance provocatively. She was an icon of cross-dressing-crossing from girl to woman, from child to plaything. The month after her death, a photographer named Randy Simons, who had been hired by the Ramseys in June 1996 to take photographs of JonBenet in her pageant clothes, sold his JonBenet portfolio to Sygma Photo Agency for $7,500. A year later, he was arrested for walking naked in the street, crying, 'I didn't kill JonBenet!' He was hospitalized, and not considered a suspect.

Judith was out of town when the murder took place - which was just as well, she now says, 'because I would have been blamed. They blamed everybody. They blamed Fleet White-their best friend! When we came back to Boulder, nobody was talking to each other-everybody was afraid to discuss anything with anybody. I felt like I was in a Robert Ludlow novel.' Gradually, many of the Ramseys' friends fell away in the swell of suspicion. The Ramseys fought with the Whites at JonBenet's funeral; the Whites urged the governor to appoint an independent prosecutor."

'It's a sickening, sickening, sickening thing!' Doc Miller starts to shout. 'That little girl was murdered. And billions of dollars have been spent covering up her murder, unfortunately, by the press. You're as guilty as that woman if you print the goddam intruder theory. You're just taking more blood out of her. You'll come out of here with blood on your hands, Gaby!'

"Judith gives me a copy of her latest coffee-table book, uncannily entitled, "Scream, Baby, Scream," and takes me into every room of the house but one. Glancing into this last, I see two rows of Sig-Sauer rifles, laid side by side on a double bed. There are so many guns that not an inch of bedspread is visible beneath."

"One of the most immediately striking aspects of the Ramsey investigation was the dispute that broke out between the police department and the DA's office. The police detectives were led by Steve Thomas, who believed that Patsy had accidentally killed JonBenet in a bed wetting incident, and that the Ramseys had then staged it to look like a murder. The DA's office called out of retirement a legendary investigator from Colorado Springs, who had solved over 200 homicide cases: Lou Smit. Smit believed the

Ramseys were innocent, that an intruder had entered the house and lain in wait in a nearby bedroom. He could be found, Smit thought, if DNA evidence was carefully considered. Foreign DNA was found under JonBenet's fingernails: 'I think she got a piece of her killer,' Smit said.

Two weeks after the murder, the results of a DNA test came back to the police. A drop of JonBenet's blood found in her underpants was mixed with the DNA of a Caucasian male, and no member of the Ramsey family was a match. It was six months before that report reached the DA's office. In August 1998, Steve Thomas resigned from the police department over the way the Ramsey case had been handled. In September 1998, Lou Smit resigned from the DA's office on the same grounds.

In 1999, just before the grand jury was about to be sworn in, the internationally recognized forensic expert Henry Lee was brought in. Yes, he suggested, the DNA in the underpants was not the Ramseys', but who was to say it was the murderer's? It could have been left there at any time, from the point of manufacture onwards.

They were going to test all the Bloomingdales factory workers in Hong Kong, until they realized it wouldn't have made any difference,' says Bob Grant, former District Attorney for Adams County and adviser to the grand jury. 'I can make the whole argument-it came from the factory, it came from the cleaners, it came from the pants being placed in a hamper with other clothes that had other foreign DNA on them - it could have come from any number of places. But as a prosecutor, I've got to prove beyond a reasonable doubt. And foreign male DNA mixed with her blood in her underpants: that's reasonable doubt, by definition.

The grand jury voted not to indict the Ramseys. At this point, for the prosecutors, the case was over; it was, as Grant realized early on, an 'unprosecutable case. But the public battles continued. Steve Thomas wrote a book that laid the blame squarely on Patsy, and the Ramseys wrote a book listing other suspects. Both came out in 2000. The Ramseys sued Thomas, and settled. That year, Chris Wolf, one of the suspects listed in the Ramseys' book, sued them for defamation. But in order to prove his own innocence, he had to prove Patsy's guilt. In dismissing the case, federal judge Julie Carnes said that the evidence presented in that civil case suggested an intruder was more likely to have committed the crime than Patsy. In the Ramsey camp, it was widely thought this meant they had been cleared.

It has been pointed out even by those who once suspected them that in the past 10 years the Ramseys have not behaved as guilty people might. They wrote a book, which locked them into a version of the story; they sued Steve Thomas, which could have brought them into a courtroom; in 2004, John Ramsey ran for the state legislature in Michigan, where they now live-why would a guilty man do that knowing the scrutiny to which politicians are routinely subjected? And from time to time, when they pass through Boulder, the Ramseys meet with the DA to find out how the investigation is coming along. Those who have been in touch with them recently say the Ramseys are devastated and broke. 'They've been badgered and kicked and everything else,' said one acquaintance. They were contacted for this story, but remained silent.

I meet Michael Tracey in a place he refers to as his 'downtown office-a bar called the Hungry Toad, which is owned by a Brit and is the only place in Boulder where you can buy a pint of bitter. Tracey is a professor of journalism at the University of Colorado; he has made three documentaries about the Ramsey case, is currently at work on a book about it, and has the ear of John and Patsy Ramsey, in whose innocence he firmly believes. He arrives with a manila envelope and tells me knowingly that he feels very close to solving the case. He can't say why, but he tells me that the DNA from JonBenet's underpants has now been tested accurately enough to be logged in the FBI system. Which means that anyone in any part of the country who has committed any crime for which a DNA sample is taken will automatically be cross-checked. Any day now, the FBI may find a match."

'This was not a staging,' Tracey says, pulling a photograph of JonBenet's neck out of his envelope. 'This was a vicious attack. There's no question in my mind now that someone came in who kind of knew them, who got off on little girls, extremely violent. She was asphyxiated-that begins to explain why there's no blood in the head-and he's getting off on this. I think they wanted to play with her. I think it was a very sick game by a very sick person.'

"JonBenet's death gripped America, Tracey suggests, because it had everything going for it: 'Sex, sleaze, the rich father, the American dream gone bad. It was a combination of voyeurism, resentment, anger, irrationality, a cultural viciousness. It was Greek-a lot of people focused on it as a kind of catharsis.'

Where is the catharsis, I ask, if the case is unsolved? 'It's in the hate. Hate the Ramseys, you feel better. This was pretty close to a conspiracy.'

When Tracey pulled the image out of the manila envelope, I thought it was one I had already seen a close-up of JonBenet's neck, designed to show the garrotte and the marks thought to have been made by a stun gun. But I noticed Tracey only pulled half the picture out of the envelope. The photographs I had seen were not close-ups but crops of this one. On instinct, I reached for the photo and pulled it out a little further. JonBenet's face came into view. She was lying down, and shot in profile. Her mouth was slightly open, her eyes were closed. If the photo had been in black and white, so that her skin's bluish tinge was invisible, you might have thought that she was merely asleep-until your eyes were drawn down to the fine blonde hair trapped under the cord with which she had been strangled. I looked at this photograph only briefly; in an unforeseeable split second I felt suddenly, swimmingly sick. Tracey's voice became background noise.

Come on, I told myself, you're not squeamish. But back she came, the seemingly sleeping child. I started to sweat.

Later, I realized what it was about the photo that had haunted me: it was so ordinary. Over the course of many conversations, I'd become accustomed to hearing of 'the garrotted neck, the fingernails, "the blood in the underpants; these things were never hers." And the infamous pageant photos, haunting in their own perverse, made-up way, put her at several removes from herself. So in our minds she seems to have gone from icon to crime-lab fodder without passing through the most obvious and fundamental incarnation. I expected her body to look unrecognizable in some way, to be bloody or obscured or overly clinical. The last thing I expected it to be was what she was: a little girl.

The sign on Frank Coffman's door reads: 'The Crypt. Ring twice for best results.' Coffman makes horror masks for a living. He lives a few blocks away from the Ramseys' old house, and first became interested in the case because he lived nearby. Ten years ago, he was a regular Columbo, bumbling around, discovering where the cord and duct tape had been bought, befriending every nanny and cleaning person who had ever worked for the Ramseys.

He has photographs and floor plans of the house. He has samples of Patsy's handwriting. 'A lot of people thought I had a kind of encyclopedic knowledge of the case,' he says, on the phone.

Later, as he leads me into his apartment, Coffman tells me he likes murder mysteries. 'I like books about the Lindbergh case, things like that. I know everything about the Kennedy assassination - that's pretty obvious really, when you look at the evidence. The Ramsey case has a lot of curlicues-it's still puzzling, even if you think you know who did it.

As we wander down Boulder's central shopping street towards a coffee shop, Coffman tells me of a parade JonBenet took part in here just before the murder. She was dressed up 'as Little Miss

Christmas, or something like that'. It was a tradition - the previous year she had sailed down the high street as Shirley Temple,
singing The Good Ship Lollipop. Then Coffman stops and tells
me something that became lost as soon as the media frenzy
began. 'She wasn't famous in Boulder, you know,' he says. 'I never
heard of her before the murder. You get the impression that she
was some kind of celebrity here. She was totally just another kid.
Even though she was in that parade, nobody knew her. It's not
like she was a target for a stranger. Her name never appeared in
the newspaper before her murder. Her mother maybe wanted her
to become famous, and maybe she was famous on the pageant
circuit, but who the hell even was aware of that? Well,' he adds
more slowly, she's famous now.'

I come back to my hotel and leave a message for Lou Smit.
I've tried him through the DA's office for months without success, but now I have a number for his home in Colorado Springs
and, although it's late, I can't get out of my mind the idea that so
much of this hangs on him, whichever way you look at it.

If some of Smit's former colleagues are to be believed, he was
swayed by his own religious convictions into believing the
Ramseys were innocent. District Attorney Alex Hunter later said
Smit got too close. Bob Grant, who had worked with Smit on a
number of difficult homicide cases in Colorado Springs, says that
in the Ramsey case 'people thought Lou was set up. The first
time he met the Ramseys there was some kind of prayer group or
something, and Lou's a very religious man. He got more so
during his employment in Boulder. Patsy asked him to pray with
them at the house-it felt natural to Lou. It should not have. I'm
not saying it coloured his objectivity, but it certainly lends itself
to that appearance.

On the other hand, here was a man who had solved over 200
homicide cases, while the detectives in Boulder had not even investigated one. By the time he was called out of retirement to
work on it, the evidence gathered was not as he would have
wanted it. He told Michael Tracey, for instance, that had he been

the first detective on the scene, he would have brought a dog in, which would have found the body in 30 seconds; he would have separated the Ramseys, asked them to come down to the station to give hair samples and blood samples; he would have taken their clothes and conducted initial interviews. Had they refused, he told Tracey, he would have arrested them. This from the man who believes most strongly in their innocence: an arrest would at least have given them the chance to clear their names.

There was another detail. In 1996, the year of JonBenet's death, Smit had solved one of Colorado's most puzzling crimes-the kidnap and murder of a 13-year-old girl called Heather Church. The trail had gone cold, Smit had been brought in and he'd solved the case on the basis of a latent fingerprint submitted to the FBI-years after the crime had taken place. Now he was suggesting that the Ramsey case could still be solved, 10 years on, using DNA evidence. Maybe he knew something others didn't.

Last year, Patsy's cancer recurred so aggressively that it was assumed she would die. Smit drove up to Michigan to visit her. Tracey speculates: 'I think he went to see her just in case.' In case of a confession? I asked. But why? He's on their side. 'No,' said Tracey, 'he's on the side of JonBenet. Now, does Lou Smit think the Ramseys killed JonBenet? No. But, would he just... a final...you know, just in case? Sure. That's how good he is.' In the letter of resignation he sent to Alex Hunter in September 1998, Smit wrote: 'Shoes, shoes, the victim's shoes, who will stand in the victim's shoes?'

The following morning, Lou Smit rings while I'm having breakfast. With direct, old-fashioned charm, he tells me he can't talk about the case because he is officially back inside it, and wants to remain that way in order to solve it. The DA, who has rehired him, has a strict policy of no publicity. But he does say he's hopeful, and tells me of others who are working on the case separately.

Ollie Gray and John San Augustin were hired by John and Patsy Ramsey in 1999. When the Ramseys ran out of money to pay them, the private eyes kept going. But it's hard. They needed the police to co-operate, and now that the police files have been handed over to the DA's office, they need the DA to co-operate.

'If they had put as much energy into investigating the crime itself as they did in trying to persecute the Ramseys, this thing would already have been put to bed,' says Ollie Gray. 'I'll bet you a nice steak dinner and a good bottle of wine that they have a bunch of evidence they have never processed. I think they have reports that basically prove that the Ramseys are innocent.'

On my last morning in Colorado, I go to meet Bill Wise, Alex Hunter's former deputy district attorney, at his home. His big white husky greets me at the door. Wise tells me that he was taken off the case for complaining about the police department's incompetence. I ask him why he thinks Smit has always believed in the Ramseys' innocence. 'I don't know,' he says, taking a deep drag on his cigarette. 'It would be because he is a much better investigator than me, and he sees things I don't see. He's a hell of an investigator. And if you can get a match anytime-murder has no statute of limitations...with all these databases that have been put together, there's a pretty good chance that DNA's gonna turn up sometime.'

In a corner of Wise's house is a framed Victorian picture. On the frame, it says it's a puzzle picture but, try as I might, I can't see the image two ways-all I can see is a pleasant pastoral scene. Eventually, I give up, and ask Wise to show me how it works. He laughs, and points a smoky finger at various details. 'There, see? That's a cat in the shrubbery,' he says, 'and there's a face there, and a crocodile down there.' Gradually, the whole hidden flip side comes into view-the English country scene is replaced by a fleeting kind of zoo. 'You can find them,' Wise says. [i]

Getting away with murder: THE AUTHOR'S COMMENTS: It was the savage killing that gripped America-the six-year-old beauty queen found strangled in her parents' basement, a bizarre ransom note left on the stairs and an extraordinary cast of suspects. But 10 years after the death of JonBenet Ramsey, her killer remains at large. Gaby Wood travels to Colorado to meet the investigators still trying to solve one of the most notorious murders of the 20th century.

Sunday June 25, 2006, The Observer: The house on 15th Street isn't quite the house it used to be. Indeed, some effort has been made to claim that it no longer exists at all. Five years ago, the number was officially changed from 755 15th Street to 749. There is no 755 any more.

'The owners are anxious to sell it,' says the estate agent in charge of the empty mansion. 'It's been on the market for a while.' The house has five bedrooms and seven bathrooms. It's in a wealthy part of what is often referred to as a 'perfect town' just by the university campus and near the foot of the Rocky Mountains. The views are breathtaking. Nevertheless, I suggest, perhaps at $1.5m it's too expensive. 'Oh, it's worth the money by far,' says the estate agent. 'It's worth $2m. It's just that there's some history that has to be sorted out by whoever buys it ...He tapers off, then adds: 'But I mean, it's been sold three times since the event.'

Author's comment: *The house on 15ᵗʰ Street: will forever be etched in the minds and the hearts of those of us who feel that JonBenet Ramsey, a once sparkling beauty queen who lost her life there, this house will never be the same ever again, no matter who lives in it. It will always be a place where JonBenet Ramsey was brutally murdered by the very people she loved so dearly, and by the very people she trusted unreservedly.*

The house on 15ᵗʰ street, holds the ghastly truth to whatever went on at this residence the night JonBenet's life was so un-mistakeningly, and so brutally taken. Her beautiful smiling face will never again shed the radiant glow of laughter that would almost light up a Christmas tree, no more forever. No more forever, will the sound of her talented young voice be heard in the house on 15ᵗʰ street. Her favorite dancing shoes she loved to wear, will no more forever fulfill the pettiness of her little feet. No more forever, will this young child wake-up to the chirping sounds of birds ushering in the dawning of a new day. No more forever, for this amazing beauty queen will the house on 15th street set the backdrop for what could have been a life so full of happiness, peace and joy.

The house on 15th street will always serve as a reminder of how cold, calculating, heartless and demonic some people can be. If one could speak to death in a very straight forward way, one would probably say to death: "death how could you unremorsefully take the life of this amazing star of beauty who had only existed on this earth six years?" "Death, how could you allow two cold hearted and heartless people (John and Patsy Ramsey) to methodically plan, methodically execute the travesty of innocence?" And then, to add insult to injury, Death, you allowed this star of beauty to be assaulted by the same people who took her life. Death, the author asks you once more, "how could you do it?" This is what the author would like to know!

At 1:05pm on Boxing Day 1996, the body of six-year-old beauty queen JonBenet Ramsey was found by her father in the basement of this house in Boulder, Colorado. Her arms had been pulled up over her head and tied together at the wrists. A broken paintbrush had been used to tighten a garrote around her neck. Her skull was severely fractured, but there was no blood. Her mouth was covered with duct tape. Her body showed signs of sexual abuse. She was blue, rigid, half-wrapped in a blanket, and stuck to the blanket was a pink Barbie doll nightie. John Ramsey pulled off the duct tape, untied some of the cord, picked up his daughter and ran, screaming, up the stairs. He put her down in the front hallway, at the base of the Christmas tree. His wife, Patsy, threw herself over the child's body and cried: 'Jesus, you raised Lazarus from the dead, please raise my baby!'

Author's comment: The irony of it all: Is it a simple coincident or just a mere happenstance that the father found the body of his daughter in the basement and his wife Patsy just happened to stumble upon the ransom note at the foot of the stairs the morning of JonBenet's death? This is worth repeating again, if the ransom note, the intruder theory, and the erroneous kidnaping are fallacies of the real truth, then who placed the ransom note at the foot of the staircase? If the author had worlds to give, the author would hedge them on the deceased Patsy Ramsey.

The police had arrived early that morning. They had been called at 5:52am, 20 minutes after Patsy had woken up and found a three-page handwritten ransom note at the foot of the stairs (the Ramseys were up early; they were due to leave for Michigan in their private plane at 7am). Strange as the ransom note was-long, literate, over-familiar, written with a pen and paper found in the kitchen and demanding a ransom that was the exact amount of John Ramsey's Christmas bonus-it was taken at face value.

Author's comment: The irony of it all: The coroner had not officially pronounced the child dead, but yet Patsy was expecting a miracle from Jesus. The irony of this is, she can hide the fact that she had nothing to do with the death of her daughter from the public, but it is most assured she cannot hide the error of her way and the fact that she killed her daughter from God or Jesus. After the way this little child was paraded around like a little lady, it is hard to believe that God is not aware of who killed His little child. And this woman has the bold audacity to ask Jesus to bring the child she killed back from the dead. "Somebody give us all a break." Though the short life span of this beautiful little child met with a tragic end, there is one thing for sure, she does not have to be concerned about her father molesting her anymore and she does not have to engage in insults with her mother anymore. Why? Because her soul is safely resting in the arms of God and Jesus Christ.

People were anxiously milling about, waiting for the kidnappers to call. Along with police officers, John and Patsy Ramsey had been joined by two sets of friends-the Whites and the Fernies - and Reverend Hoverstock, the Ramseys' pastor. Their nine-year-old son, Burke, was taken to a friend's house. Priscilla White started cleaning the kitchen, not thinking she might be destroying evidence. Just before one o'clock Detective Linda Arndt dispatched John Ramsey and his friend Fleet White to search the house again. And that was when, in the labyrinthine basement, **behind a door that had been bolted shut,** John found his daughter. White, who was a few feet behind him and claimed to have searched that room earlier, **felt sure Ramsey had shouted, 'Oh my God!' before turning on the light.**

Author's comment) *"Oh my God!" The author is inclined to believe the report of Mr. White shortly before they entered into the room where the body of JonBenet was found, in other words, what Mr. White is saying, John Ramsey knew his daughter's body was in the room even before they entered the room. How did he know that? He knew that because he was not the one who placed it there, but he knew that his wife had earlier dragged the little child's body and left it there.* *"Behind a door that had been bolted shut:" In the aftermath of this child's death anything left behind a bolted door was deliberately and purposely put there. Whether or not to further assuage the idea of personal involvement relative to JonBenet's parents: or to try and fool the public and to create a disingenuous air of alien hostility.*

So far this little stunt by the Ramseys has managed to altercate the demeanor of some of the best minds in criminal law; even the highly acclaimed Lou Smit. A person unconcerned about getting caught would place the body of a dead child behind a closed door and then take his or her own good time bolting it shut. Out of remorse, a child's mother would do that; and go somewhere to sit down and write a long 3-page ransom note. John and Patsy Ramsey knew that during the whole fiasco of their daughters death that time would be on their side. And, to their great expectation not only was time on their side but the entire city of Boulder Colorado, its police precincts, and what could have been a great team of precinct prosecutors were on their side also. With high profile personalities of this caliber on their side, it became almost impossible for the Ramseys to be righteously prosecuted in the town of Boulder, Colorado.

Linda Arndt called headquarters and revised the initial report. **It was not a kidnaping. It was a homicide.** And the evidence had been smeared and left lying all over the place. JonBenet Ramsey was the only murder in Boulder that year. None of the Boulder police detectives who went on to investigate the case had ever dealt with a murder before, and this was the day after Christmas.

Author's comment: *It was not a kidnaping. It was a homicide. From a kidnaping to a murder, how ironic again, the ransom note is for a fact not worth the money it was written on. If the child's body was found in the afternoon, and the ransom note in the early morning hour, and no one relative to/in association with the kidnappers had entered the house to leave the child's body in the secluded area in the basement says more things than one:*

1. *There was no kidnaping of JonBenet Ramsey*
2. *There was definitely no intruders in the house*
3. *The ransom note is just words on a piece of paper*
4. *No one other than the Ramseys were in the house that night*
5. *The child was murdered by her parents/mother*

Undetermined Time of Death/Partial Autopsy: In light of the latter numbered statements and the false assertions of each, there remains no other alternative but to focus complete attention on the fact that John and Patsy Ramsey were the only ones, not could have been the only ones in that house to cause the death of innocence.

The coroner didn't get there until after 8pm, and by the time he performed the autopsy the following morning, he was unable to determine the time of death:

Author's comment: *"Deliberate Crime Scene Contamination!"* *The entire crime scene and the area where the child died, was deliberately and completely contaminated by people and outsiders who were purposely invited in, further contaminating the crime scene to prevent any positive assessment of the true time of death, which could only circumvent a partial, incomplete autopsy. The deliberate contamination of the crime scene was also designed to lessen the suspicion of the involvement by the Ramseys in the death of their daughter, JonBenet.*

Even though the exact time of death could not be determined with preciseness, one positive note comes to mind. The child did not die between the time the ransom note was found, and the time her father recovered the child's body from the basement. So one thing is for sure/fact, JonBenet Ramsey was killed sometime between the time she was put to bed and the time the ransom was found in the early morning hours at the foot of the stairs by her mother, Patsy Ramsey. This statement once again invalidates the ransom note. Without the ransom being valid, what purpose does the intruder theory serve? The ransom note mentioned a kidnaping, which is also invalidated when John Ramsey found his daughter's body in the basement shortly after 1:00 PM, the same day of the child's death.

A complete and thorough autopsy would have proven many things; the time of death, the exact cause of death, was the child strangled before or after she was dead? How much resistance did she put up or did she try to fight back? How much effort/struggle did she put up to try and get the cord from around her neck, or was the little girl even alive when it happened? Nothing more than the little DNA found under her fingernail, and on her panties was certainly not enough evidence to convince the authorities to charge someone with the death of innocence, let alone John and Patsy Ramsey or anyone else for that matter. By no means is the latter statement a defense of the Ramsey's involvement in the death of innocence.

Did the child have an enlarged vagina, customary from having sex with an older person? And if so, was an enlarged vagina the result of having regular sexual encounters with the same person or multiple partners? And was the effects of an enlarged vagina due to objectivity or vaginal intercourse or both? Did the killer of JonBenet Ramsey deliberately use an object in her body to try and hide the fact that the child was having regular sexual intercourse with a male person; "namely her daddy," since no one else could be remotely proven to have entered into the home? What other reason would the child have been objectized, if not to hide the fact that her daddy was a regular sex partner, which also made her mother (Patsy Ramsey) go into a jealous rage because John Ramsey was showing more affection toward his daughter than he was for his wife? Because such was the case, and the only way John Ramsey could hide the fact that he was having sexual intercourse with his daughter, the object used to over-enlarge her vagina was also deliberately done to hide his guilt of child molestation?

John Ramsey is guilty of objectizing his daughter to assuage the fact he was having regular or routine sex with her, which after the passing of time, became an repugnant irritant to her mother. This is one more of the reasons John and Patsy Ramsey would not allow a complete autopsy to be performed on their daughter. They would run the risk of being exposed and their little secret would eventually be out in the open. "Which meant certain jail time, or the needle by way of lethal injection."

The Murder of JonBenét Ramsey
by J. J. Maloney & J. Patrick O'Connor
Related Story: Solving the JonBenet Case by Ryan Ross. (04/14/03)

A bombshell in the case was the autopsy report, finally released to the public following a lawsuit by the national and local media. The major findings of the autopsy, however, were that she died of ligature strangulation, with a furrow surrounding her neck, and cranial damage–including an 8-inch long skull fracture, with a piece of skull nearly an inch square broken loose. However, there was no laceration of the scalp, as would be expected if she was struck with a flashlight or a golf club (as had been speculated). The wound would be more likely the result of her head being bashed against a toilet, a sink or a bathtub. It was determined that the strangulation was accomplished by the murderer using part of the handle on one of Patsy's paint brushes to tighten the cord around JonBenet's throat to choke her to death. There were also abrasions on her back and legs consistent with her having been dragged (see autopsy report).

There were also indications of chronic sexual abuse. The Ramseys heatedly disputed the possibility of this, as does the family doctor. However, there was not only chronic inflammation of the vaginal tract, but a 1-cm by 1-cm opening in her hymen. There were traces of blood in the vaginal area and in the crotch of her panties. Thomas reports in his book that a panel of pediatric experts from around the country concluded that the trauma to her hymen and chronic vaginal inflammation were "evidence of both acute injury and chronic sexual abuse."

One expert widely quoted is Dr. Cyril Wecht, coroner for Allegheny County, Pa.: "There's absolutely no question she was abused," Wecht said. "There's blood, and contusions (in the vagina,) and the hymen has been torn."

As these revelations became public, the standing of the Ramsey family in Boulder began to plummet. [ii]

The Gash in Her Head! A narrative of sorts: The big gash in the young child's head was purposely put there for more reasons than one. A. One of the reasons is this, was the large gash in JonBenet's head deliberately done to take away some attention related to the fact that the child was sexually molested? Which would have also pointed to John Ramsey having had regular sexual intercourse with his daughter? And there is a very strong possibility that both of them (her parents) were engaged with sexual intercourse with JonBenet. Somehow, it appears that one could not tell on the other. B. The Ramsey's did not realize they made a serious blunder, a mistake of very significant proportion when they realized they had not done anything to alter evidence denoting that the child had been molested numerous times in the past. C. They had to create a diversion away from the initial point of interest that would have proven that John had violated his daughter on several occasions before her death, and the strong possibility that both of them (he and Patsy) were having sex with her. One could not tell on the other, (amounting to a self imposed gag order) even more so after the child had been murdered.

It was at this moment that Patsy Ramsey stood over the lifeless body of her dead child, in a kind of tired and overly stunned stupor gazing at what she had done just a few seconds ago. Well, John, you have managed to F¼.K-UP a wet dream again, you and your small-no brain self, "what did I tell you about trying to grow a brain, John!" All these years and you haven't grown a brain yet. John, we cannot allow the dead child's body to be seen by the coroner without first destroying the evidence showing you were having routine sex with her. If you had only heeded the first warning to both of you, the child would be living and you would not have gotten yourself caught in this mess, and I could be getting her ready for her next pageant! No, but you just had to have your little afternoon delight, and look where it has landed all of us. Misery for the rest of our lives, and one dead child to show for it. The fact that you have been having sex with JonBenet adds all the more to a difficult situation. Should the authorities come to the conclusion, if they should do a thorough autopsy, that you have been having sex with your own daughter, the whole ball game is over. All the other missing pieces of the puzzle will automatically fall into place; the end result of what could land us in jail for the rest of our lives or on death row.

*Crack the child's skull, tie a garrote around her neck and strangle her again, but much tighter this time. Take a cylindrical object and do all that you can, to enlarge her vaginal area: **A.** to show that an outsider did all the damage to her body. The coroner will see that the crime scene is so hideous and the child is so badly disfigured, he will not waste a lot of time examining the child in an autopsy, grant us our wish and allow a quick memorial and burial service for JonBenet. **B.** The coroner will be so preoccupied with other areas of the child's body until very little attention will be given to the fact that the child had been engaged in previous sexual activity. When we are finished with that little heifer's body, the public and the media will think that some loose screw, crazed maniac got a hold of her and turned her body into a despicable display of human carnage.*

Every one will be so caught up in the hoopla, until not much or very little attention will be given to the fact that the child was repeatedly molested, time and time again by you, John. And, by the time the authorities figure out who did it, we will be old and gray, and all of this mess will be long since forgotten. After a year or two, the entire issue of JonBenet's untimely but timely death will have faded into the archives of time past and gone forever into the corridors of time and chance. "We will have planned a perfect murder in a perfect town."

Did the child bleed out? Were there ligature marks on her hands to show that she struggled to try and remove the garrote from around her neck? Was the child awake or was the child killed in her sleep. No blood was found near the child's body as a result of the gash, where did the child bleed out. Was there enough blood left in the child's body to show that she retained or lost any blood at all. And if the child did bleed out where is the lost blood or the blood residue?

Did she even have a chance to fight back? How long did it take for the child to die and was death instantaneous? Note: no intruder in his right mind would write a three page ransom note, especially when the child was already dead; trying to make sense of nonsense only points more vividly to the parents taking the life of innocence. Did the child's body show any signs of more than one person other than her father and her mother having contact with her body? Did the child's body show signs of sexual activity on a continuous/ongoing basis? This latter statement strikes fear at the very core and the very heart of John Ramsey. The last thing in the world he would want people to know is that he was having sex with his little six year-old daughter. And because of it, this beautiful little child is dead. And the fact that a jealous wife, found his relationship with his own daughter, had reached an unbearable moment of deranged jealousy. The same jealousy prompted Patsy Ramsey into such a jealous fit of rage that for ten brief, quick seconds she lost her mind and murdered her daughter, her precious love child. Another reason why, in his heart, he had hoped that John Mark Karr would have been found guilty of the murder of JonBenet.

A complete and thorough autopsy would have proved all of the above and if the Ramseys were innocent. They would not have had anything to lose or to be afraid of. On the contrary, they would have everything to gain, up to and including freedom from further prosecution and slanderous assaults on their personal and private lives. Was JonBenet's execution conducted by one person or two or more persons? A complete and thorough autopsy could have shed more light on the possible culprits behind the travesty of innocence. But the Ramseys would not allow it WHY? And, no court of law would insist on it, seeing that a very serious crime on the life of a little child had been committed. Were the Ramseys afraid that a complete and thorough autopsy would have pre-

sented/revealed further evidence positively pointing to them as JonBenet's executioners?

The real truth of this whole murderous episode of a young girl's death, lies in the fallacy of primarily Three Things, and is worth repeating:

1. *The Fallacy of the Ransom Note Theory*
2. *The Fallacy of the Intruder Theory*
3. *The Fallacy of the Kidnap Theory*

It is no irony of thought or even of the imagination, the latter numbered statements of truth are now proven facts, that none of the above ever occurred (no intruder, no valid ransom note, no kidnaping took place) within the Ramsey home the night JonBenet Ramsey was so brutally murdered by her mother and her father. The mother because of jealousy, the father because he was sexually molesting his daughter. Of the which neither one of them wanted to get caught.

The above theories once again, have been proven without the slightest of doubt to be inferences of circumstances that never took place in or outside of the Ramsey home. The ransom note was not worth the paper it was written on; the kidnap theory turned out to also not be worth the paper it was written on, and the kidnap theory only existed in the minds of John and Patsy Ramsey, and the intruder theory is good for nothing but to be thrown in the toilet and flushed out into the pipe-dreams of wasted time. Without the validity of the ransom note, the intruder theory, and the kidnap theory, the Ramseys do not have a leg to stand on, the guilt is now so vivid and clear, any court in the land should be able to convict them. "It doesn't get any clearer or plainer than this, and you don't have to be a rocket scientist to see through their camouflaged rhetoric."

Within days, this was to become one of the most infamous murders of the 20th century. Pandemonium descended on the house, and on Boulder. One TV channel alone sent 20 people. Money started flying around-supermarket tabloids were offering to hire informants for vast sums and trying to buy copies of the ransom note for tens of thousands of dollars. A photo-lab technician stole autopsy photographs and sold them to The Globe newspaper. In 1996, 804 children were murdered in America. But the country didn't care about any of them as much as it cared about JonBenet.

Author's comment: A Strong Spiritual Impact! *Whether or not one would want to believe it, the death of JonBenet Ramsey and the travesty of innocence has* **a strong spiritual impact** *to it. All the world wants to know exactly how this child's life was so brutally taken. "Who were the people responsible or behind the travesty of innocence?"*

This little child's death has not only impacted the world, but this brutal travesty of innocence also illumes the spirit world. It is for this reason the author believes that the truth surrounding the death of innocence will soon be revealed as a result of divine intervention. Some might say, what has God and divine intervention got to do with it? And what makes God so interested in this particular person's death? It would be very naive of humanity to think that heaven is not concerned about what goes on with people and situations of circumstance associated with mankind and the earth! Do you think that Creation would just abandon its handiwork to the works of darkness and the evils that prevail upon it? God forbid that such should be the case for even the slightest degree of divine ineptness. It may seem like the Prince of this world and the air is in control of things, not so in the lease. God is still in charge of his creation, the earth, and everything therein is. The fallacy of thought is not with God the Suffering Savior but indeed lies with us and fallen humanity.

Though so many of us have forgotten from whence we came, how we came and who brought us, and the great struggles encountered to make this nation the only sustained superpower to come to the forefront of creative existence to date. Well, if most of you have forgotten, let the author briefly remind you, "it was divine intervention behind us every step of the way."

JonBenet Ramsey Speaks: *If JonBenet could speak from heaven via her spirit from the grave, what do you think she would say? "Certainly I am appalled at my parents for bringing me down that particular* *road of life. And trying to make me grown before my time. And how they allowed their weak consciences to overpower their will to do the right thing which ultimately resulted in death of innocence falling on both of their hands.*

Because of Glory Bright I have to forgive you, but in light of your guilt and the destruction of your own flesh and blood, can you forgive yourselves for the Travesty of Innocence? Daddy, mother may not be with you now, I want to prayerfully let you know, it's not too late to be a real man and own up to the error of your way and ask the Lord to forgive you and bring to an end your internal suffering-so you and mother can be with me in heaven. In sprite of all the circumstances and the fact that my murder has not been solved, I still love you! Yours in the Lord, little JonBenet."

P.S. Oh, Yes, "It's not to late for salvation and the truth to come to both of you, even though mother is deceased and awaiting the judgment bar of Creation; just like God has forgiven me for all my sins, "He can do the same thing for you, too!" Love you, JonBenet."

A high metal fence now cuts across the front lawn of 749 15th Street, and fortifies the entire property. Recently planted trees shade the mock-tudor building from potential voyeurs. At the back of the house is a public alleyway that runs the length of the block. Local kids used to ride their bikes here, and if you look up you'll see a sign, a little obscured by overgrown branches: 'Children At Play'. Ten years ago, you used to be able to walk right into the Ramseys' back yard. Now, where the fence has been erected, a large, indelible letter has been carved deep into the bark of a big old tree. A capital letter for the capital crime that refuses to be forgotten: 'M' **'I'll always remember that day.** Shortly after dinner I got a call from my office saying that there was this kidnaping situation at a home in Boulder, nearby, and could I get over there.'

Charlie Brennan is a reporter for the Rocky Mountain News. He was the first journalist to arrive at the Ramsey home on 26 December, and he is perhaps the only one who has followed the story consistently for the past 10 years. In 1997, Brennan teamed up with Lawrence Schiller, who had written a bestseller about O.J. Simpson, and conducted almost 600 interviews for a book that was to become the most authoritative on the Ramsey case, Perfect Murder, "Perfect Town." Over breakfast in downtown Denver, he recalls those first days.

'Before I left home I called one source I had at the DA's office, and I was told that yes, it's a kidnaping, and the child is inside the home. And I thought, these facts do not belong in the same sentence. It sounded like the craziest kidnaping I'd ever heard of, and my source agreed, and said it did not add up.'

Statistically speaking, in cases where a child's body is found in the family home, the culprit is almost always a 'family member/perpetrator. Early on the morning of the 26th, when the Ramsey case was thought to be a kidnaping in a wealthy neighborhood, the Ramseys were treated as victims. As soon as the body was found, they became prime suspects. Except that they were never exactly declared to be suspects-the foggy phrase 'under the umbrella of suspicion' was used. Police, however, appeared to have made up their minds. They thought, in the words of one ex-officer, that 'it was a slam-dunk case, and they would question people with the opening line: "The Ramseys say you did it." You don't say that to someone who could possibly be a suspect! When you focus on the Ramseys, you taint whatever you're going to get from other people.'

But the press went with them. It wasn't long before the police leaked the following: there were no footprints in the snow, and no signs of forced entry. **Author's comments:** *No foot prints in the snow, going back to the ransom note and the number of individuals mentioned there, two at the least, three at the most, poses a fact of interest-overlooked by almost everyone. How in God's name could anyone the night of the child's death, enter into her home in the dead of night with snow on the ground all around the house and not leave any form of trace evidence, not even a foot print. It is simply not possible by any standard of practicality; impractical would be an accepted rule of* *thought. No signs of forced entry, further exacerbates the fact that the intruder theory was nothing more than an illusion of thought, having no verifiable significance. If anything, the intruder theory was to serve as a deterrent, especially when the body of JonBenet Ramsey was discovered, the ransom note and the kidnap theory fell through the cracks of nothingness. This state of nothingness was heavily fortified by lies and false innuendoes to hide the real truth about what really went on in the Ramsey house the night their daughter died so brutally.*

The perfection of criminal intent-straight from the notorious mind set of Patsy Ramsey. The ransom note, the intruder theory, and the false/bogus kidnaping, only existed in the minds of John and the late Patsy Ramsey. The guilt of John Ramsey and his wife is so obvious, a little child would not have trouble finding them to be the culprits of the travesty of innocence.

The garrote was an unusual method of strangulation, though one which was common in the Philippines, where John Ramsey had once been stationed at a naval base. **The geography of the house was so complicated you'd have to be extremely familiar with it to know which was JonBenet's room and how to get to the basement.**

Author's comments: *Apparently, someone who was very familiar with the Ramsey home had to perform this dastardly deed of murder and mayhem. Since the ransom note is invalid and the intruder theory made of non-effect, and since it has not been proven beyond reasonable doubt that anyone else other than the Ramsey family was in the house that particular night, the only other possible culprit for JBR's death had to be her mother, and John Ramsey as an accomplice.*

Both John and Patsy Ramsey told police that Burke was not awake when they called 911, but when the tape was analyzed a third voice was heard in the background, and it sounded like Burke. Midway through the afternoon, John Ramsey insisted that he had to catch a plane. The ransom note, with its mysteriously precise sum and in-joke about John Ramsey's 'good southern common sense' (Ramsey was not from the south, Patsy was; that he had a more 'southern' character than she had was a family joke), was so long it was referred to by one FBI profiler as "the War and Peace of ransom notes." Clearly, whoever had written it on the Ramseys' notepaper had no fear of being caught in the act.

Author's comment:*The absence of fear and the fear of being caught for wrong doing, will eventually find you out. If what the Ramsey's did or didn't do that night their daughter was murdered, doesn't come out in the wash, by the grace of God, it will come out in the rinse. Clearly there was no fear of being caught in the act because the ransom note itself was pre-written before the child's death took place. In other words, the ransom note was a premeditated act of correspondence impossible to be written the night of the incident because the note was carefully thought out and planned by a clever minded person. One of the reason being, Patsy Ramsey, the person who wrote the ransom note, had what appeared an extensive background in criminal intent for one thing. And then secondly, the ransom note has continued to baffle some of the best minds to date in criminology.*

Another reason, the writer of the ransom note (Patsy Ramsey) had no fear of being caught was primary because she felt like she was out of or beyond the perimeter of being caught. One would have to admit, that neither Patsy nor John Ramsey were dummies, not by a long shot. They should have been offered employment with the local authorities and perhaps even the FBI. Because of wealth and prestige, they have been able to make ass-rags of them all. And, to add insult to injury, so far, they have gotten away with the senseless murder of innocence. Together, they have made a mockery of some of the smartest people in the world, the American criminal justice system.

Someone said of two children playing, who heard of JonBenet Ramsey and how she was so ruthlessly killed, knew also that the Ramseys were very wealthy people, and up until this point in time had not been prosecuted, said unashamedly, (and the fact that no one had been apprehended for the crime). "See what money can buy you!"

Charlie Brennan arrived to find a macabre scene. Patsy Ramsey's over-the-top Christmas decorations were still in place-red and white striped candy canes dotted along the walkway, white lights around the doorframe, an illuminated Santa in a sled on the snow-strewn front lawn. And all around the house, crime scene investigation tape, investigators' vans and police cars. There was only one other reporter there that night and Brennan thought: 'Where is everyone?' When the body was brought out, he remembers thinking, 'that's the most bizarre name. And I thought: this is going to be an unusual case.'

Eventually, other details emerged which competed with the original picture. Though there was no sign of forced entry, there was that small broken window into the basement that had been left open. Though there were no footprints in the snow, there was no snow on the part of the lawn that would need to be crossed to get in through the window. There was a footprint near the body left by a Hi-Tec boot. There was a latent hand print on the doorframe that didn't match any of the Ramseys'. If you looked closely, there were marks on the child's back and neck that were consistent with the use of a stun gun. The garrote was viciously tightened: would a parent kill their child that way?

Author's comment: *Would a parent kill their child in such a way? "The answer the author think, is yes!" In a fit of rage anything can happen. The rage to kill can reach an apex in a split second and in another split second engender utmost remorse. An insanely jealous Patsy Ramsey in a fit of rage would have no problem at all killing. That same fit of rage could be quite possible in any one, provided one's evil temperament has reached the apex of endurance. The same thing could happen to any one of us, at any given moment absent of incontinency/self control. Insane jealousy and abnormal hatred and malice toward a supposed love one can also be the culprit of outrage and murder so heinous as to what happened to JonBenet.*

The other side of the coin is this, it is extremely hard to believe that anyone other than an overly enraged mother, infused with insane jealously, could kill a little child in such a hideous way, and then try to cover up the psychic monster within her demeaned personality by trying to point the error of her mean-spirited intent in another direction of blame. An unproven intruder theory and the ransom note, a bogus kidnaping are oftentimes the mindset of a deranged person to assuage the error of his or her guilt.

On New Year's Day 1997, Patsy Ramsey went on CNN. 'Hold your babies close,' she said. 'There's a killer out there.' (**author's comment**) *If there is any truth to the statement Patsy Ramsey made, why hadn't the killer struck again? The reason being, the killer is only in the mind of Patsy Ramsey, she herself knows the truth along with John Ramsey. It is a shame that walls cannot talk, and doorknobs are not cameras, "the truth the whole truth and nothing but the truth would be told!" Patsy Ramsey would have died in jail and John Ramsey would be turning out license plates.*

Ten years on, the case is still open. Judith Phillips had known the Ramseys since before they moved to Boulder. They had lived in Atlanta together, Patsy had been a colleague of Judith's then-husband, the two women had been pregnant at the same time. Burke Ramsey and Lindsey Phillips were born a month apart.

Judith brings down a black and white photo she took of Patsy, Burke and JonBenet in the year before the murder. 'It haunts a lot of people,' she says. 'A lot of people have said they see a lot of evil in Patsy's eyes.

Author's comment: *Sometimes the true nature of a person or a person's personality is hard to hide, and add to this scenario in regards to public opinion, the truth oftentimes prevails in the overall sense of things. Guilt or a guilty conscious is also very difficult to hide, it is like that old cliché, "you can fool some of the people some of the time, but you cannot fool all of the people all the time."* She pauses and fiddles with that opinion for a second. 'I'm too close to it, I don't know.

In the photograph, Patsy is wearing a dramatically ruffled cream blouse; Burke is seated on her right; JonBenet is draped over her left shoulder, looking at the camera with hooded, seductive, melancholic eyes. It is the pose of a much older woman, a worn-out temptress, and she is heavily made-up with great sweeps of powder and shadow and dark, fifties eyeliner. Later, when pictures of JonBenet as a miniature prom queen began to circulate in the supermarket tabloids, John Ramsey would say that they had been retouched. Yet here was the black and white truth of how Patsy wanted her children to be seen.

Author's comment: *Here is the black and white truth of the whole matter, had Patsy Ramsey not taken such an overly concern for her daughter looking so grown up and lady like, the chances are she, JBR, would be living today. Patsy Ramsey would not have become an obsessed mother over the fact that her husband was having an affair with their daughter. And the fact that one or both of them had an intimate relationship with the little girl, would only make a bad situation worse, and in all probability, would not have occurred. In the provocative attire and the way in which JBR was dressed, and made to look like a little lady, (a pedophile's delight) was a death sentence neither of the parents anticipated.*

In the year of her death, JonBenet Ramsey had been crowned Little Miss Colorado. She had also been America's Royale Little Miss, National Tiny Miss Beauty, and Colorado State All-Star Kids Cover Girl, among others. In her youth, Patsy had been crowned Miss West Virginia, and so had her sister Pam. A special display case was made to house JonBenet's pageant trophies. Once, when Judith's daughter Lindsey Phillips asked JonBenet about these, she said: 'They're not really mine. They're more my mom's trophies.' JonBenet was dressed in outfits reminiscent of a Vegas showgirl; she wore tiaras and lipstick; her hair was lightened and curled; **she was taught to dance provocatively.** She was an icon of cross-dressing-crossing from girl to woman, from child to plaything.

Author's comment: *A child marked for death: Instances, wherein a little child is dressed in the provocative attire such as this young beauty queen, the avoidance demonic forces of evil are almost always covertly lingering in the background, ready to pounce on this young* *child the moment a fool would lose sight on reality. And such a fool was her father. This is why Patsy hated both of them, even though she may have instigated the sexual attraction between the two of them. And if she could have killed both of them and gotten away with it, she would have done so. Her dress attire was an open invitation to attract a deranged pedophile, including her own daddy. The child's over personal relationship with her father would sanction the outraged jealousy of Patsy Ramsey-her mother. After the rage, Patsy Ramsey's jealousy would eventually turn into a murderous assault on JBR. The author feels that from the very first moment this child was attired to look like a little woman, she would inevitably be marked for death; the result of a pedophile's delight.*

The month after her death, a photographer named Randy Simons, who had been hired by the Ramseys in June 1996 to take photographs of JonBenet in her pageant clothes, sold his JonBenet portfolio to Sygma Photo Agency for $7,500. A year later, he was arrested for walking naked in the street, crying, 'I didn't kill JonBenet!' He was hospitalized, and not considered a suspect. Judith was out of town when the murder took place, which was just as well, she now says, 'because I would have been blamed. They blamed everybody. They blamed Fleet White, their best friend! When we came back to Boulder, nobody was talking to each other-everybody was afraid to discuss anything with anybody. I felt like I was in a Robert Ludlow novel.' Gradually, many of the Ramseys' friends fell away in the swell of suspicion. The Ramseys fought with the Whites at JonBenet's funeral; the Whites urged the governor to appoint an independent prosecutor.

Author's comment: *In the midst of things, the blame game seems to always point away from the real culprits, apparently the Ramseys blamed everyone but themselves for the death of JonBenet. For all that the Ramseys cared, President Bush (though Bush was not president at the time) or President Clinton could have killed the child, as long as the evidence did not point to them. John Ramsey wanted a fall guy so much after his wife died, (to take away the suspicion of being a pedophile) John Mark Karr could have taken the rap for all he cared.*

And, it appeared he was willing to allow Karr to go to jail for the murder of his daughter, when he knew from jump street that John Mark Karr was no where near the Ramsey home the night JonBenet was killed. John Ramsey did not voice an out right opinion of whether or not Mr. Karr was guilty. But down in the deep recesses of his heart, and in his exterior mannerisms, the camera could visibly show how emotional he was that someone other than him and his deceased wife would take the rap for the murder of JonBenet Ramsey. As fate would have it, all of his hopes and expectations again fell through the cracks, when the authorities found out that John Mark Karr was innocent, because his DNA did not match.

For John Ramsey, it was back to the drawing board in search for another stoolie, because he knew in his heart that his dead wife had premeditatedly killed their daughter. Should the authorities find two or three more persons who could fit the bill, even remotely close to someone who could be proven guilty, John Ramsey, here again, knew in his heart who killed his daughter.

'It's a sickening, sickening, sickening thing!' Doc Miller starts to shout. 'That little girl was murdered. And billions of dollars have been spent covering up her murder, unfortunately, by the press. You're as guilty as that woman if you print the goddam intruder theory. You're just taking more blood out of her. You'll come out of here with blood on your hands, Gaby!'

One of the most immediately striking aspects of the Ramsey investigation was the dispute that broke out between the police department and the DA's office. The police detectives were led by Steve Thomas, who believed that Patsy had accidentally killed JonBenet in a bedwetting incident, and that the Ramseys had then staged it to look like a murder.

Author's comment: *The premeditated murder of JonBenet Ramsey was no accident, and the belief that her mother killed her for bed wetting is highly unbelievable as is the intruder theory and the ransom note, as well as the bogus kidnap theory. The death of innocence was planned and orchestrated and carried out by a very clever person, who* *was well aware of the Ramsey home and well aware of every thing that went on in that house, the night and the morning of her death. The Ramseys did not have to stage the incident to look like a murder, "because that is exactly what it was—-a murder!"*

This murder was the un-amiable and the unenviable results of jealousy and hate. An accident would have been less violent than what happened to this young child in her parents house, the night her life had so tragically ended. The author believes that if JonBenet's death was an accident, the parents, the real culprits of the child's demise, should have come clean with the authorities and made a true assertion of their guilt. From the way this little girl was bludgeoned, choked with a garrote, hands tied, dragged, and not to mention sexually assaulted, it is virtually impossible to say that her death was an accident.

The DA's office called out of retirement a legendary investigator from Colorado Springs, who had solved over 200 homicide cases: Lou Smit. Smit believed the Ramseys were innocent, that an intruder had entered the house and lain in wait in a nearby bedroom. He could be found, Smit thought, if DNA evidence was carefully considered. Foreign DNA was found under JonBenet's fingernails: 'I think she got a piece of her killer,' Smit said.

Two weeks after the murder, the results of a DNA test came back to the police. A drop of JonBenet's blood found in her underpants was mixed with the DNA of a Caucasian male, and no member of the Ramsey family was a match. It was six months before that report reached the DA's office. In August 1998, Steve Thomas resigned from the police department over the way the Ramsey case had been handled. In September 1998, Lou Smit resigned from the DA's office on the same grounds.

In 1999, just before the grand jury was about to be sworn in, the internationally recognized forensic expert Henry Lee was brought in. Yes, he suggested, the DNA in the underpants was not the Ramseys', but who was to say it was the murderer's? It could have been left there at any time, from the point of manufacture onwards.

Author's comment: *It is very feasible to say that the Ramseys would have exercised a bit of stupidity had their own blood DNA had been found on their daughter's underwear. Whoever the foreign DNA belonged to, they certainly had to put it there. If it had been left there from the manufacturer on, it should have been noticed during the washing cycles, if her underwear was not brand new. Like the ransom note, the bogus intruder theory, and a false kidnaping, the blood spot on JonBenet's panties could have been placed there by the Ramseys to further undermine the investigation. It certainly appears to be a strong probability.*

All of the latter points ever so discreetly to the same fact of interest, the killing of JonBenet Ramsey was planned at least several days before her death. It would have been virtually impossible for the so-called intruders/kidnappers to have found everything he/they needed to write a ransom note, the strangulation materials, plant bogus evidence all in one night in the dark, not knowing the floor plan or even how to successfully maneuver themselves in the Ramsey home. Only persons familiar with the home could remotely attempt the latter. No child could have planned such an elaborate crime scene with all these little intricacies, certainty not Burke Ramsey. The DNA may not have been the Ramseys but the Ramseys (the murderers of innocence) certainly placing it there is also a strong probability.

"The grand jury voted not to indict the Ramseys. At this point, for the prosecutors, the case was over-it was, as Grant realized early on, an 'unprosecutable case." **Author's comment:** *The author would have to beg the differ in all due regard, the only case that is unprosecutable, is a case that never took place, or an incident of prosecution that never happened. Favoritism sometimes plays a big role in whether or not some criminal cases are prosecuted or not. In Boulder Colorado, the Ramseys are among the elite in the socialite circle and are well thought of as people of wealth who have in their hands the pulse of the community. For law enforcement to prosecute the Ramseys* *would be tantamount to putting Jesus in jail. Now ask yourself, how eminent or how likely is that happening?*

Prestige, wealth, and notoriety has its place in life, but these same criterias seem to run amuck with some people. John and Patsy Ramsey just happen to be in that elite class. It alone has been the primary point of interest that has kept them out of jail. Because JonBenet had been sexually molested which in turn borders on pedophilia, immoral sexual behavior at best, and because of the way society supports the same, John Ramsey has a lot of that same nature of immorality supporting him. Under these circumstances, how can he lose.

No one may ever questioned how the Ramseys were able to escape prosecution, but one thing stands out very clear and resonant, the Ramseys had the grand jury, the prosecution, and the whole town of Boulder, Colorado in their back pocket. The way things went on after the death of innocence, it was as if John and Patsy owned the entire town, including control over the Boulder police department. They did what they wanted to do, whenever they wanted to do it, however they wanted to do it and with whomever they wanted to do it with. It was as if the Ramseys were a deck of cards. "They had all the aces, and the deuces were wild." In all of the author's 61 years of life, I have never seen the likes of this murder case wherein two people have not only gotten away with the adulterated murder of a little child, but have managed to rape an entire town of its decency and respectability by controlling the entire constituency. They were not worrried in the least about going to jail for the crime of voluntary manslaughter. Why? **Boulder was and still is, in their back pocket.**

Judge Dismisses the Case:
Federal Judge: 'No Evidence' That Ramseys Killed JonBenet
Judge dismisses a defamation suit against Ramseys, suggests intruder may have slain their daughter

R. Robin McDonald
Fulton County Daily Report - April 7, 2003
Atlanta attorney L. Lin Wood Jr.image: Catherine Lovett/Fulton County Daily Report

Through the prism of a defamation suit, a federal judge (Julie E. Carnes) in Atlanta has examined the 1996 murder case of 6-year old Boulder, Colorado beauty queen, JonBenét Ramsey, a talented young aspiring star of stage and screen, determined on July 7, 2003 made a decision suggesting that there is "hardly any or enough evidence" to support theories that John and Patsy Ramsey had anything to do with the death and the murder of JBR.

U.S. District Judge Julie E. Carnes, being a former federal prosecutor herself, made a decision that there is "substantial evidence" to support the accusations by the young child's parents, John and Patricia Patsy Ramsey, "that an intruder entered their home at some point and time during the evening/night of Dec. 25, 1996, and killed JonBenet Ramsey in stark cold blood." An assertion of innocence the author just doesn't agree with.

Judge Julie Carnes made a decision the writer thinks was not based on sound, unequivocal unbiased and rational judgment. And, because of her biased and irrational decision, she has allowed the persons responsible for the death of innocence to go free and unchallenged for the error of their aberrant and murderous behavior. The fact that the Ramseys said that an intruder entered their home and killed their daughter is nothing but unsubstantiated lies and false unprincipled innuendoes.

And, this writer would stand on a stack of Bibles, if it were possible, and say unequivocally that this judge was wrong and did not give attention to thoroughly examine the ransom note, and the intruder theory to properly give judgment to the fact that the home of the Ramseys was never intruded upon by any alien source other than the immediate family. For this judge to agree with the intruder theory, which is a proven fact by the author that such never existed/occurred before or after the death of JonBenet, is surely an act of bad judgment. Her decision to set the Ramseys free, to let them off the hoof, was based solely and entirely on an opinion associated with her fondness towards the Ramseys and not the truth. And, here again the truth substantiated by proof is that the Ramsey home was never at any time compromised by an alien source. Especially not by at least two or three persons so mentioned in the fictitious ransom note. "And, this is the truth, the whole truth, and nothing but the truth, so help us God!"

Judge Julie Carnes also lists a series of largely uncontested facts that suggest an intruder entered the Ramsey home and murdered JonBenet. Among them:

Note: all these things can be positively refuted by the writer in the proof positive and without the slightest of doubt, "God being my Judge."

PROOF OF AN INTRUDER: · At least seven windows and a door in the Ramsey home were found open or unlocked after JonBenét disappeared. The alarm was off and windows were accessible from the ground level, including three that opened into the basement. *Fact: JonBenet never disappeared, her dead body was found in the basement where Patsy Ramsey dragged it earlier the night before. Fact: It's just not practical to have windows open when its ten degrees outside, that's cold, especially seven windows. Also the cost of heating oil, no matter how wealthy some people are, here again, having windows otherwise deliberately open is for the most part, impractical.*

It must have been cold in that basement before the body was discovered by John Ramsey with three windows open leading to the basement. No mention was made about how cold it was in the basement, especially when the temperature was somewhere around the ten degree mark out-side the home, and with snow on the ground.

When the child's body was found, the report was that rigor mortis had already set in. With at least three windows open leading to the base-ment, it should have been freezing there, but the basement was just as warm as any other part of the home because rigor mortis sets in quicker in warmth than it would in cold. Those windows had to have been open after the child's body was discovered or not long after the ransom note was found, or they were never open at all, which means that the information the judge got were all lies.

How ironic it is that the alarm just happened to be off, when reports of break-ins were taking place in and around the entire community. These latter innuendoes appear to be all lies with the primary intent to dispel any idea that the Ramseys had anything to do with JonBenet's death, and to convince the judge of the same. These impractical innuendoes, though not convincing enough to the author, were more than convincing enough to Judge Carnes. She set them free to momentarily rejoice over the fact that they, planned, plotted and killed their daughter and got away with it.· **Evidence suggested that an intruder climbed through a basement window and walked through the room where JonBenet was found.** *Fact: Coming from the outside, where snow/ice and dampness blanketed the ground, the fact that there were several persons mentioned in the ransom note, why wasn't there ample footprints found in the home? "Did the intruder/intruders clean up after themselves?" "The author doesn't think so." Fact: If an intruder/intruders entered the Ramsey home through the basement window, then they would have to go up at least two flights of stairs to get JonBenet's room, which was on the second floor, excluding the basement.*

Fact: According to the ransom note, it made mention of possibly three people compromising the Ramsey home. It would again be virtually impossible for one to three persons to enter the home through a small basement window, go up several flights of stairs to the second floor, molest, strangle, garrote this child, come back down two flights of stairs to the basement with this dead child, and the only evidence that they had been in the home were token items, a shoe here, a bat there. Anyone could have placed these items where they could be easily found. After all, the Ramseys had a big Christmas party the week before the murder. But there was no real profound tangible-verifiable evidence like the same shoe/footprints all over the carpeted area of the home, leading to JonBenet's room to truly prove that quite possibly three persons could have killed this child. Does not make any sense in the least. Neither could the Ramseys prove with any degree of probability the latter falls within the perimeters of the truth.

For anyone to believe this concocted lie (an intruder entered the house) is just as gullible as those who show unreasonable compassion for the Ramseys and even the Ramseys themselves are just as guilty of gullibility to think that sensible people would ever believe a lie or lies of this caliber. Now, what a sensible person would believe is that these token items of an intruder were convincingly placed where they could be convincingly found and believed.

The truth of the whole matter is, "none of these things ever happened because the ransom note once again is a lie, the intruder theory is a lie, and for purpose of further truth, the kidnap theory is a lie, Judge Carnes!" Fact: JonBenet's room was not in the basement, for an intruder to get to her room, he had to know where her room was, not practical in a complicated floor plan of the likes of the Ramsey's home.

As far as the spider web is concerned outside the window, spiders cannot live in ten degree weather, therefore the spider web outside the basement window was undisturbed and had been there for quite sometime. Which also means that no intruder passed that way relative to a break-in. These token innuendoes of evidence had to have been placed there for the same previous reason to take away the guilt of murder from JonBenet's parents. Judge Carnes bit the bait, hook, line, and sinker. She may not know it, because she did not consider the facts in its entirety concerning this awful murder mystery. And, by dismissing the case against the Ramseys, she may have become unknowingly an accomplice in the death of innocence, not by criminal intent, but by sympathetic apathy. She based her final decision on the supposition that an intruder entered the house and killed the Ramseys little beauty queen.

The word intruder in the singular means one, the ransom note mentions at least three persons, "the writer of the ransom note, and the two men who have your daughter," adds up to three persons in anybody's mathematics, and leaves no doubt in the mind of the author, provided the ransom note was actual truth, which it wasn't, that only one intruder entered the home, killed the star of innocence without leaving any worthwhile evidence that they had been there. Here again, the bottom line is nothing but lies on top of lies, which Judge Carnes overwhelmingly fell for.

Based on the truth factor, the home of the Ramseys was never, again and its worth repeating, invaded or compromised by persons contained in a fictitious ransom note. "Because the persons of the ransom note never existed, and that's the God's heaven truth!" The author, not being a duly licensed person of law, could readily see the fallacy of the ransom note including the unproven-unsubstantiated intruder theory. Judge Carnes should have been able to do the same.

Since she is a better trained person of law than the author. Sometimes in a murder mystery of this caliber, common sense makes a good advocate of the truth in edification. Good common sense ethics goes a long way to arrive at the truth of some issues in life. A PhD is not to be weighed against good common sense at any time, according to the author, relative to a highly complex issue of seemingly unsolvable situations.

· JonBenét's body was bound with complicated rope slip-knots and a garrote that the order described as "sophisticated bondage devices" by someone "with an expertise in bondage." No evidence suggests the Ramseys knew how to tie such knots. (1) *John Bennett Ramsey: A distinguished naval officer, he holds a pilot's license and owns two planes. (2) In 1989, late in his military career, he formed the Advanced Product Group, one of three companies that merged to become Access Graphics. After mandatory military retirement, he became president and chief executive officer of Access Graphics, a computer services company and a subsidiary of Lockheed Martin. (3) In 1996, Access Graphics grossed over $1 billion, and he was named "Entrepreneur of the Year" by the Boulder Chamber of Commerce.*

"No evidence suggests the Ramseys knew how to tie such knots." *The author being a former United State Navy Petty Officer (enlisted person) very much would like to beg the differ on this statement. One requirement for being associated as naval personnel is being able to tie various and different knots. And, learning how to tie intricate knots, such as a slip knot, is one of the perquisites to learning how to perform in sea worthiness endeavors. At one time or another all Navy personnel, enlisted or officers, had to learn how to tie various kinds of knots in conjunction with other duties pertaining to rope maneuverings. A slip knot is the most common knot to tie in the United States Navy.*

So, therefore, John Ramsey knew how to tie a slip knot, or he had an acquaintance with someone who did . He may claim that he had forgotten, but at one time or another, in his naval military career, he had some knowledge about the intricacies to tying a slip knot in conjunction with various other knot tying skills. The author might also conclude with this statement of fact: it is very hard and inappropriate to be U S Navy Military Issue and not have some experience with tying knots. Judge Carnes, more in depth research would have found that out before arriving at such a drastic decision to let the Ramseys off the hook.

· **Black duct tape found on JonBenet's mouth was never found in the Ramsey home, although evidence suggested "it came from a roll of tape that had been used before."** *Finding the black duct tape may have been a simple oversight in the middle of everything else going on. The duct tape may have had on it incriminating evidence, such as finger prints, DNA etc., that would certainly have pointed to who the killer/killers were. The use of duct tape has a great tendency to leave sticky incriminating evidence. There could also be any number of reasons the duct tape was not found. The finding of duct tape could also have been the last thing on the minds of those who were trying to get to the bottom of this murder mystery.*

The author feels that not finding the black duct tape should not have been a perquisite for dismissing the case against John and Patsy Ramsey. "They simply did not want to be caught in a sticky situation, Judge Carnes!" How ironic the duct tape was never found, but just about everything else used to slay this child remained at the crime scene. Also, the duct tape came from another source other than the Ramsey's home, and could have revealed the source from which it came, not meaning that another source had anything with the death of innocence, but could have told where the Ramseys got it from, dispelling the intruder theory, possibly shedding light on them as the real culprits of JonBenet's death. Since no intruder has been proven to have occupied the Ramsey home the night of JBR's death, the duct tape had to have come from the Ramseys and discarded because of its revealing evidence towards the Ramsey. Without a doubt the lost duct tape had to belong to the Ramseys, not an intruder.. Or else the tape should have been found somewhere in the home. The Ramseys managed very skillfully to discard the tape, perhaps early in the morning of the incident itself.

There are other reasons that they were avoiding any chances of being caught in a sticky situation. They had everything well planned and fixated to the exactness of confounded intent. Even today, there are those who are still trying to figure out what happened in the Ramsey household the night of the grotesque murder of JonBenet Ramsey. Because of divine intervention, the truth is finally coming to light, and John Ramsey will soon be going to jail for his part in the travesty and the death of innocence.

Now the other side of the coin is this, if they felt the duct tape would help to vindicate them, why wasn't it left in the house like the other evidence found at the crime scene? Answer, they did not want to take any chances on the duct tape possibly incriminating them. The response to some of these intricate details, if one wants to call them that, and the fact that thus far no one is held accountable for JBR's death, most assuredly says that this child's demise was preplanned and a premeditated act on her life, long before the murder incident happened. And to the author, all the preplanned intricacies points to the mother and the father of the dead child. But one thing is for sure, this plot of murder and mayhem was not, the author repeats, this plot of murder and mayhem was not an overnight thing. It is virtually impossible for this incident to have been planned and plotted in one night.

The Coin Has Many Faces: *The entire crime scene was meticulously and painstakingly set up by the Ramseys. It takes a lot of planning to almost criminal proof a murder mystery and the travesty of innocence. Its no telling how long the Ramseys had planned on killing this child. There is a strong possibility that the Ramseys started out on their sinful escapade when JonBenet started participating in beauty pageants. But, they had no knowledge or even the remotest idea, it (the beauty pageants) would turn out to be a situation of death, jealousy, and child molestation.*

John Ramsey said on national television, that when his wife was diagnose with ovarian cancer, it was her desire to spend more time with her daughter who had not yet started participating in beauty pageants. In 1993, the same year that Patsy Ramsey had developed ovarian cancer, according to John Ramsey, they started entering JonBenet in beauty pageants. In light of all this Patricia Ramsey knew that she did not have long to live; and it is for this reason they, together, decided to enter their daughter into pageant competition. These thoughts were before any remote inkling came to pass to kill their daughter

Things that possibly triggered the Ramseys to kill their daughter:
1. The beauty pageants: Something went terribly wrong on the way to the forum. John Ramsey's suggested idea of a beauty pageant was the straw that would eventually break the camel's back. The works of incest and the lewdness of pedophile behavior became an uncontrollable urge to sink further into a world of sin and adulterated mayhem. The decision to enter their daughter into highly acclaimed beauty pageants arose out of the announcement of Patsy Ramsey's ovarian cancer episode. They made their little daughter into a pedophile's afternoon delight, even unto her own father, and quite possibly, her own mother.

2. Her inability to perform her wifely duties: When Patsy learned of her ovarian cancer, it triggered a lot of mechanisms in her family. One was that she was no longer able to perform with genuineness her wifely duties with her husband. And, she did not want John to go to someone else for sexual fulfillment. Her feminine instinct told her that her husband appeared to exemplify a pedophile arousement whenever he saw little JonBenet in her provocative clothing. She allowed John Ramsey to assist her in dressing and undressing this little child. And, in doing so, another problem was created. Intimacy began to come into play that created such jealousy in Patsy until this little child was no longer the envy of her heart. The fact that she was also dying of ovarian cancer did not make the situation any better, in fact it made the situation worse.

3. JonBenet became a victim of circumstance-a sexual play toy: In JonBenet's autopsy, this little child had been sexually molested. The proof is in the pudding. Why would someone take an object and literally rupture her virginal area, if they were not trying to destroy evi-

dence that would have proven she was having regular sex with someone, who was more than likely her daddy. Fact: The Ramseys adored this child so much, it is highly improbable that they would allow anyone other than themselves to remotely get that close to their daughter. One day she would grow up and tell the truth about what her parents had done to her, another reason and point of inference why she was marked for death.

4. The fact that Patsy's life was limited to death-jealousy of JBR crept in: No one in his or her right mind would relish the likely hood/the possibility of death and by the same token, no woman in her right mind could appreciate to any degree the fact that her husband is having regular or routine sex with her daughter, no matter what her sickness might be. Sooner or later the dam will burst, especially if it has a hole in it. Patsy Ramsey had taken all she could take, and her greatest desire was to see this child dead, especially now that ovarian cancer would soon take her life. As a result of this devastating news something inside of her triggered the dark side of her demeanor that only death and mayhem could satisfy.

5. Patsy Ramsey encouraged John Ramsey to molest JonBenet: Because she knew she was going to die. She could not stand to leave both of them alive to continue their sexual escapades. If JonBenet was dead, it would leave only John Ramsey to deal with. And she also knew that someone would come along and find out the truth. John Ramsey would either end up on death row or he would spend the rest of his natural born life in prison. John Ramsey did not have the sense to figure out what his wife was doing. She would get rid of two birds using one stone, the uneventful death of JBR would also lead to the eventual imprisonment or the execution of her husband, giving her the peace of mind she sought in death via her ovarian cancer.

6. The ovarian cancer went into unexpected remission: Is probably why she didn't take a gun and kill them both before the remission occurred. She thought that her ovarian cancer was gone for good, and still her hatred for JonBenet would be accomplished in the child's death. Someone had to remain behind to take care of the surviving children. Here is how the entire situation came to fruition. First the ovarian cancer, and with it, the Dr.'s report of his terminal diagnosis. Then the beauty pageants followed, suggestive of John Ramsey to ease the burdensome stress that Patsy Ramsey, his wife was now encountering. From this point, the author believes that dressing and perhaps helping to undress the little beauty queen created the uneventful/unethical situation of pedophilia, and then came death and the travesty of innocence.

·**Nothing in the Ramsey home matched dark animal hairs found on the duct tape and JonBenét's hands.** *The author believes that the animal hairs found on the duct tape was purposely placed there by the Ramseys to further augment the intruder theory as a way of misleading the criminal investigation by authorities in association with the crime scene. This was a very smart move on the part of the Ramseys, it succeeded in throwing the entire investigation off tract. And, it has been that way for almost ten years. "Shame on you America."*

The only way the duct tape could have gotten in the home is that the Ramseys brought it into the home for the same purpose in serving as a decoy to mislead the investigation. The duct tape is also part of the humongous lie about the intruder theory which also was a lie simply because there was no intrusion into the Ramsey household by anyone other than the Ramseys themselves. Animal hairs and the duct tape itself is not a proven fact of probable cause that validates any intruders/intruder had compromised the home of JonBenet. Black duct tape with brown dog hairs on it only says that this murder scene was carefully planned and orchestrated by John and Patsy Ramsey long before the actual incident ever took place. Which only says again, "JonBenet Ramsey was marked for death!" And, that's the God's heaven truth, Judge Carnes.

Judge Carnes, by now, you should understand that Patsy Ramsey is no joke when it comes to altering the crime scene to make it look as though intruders had entered her home and killed JBR in cold blood. Patsy Ramsey knew she was going to die from the ovarian cancer even before it reoccurred, it was only a matter of time, even if it was in remission almost ten years. Because of her ovarian cancer which was also diagnosed to be terminal, she did not want to leave this world knowing that her husband and her daughter engaged in sexual concupiscence. The very thought of dying and these two engaging in a life of molestation and sexual bliss was so disturbing until she could not think of dying and leaving these two behind to carry on this escapade of sexual indulgence.

· **Newly made, unidentified shoe prints, including one with a HI-TEC brand mark, were found on the basement floor. None of the Ramseys' shoes matched those prints.** *One of the reasons Judge Carnes, the Ramseys didn't get any sleep the night before (evidenced by Patsy Ramsey having on the same clothes) is because they were so busy setting up the crime scene in a specific order so that the evidence itself would seem as though an intruder had entered their home and committed the murder of JonBenet. And, to add insult to injury, they seemed to have put forth a very convincing effort to even fool you, Judge.*

Here's something else for you to think about Your Honor, since when did wealthy people start wearing the same clothes two days in a row, if they were not preoccupied with something else more important than changing clothes? It is simply unheard of among the rich and the famous. The other side of the coin is this. They could have been wearing outer garments to cover their other dress wear. Which makes a lot of sense, if one is going to be involved in a murder situation and falsifying a deadly crime scene. Maybe this is why John Ramsey had to leave the house early that morning to discard unwarranted evidence.

Now, if these same shoe prints were found by going back and forth to the young child's room, the author would have more than a little reason to believe this report. This alone would been have convincing enough to the writer that the Ramsey's home had been truly compromised and broken into. Proven evidence says that there were no intruder/intruders in the home that night the murder took place.

The shoe prints should have been reflective of at least two to three persons given to the so-called intruders being in the home. Also, these same shoe prints should have been traceable to the upstairs bedroom of JonBenet, especially when snow and ice was on the ground outside the home. Judge Carnes, it is highly unlikely that intruders entered this home under these sordid conditions and only left token traces of evidence that they were there. Judge Carnes, here again, it doesn't make much sense at all. This is the way they planned it, "given to the acrimonious mindset of Patsy Ramsey!" And, the sad part of it all, Judge, Patsy had very little and perhaps no trouble at all convincing you of pre-positioned falsified evidence.

· **A palm print on the wine-cellar door where JonBenet's body was found does not match the Ramseys' palm prints and has never been identified.** *Judge Carnes, in the absence of sound judgment, the writer would have given you more credit than that, the people who were in and out of the house, one palm print is not enough or justifiable evidence to allow the Ramseys to slip off the hook. Neither is one palm print convincing enough to say an intruder was part of a crime scene where-in death had recently occurred. An unidentifiable palm print can only mean that the palm print itself had to have been tampered with by someone more than likely proving it for identification purposes. A mistake that could have easily taken place.*

· **A baseball bat found outside the house with fibers consistent with fibers found on the carpet in the basement where JonBenét's body was found did not belong to the Ramseys.** *So then, Judge Carnes, you are attributing a baseball bat as being part of the evidence suggesting that an intruder compromised the home of the Ramseys, when no intruder has actually been proven to be inside the Ramsey home. Only lets the author know most assuredly that Patsy Ramsey, in her attempt to hide evidence, that she and her husband had nothing to do with the death of JonBenet; exacerbates the fact that this tragic incident, in conjunction with all the other pre-planted paraphernalia, serves to suggest an intruder (who never existed before-during-or after the death of innocence) entered the home and killed this beautiful child. The fact that none of theses things belonged to the Ramseys was more than enough for Judge Carnes to dismiss the case against them.*

Why was these fibers only found on the baseball bat and on the carpet in the basement where the child's body was found, when in actuality, these same fibers should have been found throughout the crime scene?

They were not found throughout the crime scene because the Ramseys were on a failed mission to prove they had nothing to do with their daughter's death. They also knew that the investigation would be compromised by these token innuendoes.

· **Brown cotton fibers found on JonBenet's body, the paintbrush used as a garrote, the duct tape and the ligature around her neck did not match anything in the Ramsey home.** *These things did not have to match anything in the house because they had to have been meticulously placed there, since the Ramsey home had not been intruded upon. Common sense would suggest that even to this point and time, no intruder or the intruder theory is or has been proven to have actually taken place, only points to the Ramseys as being conspirators in their own deviant plan to evade any possible incrimination connecting them with the death of JonBenet. Real intruders would not have left all this evidence behind unless they wanted to get caught; or someone or somebody wanted to make it seem like the home had been entered into by an alien source in association with intruders. Smart thinking on the part of John and Patsy Ramsey to try and hide the fact that they were responsible for the death and the murder of the travesty of innocence.*

· **Male DNA found under JonBenet's fingernails and in her underwear does not match that of any Ramsey and has not been identified yet.** All the evidence so far-only suggest that an intruder/intruders violated the Ramsey home; since this time the author has proven beyond reasonable doubt that the Ransom note failed the reality test, the intruder theory failed the reality test, and the kidnap theory failed the reality test, and once again, it is now a proven fact of interest none of these incidents ever took place at any time before, during or after the death of innocence. This question of interest comes to mind after all these innuendoes have now been proven to be false and non existent, <u>"where did the DNA come from Judge Carnes?"</u>

· **A pubic hair found on the blanket covering JonBenet's body did not match that of any Ramsey.** *Only proves that someone or somebody was close enough to the child to leave "a" meaning one, pubic* *hair on the blanket used to cover the dead victim. Talking about sense and sensibility; is there no end to the uncompromising madness associated with this travesty of innocence; or what a criminal mind will do to avoid being held liable for the life of an innocent child?*

The killer deliberately left one-just one mind you-pubic hair on a blanket to deliberately alter the course of the investigation, to hopefully take the pressure off of the Ramseys and their having anything to do with JBR's murder. One pubic hair could have come from someone at the Christmas party the Ramseys held the week earlier. One thing is for sure, it did not come from an intruder; because there was no intruder or intruders in the Ramsey home at no time prior to or after the death of innocence.

· Injuries found on the child's body are consistent with the use of a stun gun, according to a forensic pathologist. The Ramseys swore they had never owned or operated a stun gun and none was found in their home. Carnes cited testimony by A. Louis "Lou" Smit, a homicide detective originally hired by the Boulder Police Department to investigate JonBenét's death but who later began working for the Ramseys. Smit has said he believes JonBenet was subdued by a stun gun.

The use of a stun gun to subdue the young child was a supposition of Lou Smit and not an actual occurrence. Only Lou Smit came up with the idea that a stun gun could have possibly been used in JonBenet's death. The truth is, Lou Smit only in the theoretical sense suggested the latter in a failed effort to avoid the fact that the Ramsey's had anything or nothing to do with their daughter's death. There were numerous other investigations regarding the death of innocence, none of them to recollection of the author made any mention of the use of a stun gun. Question? If a stun gun was used according to Lou Smit's theory, why was there nearly a seven inch gash in the child's skull? A blow to the head of that caliber has to suggest several things: 1. A stun gun was obviously never used on the child, if she was already dead from the blow to her skull. The use of a stun gun doesn't make much sense, Mr. Smit should have known this. He was too preoccupied in trying to find evidence of innocence to keep the Ramseys out of jail. Fact: The use of a stun gun to subdue the child was only a supposition of Lou Smit and never a proven possibility. 2. This child was only six-years old and less than fifty inches in height, "the use of a stun gun makes it seem like this child was a full grown person with the strength to match, how blatantly ironic!" If a stun gun was haphazardly used to subdue the child, why didn't other forensic evaluations come to the same conclusion?

The reason being, no stun gun was used on the child at any time before or after her death. Surely, at least three grown people according to the ransom note, could have easily subdued this little child without the use of a stun gun. And if the intruders used a stun gun, what was the reason of fracturing the child's skull? One strong fist to the child's head would have easily knocked her out, the rest would have been as easy as taking candy from a baby.

· Injuries found on the child's body are consistent with the use of a stun gun, according to a forensic pathologist. The marks found on the child's body may have been consistent with the object that was used to rupture this little girl's vagina. *This child was more than likely subdued by asphyxiation by the garrote or death was inflicted by an awful blow to the head. And, if the so-called intruder/intruders were men, it is unlikely that they would need a stun gun to subdue one little six year old child. Now, on the other hand, it is highly conceivable that the Ramseys would use a stun gun theory, to reflect on a given moment suggesting that their home was indeed compromised by an alien source. A ploy by Lou Smit to get John and Patsy Ramsey from under the umbrella of suspicion, according to Judge Carnes was good enough to convince her.*

A. Louis "Lou" Smit, a homicide detective and originally hired by the Boulder Police Department to investigate JonBenét's death but who later began working for the Ramseys. Somehow detective Smit must think that most of us are stupid or just plain ole naïve. The Ramseys were well known to be wealthy upstanding people. There is no way on God's green earth Lou Smit hired by the Ramseys to investigate the murder of JonBenet, would be looking for evidence to convict them. On the contrary, he would most assuredly be looking for evidence to set them free, even if he had to stumble upon evidence that made them culpable of this heinous crime. To the writer, it is ludicrous to bite the hand that's feeding you. So then, Lou Smit was bound by a financial agreement to work on the behalf of the Ramseys irregardless of the negative evidence he would come upon, Judge Carnes.

Carnes reserved special criticism for Thomas, the former Boulder detective upon whose theories the Wolf complaint was based. "Whereas Detective Smit's summary testimony concerning the investigation is based on evidence, Detective Thomas' theories appear to lack substantial evidentiary support," she wrote. *Detective Smit's testimony, Judge Carnes, was based on false evidence. Judge Carnes, evidence of any nature must be based on the truth. And the truth is, none of these theories eluding to someone other than the Ramseys were in the home the night death came and took little JonBenet. All the evidence found in the Ramsey home, the author can now say with confidence, was contrived and is unrealistic in its truth, eluding to an outside source breaking into their home. Judge Carnes, Steve Thomas may not have said the right things to please and convince you, but his concept of thought eluding to one thing in general, the Ramseys were indeed responsible for the death of innocence and now it is proven via the means of precept and example.*

The precept is the murder, the example is the proof behind the murder. Everything said so far Judge, seems to support the fact that your ruling was purposely designed to support the Ramseys, and not the dead child. Your judgment concerning this case never appeared to be coming from an objective point of view, even from the beginning. It also appeared from jump street that you were indeed partial towards the Ramseys, the result of this is, it was not a burden of thought on your part to set them free.

There is simply no real evidence pointing to or convincing enough to say an intruder/intruders killed the little princess. When time and time again, Judge Carnes, this writer has proven any so-called intruder or intruders never existed to any degree of reality."The intruder theory, the ransom note, the kidnaping were all lies, Judge. Surely you can see that by now."

There is no substantial or proven evidence that goes beyond reasonable doubt which says in essence, the Ramsey home was criminalize by an alien source other than the owners of the home. And surely, it has not been proven to the contrary that anyone other than the Ramseys themselves KILLED THIS CHILD,"your honor!"

"Indeed, while Detective Smit is an experienced and respected homicide detective, Detective Thomas had no investigative experience concerning homicide cases prior to this case. In short, the plaintiff's evidence that the [Ramseys] killed their daughter and covered up their crime is based on little more than the fact that defendants were present in the house during the murder," Carnes wrote:

It is also a proven fact that the Ramseys were the only ones in the home the night of their daughter's death. Judge, to your lack of culpable knowledge concerning a serious and profound act of murder, and your inability to discern between the truth and a lie, meaning falsified evidence in conjunction with the ransom note, the intruder theory, and the kidnaping theory, leaves you on the outside looking in with no reasonable consciousness to seek the truth; and not your personal opinion towards Mr. Thomas (in an effort to justify your decision) who is only trying to resolve one of the most heinous crimes of this century. Your response to this murder investigation shows clearly a partiality for the Ramseys and not so much for the truth, and the issues involved in arriving at the truth. Nor a concerted effort in an attempt to get at the truth. Your thought processes said emphatically that the Ramseys were innocent, and nothing else to the contrary mattered.

For all intensive purposes, your primary intent of rationale, it appears to the writer, was solely to set the Ramseys free. And that is exactly what you did by lambasting Mr. Thomas and glorifying Mr. Lou Smit. A real judge endowed in a serious conscious effort to seek the truth would not have done that. Experience plays a vital role in detective work, in this effort the author must agree, but good common sense is an attribute well worth considering also.

Judge Carnes, my name is Rev. John Henry Walker, I am a licensed-ordained minister of the gospel of Jesus Christ. I am also one semester from receiving a Bachelor of Theology Degree from the Shaw University School of Divinity, in Raleigh, North Carolina, where I majored in Theology and Ministry. Judge Carnes, the latter statement is to bluntly say that I have never had any formal training in detective work or basic criminology, but what I do have is a divine degree in basic common sense ethics, something that you seem to show little compassion for or knowledge of. By the grace of God, the author has been able to prove without a doubt that the Ramseys (and absolutely no one else) are indeed the culprits behind the travesty and the death of innocence. So, where does that leave the author in your assessment of one's ability to differentiate between the truth and a lie, Judge? Subscribe to Fulton County Daily Report

Continuation of: Getting away with murder. But the public battles continued. Steve Thomas wrote a book that laid the blame squarely on Patsy, and the Ramseys wrote a book listing other suspects. Both came out in 2000. The Ramseys sued Thomas, and settled. That year, Chris Wolf, one of the suspects listed in the Ramseys' book, sued them for defamation. But, in order to prove his own innocence, he had to prove Patsy's guilt. In dismissing the case, federal judge Julie Carnes said that the evidence presented in that civil case suggested an intruder was more likely to have committed the crime than Patsy. In the Ramsey camp, it was widely thought this meant they had been cleared.

'This was not a staging,' Tracey says, pulling a photograph of JonBenet's neck out of his envelope. 'This was a vicious attack. There's no question in my mind now that someone came in who kind of knew them, who got off on little girls, extremely violent. She was asphyxiated-that begins to explain why there's no blood in the head-and he's getting off on this. I think they wanted to play with her. I think it was a very sick game by a very sick person.'

JonBenet's death gripped America, Tracey suggests, because it had everything going for it: 'Sex, sleaze, the rich father, the

American dream gone bad... It was a combination of voyeurism, resentment, anger, irrationality, a cultural viciousness. It was Greek-a lot of people focused on it as a kind of catharsis.'

Where is the catharsis, I ask, if the case is unsolved? 'It's in the hate. Hate the Ramseys, you feel better. This was pretty close to a conspiracy.' When Tracey pulled the image out of the manila envelope, I thought it was one I had already seen-a close-up of JonBenet's neck, designed to show the garrotte and the marks thought to have been made by a stun gun. But I noticed Tracey only pulled half the picture out of the envelope.

The photographs I had seen were not close-ups but crops of this one. On instinct, I reached for the photo and pulled it out a little further. JonBenet's face came into view. She was lying down, and shot in profile. Her mouth was slightly open, her eyes were closed. If the photo had been in black and white, so that her skin's bluish tinge was invisible, you might have thought that she was merely asleep-until your eyes were drawn down to the fine blonde hair trapped under the cord with which she had been strangled. I looked at this photograph only briefly; in an unforeseeable split second I felt suddenly, swimmingly sick. Tracey's voice became background noise. Come on, I told myself, you're not squeamish. But back she came, the seemingly sleeping child. I started to sweat.

The sign on Frank Coffman's door reads: 'The Crypt. Ring twice for best results.' Coffman makes horror masks for a living. He lives a few blocks away from the Ramseys' old house, and first became interested in the case because he lived nearby. Ten years ago, he was a regular Columbo, bumbling around, discovering where the cord and duct tape had been bought, befriending every nanny and cleaning person who had ever worked for the Ramseys. He has photographs and floor plans of the house. He has samples of Patsy's handwriting. 'A lot of people thought I had a kind of encyclopedic knowledge of the case,' he says, on the phone.

Later, as he leads me into his apartment, Coffman tells me he likes murder mysteries. 'I like books about the Lindbergh case, things like that. I know everything about the Kennedy assassination-that's pretty obvious really, when you look at the evidence. The Ramsey case has a lot of curlicues-it's still puzzling, even if you think you know who did it.'

I came back to my hotel and left a message for Lou Smit. I've tried him through the DA's office for months without success, but now I have a number for his home in Colorado Springs and, although it's late, I can't get out of my mind the idea that so much of this hangs on him, which ever way you look at it.

If some of Smit's former colleagues are to be believed, he was swayed by his own religious convictions into believing the Ramseys were innocent. District Attorney Alex Hunter later said Smit got too close. Bob Grant, who had worked with Smit on a number of difficult homicide cases in Colorado Springs, says that in the Ramsey case people thought Lou was set up. The first time he met the Ramseys, there was some kind of prayer group or something, and Lou's a very religious man. He got more so during his employment in Boulder. Patsy asked him to pray with them at the house-it felt natural to Lou. It should not have. I'm not saying it colored his objectivity, but it certainly lends itself to that appearance.' **Author's comment:** *There is an awful strange awe about the Ramsey's and their persuasive personalities with others, who come into their immediate surroundings.*

Every now and then, people come along who, without the slightest bit of effort, exudes a strong air of like ability. In some instances, this kind of liability can cloud honest and sincere judgment when one has to access critical issues concerning very likable people. Most of the time when you like someone, it is very hard to find wrong in them, the situation of thought triples, when it concerns persons of the same spiritual beliefs.

The moment Lou Smit engaged the likeability of the Ramseys, he should have dismissed himself from the case immediately, because when you like someone, and your personal feelings enter in, sometimes it is hard to look for guilt in that individual/individuals. Lou Smit started this case from jump street with his mind already made up. In an instance such as this, the guilty party almost always comes out of a situation like unto the Ramseys-clean as a whistle. His objectivity was more than colored, his objectivity was never objectivity in the first place. He fell under the awesome spell of the Ramsey's charming and mesmerizing but devilish personalities, just like everyone else who had an immediate attachment to the case.

On the other hand, here was a man who had solved over 200 homicide cases, while the detectives in Boulder had not even investigated one. By the time he was called out of retirement to work on it, the evidence gathered was not as he would have wanted it. He told Michael Tracey, for instance, that had he been the first detective on the scene, he would have brought a dog in, which would have found the body in 30 seconds; he would have separated the Ramseys, asked them to come down to the station to give hair samples and blood samples; he would have taken their clothes and conducted initial interviews. Had they refused, he told Tracey, he would have arrested them. This from the man who believes most strongly in their innocence: an arrest would at least have given them the chance to clear their names.

Author's comment: In the aftermath of Lou Smit's thoughtful gestures, hindsight has little or no validity after the fact, even though sense and sensibility pervades the air of reasonable rationale. If the Ramseys were not guilty, why didn't they authorize a full and thorough investigation of the crime scene, just like Lou Smit suggested, instead everything relative to the immediate death of their daughter was in a mode like unto, quick, fast and in a hurry! One can only think that due to the fact that the latter did not take place, the air apparent appears that they had something to hide. Again, had this been the case (a full investigation) in regards to the death of innocence, and the Ramseys were innocent, the world would have gotten a reasonable portion or some small degree of the truth; their guilt apparently kept this from happening, even non-experienced policemen were on the scene. Once more, they should have suggested that the latter be done, if nothing more than to clear their names.

The author agrees with Lou Smit in several areas, the course he suggested that should have been taken from jump street, would have been a highly sensible thing to do; but as everyone can see, this was not done. Could money and the fact that they were wealthy people, and people about town, could have prevented this from taking place? Any reasonable and rational person would more than likely agree with the author.

There was another detail. In 1996, the year of JonBenet's death, Smit had solved one of Colorado's most puzzling crimes, the kidnap and murder of a 13-year-old girl called Heather Church. The trail had gone cold, Smit had been brought in and he'd solved the case on the basis of a latent fingerprint submitted to the FBI-years after the crime had taken place. Now he was suggesting that the Ramsey case could still be solved, 10 years on, using DNA evidence. Maybe he knew something others didn't.

Author's comment: Even though the magnitude of this child's death and her murder, the use of DNA of the amount discovered in this case is not always a panacea/cure all towards getting at the truth. In some instances, just some instances mind you, token DNA, a spot here and a spot there lacking more positive culpable evidence has to be ruled out. The DNA discovered at the scene of the murder was simply not enough evident to warrant the Ramseys escape from prosecution. It should have been disallowed because it had no exculpatory value, or in other words, this small but minute degree of DNA was not enough positive evidence to set the Ramseys free..

Last year, Patsy's cancer recurred so aggressively that it was assumed she would die. Smit drove up to Michigan to visit her. Tracey speculates: 'I think he went to see her just in case.' In case of a confession? I asked. But why? He's on their side. 'No,' said Tracey, 'he's on the side of JonBenet. Now, does Lou Smit think the Ramseys killed JonBenet? No. But, would he just... a final... you know, just in case? Sure. That's how good he is.' In the letter of resignation he sent to Alex Hunter in September 1998, Smit wrote: 'Shoes, shoes, the victim's shoes, who will stand in the victim's shoes?'

Author's comment: In his old age, Lou Smit seems to have a problem trying to decide who he really wanted to represent, the parents whom he said he felt were not guilty, or the murdered child, little JonBenet Ramsey. Apparently, he cannot do both, stand up for the mother and the father, and at the same time walk in the shoes of the travesty of innocence. The person who walks in the shoes of innocence cannot be a friend to the mother and the father of this little child at simultaneous moments. If the case were so, the truth can never be arrived at.

Again, the author feels, it is simply impossible to represent this little child and the parents at the same time. It just can't happen. It's one or the other, but not both. The person who walks in the shoes of innocence must be a person of deep spiritual belief and one who is deeply concerned about this child's spirit being laid to rest once and for all and the party responsible for her death brought to the bar of justice. "Only then will her spirit rest in peace." In this penmanship, the author feels justice for this little child has finally come to fruition.

Ollie Gray and John San Augustin were hired by John and Patsy Ramsey in 1999. When the Ramseys ran out of money to pay them, the private I's kept going. But it's hard. They needed the police to co-operate, and now that the police files have been handed over to the DA's office, they need the DA to co-operate. **Author's comment:** *The author thinks that it's a crying shame to impede justice that would place the killer of innocence behind bars, namely her father John Ramsey, since the real culprit of her death is dead, Patsy Ramsey, her mother. First, the police were not cooperating since the case is in the hands of the DA, now they are not cooperating. One thought comes to mind, Why? What is one or some of the reasons law enforcement is not cooperating?*

1. Money-the wealth of the Ramseys
2. The pre-innocence of the Ramseys
3. Notoriety of the Ramseys
4. Secret payoffs
5. Contributions to Boulder Colorado
6. Affinity to the Ramseys, the whole town is in love with John and the late Patsy Ramsey.

'If they had put as much energy into investigating the crime itself as they did in trying to persecute the Ramseys, this thing would already have been put to bed,' says Ollie Gray. 'I'll bet you a nice steak dinner and a good bottle of wine that they have a bunch of evidence they have never processed. I think they have reports that basically prove that the Ramseys are innocent.'

On my last morning in Colorado, I go to meet Bill Wise, Alex Hunter's former deputy district attorney, at his home. His big white husky greets me at the door. Wise tells me that he was taken off the case for complaining about the police department's incompetence. I ask him why he thinks Smit has always believed in the Ramseys' innocence. 'I don't know,' he says, taking a deep drag on his cigarette. 'It would be because he is a much better investigator than me, and he sees things I don't see. He's a hell of an investigator. And if you can get a match anytime-murder has no statute of limitations...with all these databases that have been put together, there's a pretty good chance that DNA's gonna turn up sometime. [3]

The Astrology of JonBenet Ramsey:

The murder of the six-year-old JonBenet Ramsey is a conundrum/confusing state of affairs. Many theories have been brought forward to explain the murder of the young beauty queen in her parents' house on Christmas Night 1996. Indeed the case is still open and still no one knows the identity of the murderer(s).

Lois Rodden's wonderful site, AstroData News, provides birth information for JonBenet, which allows us to speculate on the motives and execution of the crime for which there is no firm case. Indeed Rodden notes sites for virtually any possibly murderer: her father, her mother, her father and mother together, her older brother, a family friend, or the police.

Her Biography:

The daughter of a charming socialite and ex-beauty queen herself, Patricia Ann Paugh (born 12/29/1956 in Parkersburg, WV) and wealthy businessman John Bennett Ramsey (born 12/07/1943, Lincoln, NE), JonBenet had an older brother, Burke (born 1/27/1987,

Marietta, GA) and two older half-siblings, John Andrew (who lived at the Ramsey home) and Melinda. They were both out of town on the night of the murder. The family lived in a 15-room Tudor style home in Boulder, Colorado.

Called "America's Tiny Little Miss," the adorable child was a six-year-old beauty and talent contest winner, dressed in sophisticated costumes and able to model like a pro.

On Christmas night, 1996, she went to bed cheerfully. Sometime before dawn, JonBenet was killed; her skull fractured; she had been sexually molested and strangled with a cord. Duct tape was put over her mouth, and **her body was dragged downstairs** to a small room in the basement.

Author's comments: If the child's body was dragged downstairs, more than likely from JonBenet's room to the basement was at least two flights of stairs, which means, it would be a humongous task for a sickly woman diagnosed with terminal ovarian cancer. Question; why would someone drag her body downstairs to the basement? 1. Did the person who took her life not have enough strength to carry the dead child down the stairs? A man more than likely would have carried JonBenet down the stairs, no problem whatsoever. But it appears that a sickly person, a woman or a child might have a problem doing it. So more than likely, it was a woman or a child who dragged her downstairs. A child is ruled out because young Burke Ramsey has been officially cleared of any involvement in his sister's death. A primary reason for the latter, the author feels is because no child could have planned such an elaborate cover-up. A child, simply put, does not have the possession of that kind of mindset.

2. John Ramsey the father of the dead child, would not have had the slightest problem of picking his daughter up and carrying her to the basement. Reason being, when he retrieved her from the place where she was found in the basement, he picked her up without hesitation and carried her upstairs, no problem whatsoever.

3. If the body appeared to have been dragged to the basement, this would also invalidate the intruder theory, because the intruder (s) appeared to be men. Quote, "the two men who have your daughter!" It is highly unlikely that two men would drag the child's body and carefully place it in a well secluded spot in the basement, of which they were highly unfamiliar with, truly lacks the probability of sense and sensibility. The dragging of the body would surely appear to be the working of a woman, and the fact that the child's hands were above her head, sheds more light on such a possible happenstance.

She was wrapped in a blanket with her feet taped together, her head uncovered and her arms above her head. **Author's comment:** *The child's hands above her head adds further proof that she was more than likely dead as she was dragged to the basement by her mother, the deceased Patsy Ramsey. Patsy Ramsey in all probability told John Ramsey what she had done after she dragged the child's body to the basement. This is when John Ramsey found out that his little child, his beloved daughter, was dead. It was at this moment when John Ramsey became an accomplice to his daughter's murder, a presupposition.*

It was also at this moment when Patsy Ramsey placed a gag order on her husband, the reason being she knew he had been having sex with her. Which also caused her to go into a jealous rage, so much so, that she would take the life of her own daughter. 4. Question, why would an intruder (s) kill the child and hide her body in a secluded area in the basement, when it appears that the object of the intrusion was to kill the child, period, if there was an actual intruder or intruders? Since the ransom note was invalid and an intruder supposedly killed JBR, and apparently there was no so-called kidnapping, why didn't the intruder (s) just simply leave the body of the young child where the ransom note was found, seeing that at the time the ransom note was found, the child was already dead? This was not possible because the intruder theory and the ransom note would have been a direct outright lie. The Ramseys would have been also directly culpable for the death of JonBenet from jump street even.

And it is a verifiable fact that the child was already dead. The only worth while purpose the ransom note would serve was to lead the au-

thorities away from the Ramseys. Apparently this little scheme by John and Patsy Ramsey has been so successful to the point of deception until ten years after JonBenet's death, no one has been prosecuted for her murder, and that's a travesty of innocence.

Shame on America, shame on Boulder, Colorado, shame on the FBI, and shame on the United States judicial system. Shame on America for not crying out bloody murder, shame on Boulder, Colorado for deliberately botching the crime scene, and for having a love affair with the Ramseys to the point of allowing her killers, John and Patsy Ramsey, to get away with murder. Shame on the FBI for allowing the murder of this little girl to go unsolved, especially when her body was moved to another state. Shame on the judicial system for not declaring the death of JonBenet Ramsey a federal offense, subject to a federal investigation by an impartial investigative network, because her murder went beyond the lines of debarkation, automatically making her death a federal judiciary criminal offense/felony.

When her mom checked the household early the following morning, she found that JonBenet was not in her room. Patsy Ramsey called the police **at 5:22 AM,** shouting "Send help!" and saying that her daughter was missing and that a 3-page ransom note demanding $118,000 had been left by the kidnapper (s) on the steps of the back stairs leading to the kitchen.

The note read, "Dear Mr. Ramsey, **We have your daughter!** *Author's comment: We have your daughter is a statement of fact acting in the plural sense denoting more than one person. This statement alone invalidates Lou Smits intruder, meaning one person theory. Even a little child who has any concept of the English language will understand the plurality of we-meaning more than one person. Lou Smit was so conscious of getting the Ramseys off the hook, that he completely overlooked the we, stated in the ransom note. Why? Is it because he knew from being an acclaimed investigative detective, if he remotely said intruders instead of intruder, he would have placed the Ramseys at great risk of legitimizing-making real the false ransom note, when in fact the ransom note was not worth the paper it was written on?*

In other words the Ramseys would have to prove the random note to be real and legitimate. Lou Smit knew in his heart they could not do that because even he was walking on thin ice when it came to the intruder theory. He knew he was not a Mother Teresa, a person of great faith, or a magician or, even for that matter, a miracle worker who could wave a magic wand or pray a special prayer and make all the Ramseys situations of involvement in their daughter's "death just go away!"

And, it would be even harder to prove that there was more than one person in the home of the Ramseys the night JBR was so brutally murdered. And, also knowing how hard it was to prove that even one person/intruder was in the Ramsey home that same hellacious night death stalked the residence would have placed his investigation in dire jeopardy. So he stuck to his single person intruder theory.

Another point of inference *relative to the ransom note and more than one person being involved: the third paragraph mid way it reads: "you can try to deceive **us** but be warned **we** are familiar with law enforcement counter measures and tactics." Here again the ransom note eludes to the plurality of persons associated with the note itself. The words us and we relative to the ransom note and the intruder/kidnap of Jonbenet Ramsey speaks again in the plural. The statement in and of itself places a further damper on Mr. Smit's single person intruder theory.*

We-first person plural, and US-third person plural, both denotes more than one person, once again further dismissing Lou Smit's single person intruder theory. "Which again makes the ransom note and the intruder theory invalid altogether."

This (single person intruder theory) would allow the Ramseys to breathe with a sigh of relief, looking for one person/intruder took most of the attention off of them. And, the spotlight would have had to have been placed on the Ramseys if he widened his search to expand beyond more than one intruder. If this had been the case, Lou Smit would have had to start his search for the culprits with the two of them, but he took them off of the suspect list because he became very partial towards them by way of fellow shipping with the Ramseys. Under these circumstances, it would have been impossible to find guilt in the Ramseys.

From jump street Lou Smit felt like the Ramseys were not involved in their little child's death, which automatically placed his investigation in jeopardy had he found information contrary to the Ramsey's innocence. If his sole purpose was to find out the truth, perhaps he would not have overlooked the "We" have your daughter in the ransom note. Instead of looking for one culprit, he would have been looking for at lease two people, according to the ransom note. Or perhaps he should have parted with partially and set his sight on finding out the truth, "this, he did not do."

It was printed in block letters and had neat margins. It also made reference to a Navy air base in the Philippines where John Ramsey had served. Four misspellings in the note appeared to be intentional.

The case remained in the media for the following four years, with apparently no solid evidence to lead to the killer. The child's parents were the focal point of investigations, both of them leading suspects of the police investigation. The ransom note was from paper belonging to the Ramseys and fiber found on the duct tape used to bind the child was consistent with that found on Patsy's clothing. The small amounts of evidence were basically circumstantial and not enough to bring charges. Though the ransom note was similar to Patsy's writing, it could not be definitively proven.

The case was tried and the Ramseys lynched and damned by the media and the public. Whether or not the case is ever solved, their lives have moved from one hell to another. Week after week, JonBenet's exquisite features were pictured in the tabloids until the public began to cry "Enough! Let that poor child go." Six months after the murder, Patsy, John and Burke moved to a home in the Atlanta area to try to mend their lives.

The police arrived at 5:35 AM and made a brief search of the house. Two hours later, a detective arrived, and FBI agents came in at 10:30 AM. It was not until 1:00 PM that someone thought to look in the basement and John Ramsey discovered his daughter's body. He removed the tape from her mouth and carried her upstairs. She laid on the floor beside the Christmas tree until 10:45 that night, when the coroner's staff took the body to the police morgue. When John Ramsey found JonBenet at 1:05 PM, her body was completely set with rigor mortis, which indicates that she had died between 10:00 PM on December 25 and 6:00 AM on December 26.

Author's comments: *Rigor mortis* is one of the recognizable signs of death (Latin *mors, mortis*) that is caused by a chemical change in the muscles after death, causing the limbs of the corpse to become stiff (Latin *rigor*) and difficult to move or manipulate. **Assuming mild temperatures, rigor usually sets in about 3-4 hours after clinical death** [*citation needed*], with full rigor being in effect at about 12 hours, and eventually subsiding to relaxation at about 72 hours. Times for the onset of rigor mortis can vary from a few minutes to several hours depending on the ambient temperature. Factors influencing rigor mortis include the age and condition of the body, as well as the mode of death and the surroundings. For example, rigor mortis will tend to set in faster in those who were active immediately prior to death.

After looking at the time factors, the latter only substantiates the fact that the child was already dead at the time her mother found the ransom note. Looking at the real sense of logic, and the child was no longer alive, proves again the worthlessness of a bogus ransom note and the fact that again it was not worth the paper it was written on. Further declaring that the person who found the ransom note, is more than likely the culprit behind JBR's death, undoubtedly the mother, Patsy Ramsey. The child's body being completely set with rigor mortis, makes it unmistakably clear that once she was laid in the basement, sometime between 10:00 PM on December 25, and 6:00AM on December 26, the child's body was never moved again, because of rigor mortis, which means no intruder (s) and no valid ransom note.

According to the kidnap theory, had the dead child been taken outside the residence of her home, in 10-degree weather, there is a strong possibility according to clinical analysis, rigor mortis would not have set in as quickly as it did. These factors further accentuates the reasonable premise of truth further alluding to the fact that JonBenet Ramsey upon her unfortunate demise never left the confines of her home at any time prior to or after she was killed. In plain simple logic, JonBonet Ramsey was never kidnapped by any stretch of the word/imagination according to the ransom note. The only time this child left the premises of her home after her death, was the next evening when she was taken to the morgue. Therefore, the ransom note had to be written by someone in that house, either the night of the killing of innocence or sometime prior to her death.

Fact: Because it has been proven without the slightest of doubt, barring the token evidence found around the crime scene, that there was no one else other than the immediate Ramsey family in that house that night the beauty queen died, the only other resolve of conclusiveness is to say, someone in that house that very night killed JonBonet Ramsey. Whoever wrote the ransom note murdered this child. And, only two people fit the category, the culprits, John and Patsy Ramsey. The direct person of choice and guilt is the deceased Patsy Ramsey, accompanied by John Ramsey her husband.

The police committed devastating errors immediately following the crime, so grievous that some critics said. "It was as if the police were attempting to do everything possible to handicap the prosecution." They irrevocably disrupted the crime scene by allowing John Ramsey to pick up his daughter's body and carry it upstairs to cover it with a blanket. A cord attached to a wooden handle was wrapped around her neck. DNA evidence was contaminated and as well, the Ramseys were not immediately and separately interviewed.

Author's comments: *One of the primary reasons the murder of JonBenet Ramsey has not been solved or brought to a meaningful conclusion is because the partiality of the people of Boulder, Colorado towards John and Patsy Ramsey. The people associated with law* *enforcement in Boulder could have solved this murder mystery the very same day it occurred, if premeditated blunders such as those above were not willingly given to the Ramsey's unproven innocence. It is also fair to say that those who were responsible for these humongous blunders are just as much responsible for JonBenet's death as the person (s) who did it. The author believes that the spirit of JonBenet Ramsey cries out from her grave, demanding that justice be given her, "so she can finally and at last, rest in peace."*

Patsy Ramsey, former beauty queen herself, began to enter her child in pageants when she was five, donning elaborate costumes and sophisticated makeup. The quantity of glamour shots of the little girl, some as provocative as those of an adult model, helped to fuel public interest in the case.

On 10/13/1999 a Boulder grand jury wrapped up a 13-month inquiry during which it had examined 30,000 pages of testimony and evidence, bringing the $2 million investigation to an inconclusive finish. They were no further toward solving the murder than on that shocking day after Christmas three years before.

Author's comment: *There are a few words of interest relative to the previous statement, that is simply stunned, stupefied and set at naught, that the death of JonBenet Ramsey has not fully awakened the consciousness of a nation of people who find it almost impossible to solve the murder and the death of one little child who loved life just as much as any of us living today. Ten years into the travesty of innocence and no one has remotely been brought to justice or made to give an account of this senseless act of murder. Another reason the author feels this case is taking so long in solving, is because the compassion for the parents of JonBenet is greater than the compassion for the child herself or else this case would have been solved long before now, how sad! But nevertheless the window of closure the author feels is drawing closer by the moment and soon the headlines will read "Killers of JonBenet Ramsey Finally Apprehended."*

The Ramsey's memoir, "The Death of Innocence," went on sale 3/17/2000, the same day that they began a string of TV appearances objecting to their persecution in the media as being the killers of their daughter.

A. T. Mann's Astrological Take on the Case:

My astrological system uniquely includes the gestation period, and in JonBenet's case, the father and mother were in opposition (Sun opposite Moon) from the beginning about JonBenet. Originally wanted by her father (after whom she was named), her mother took over her beauty career, using the little one as a surrogate of her own unfulfilled ambitions.

The directed Moon squares the Mars/Pluto opposition at the time of the murder, and the transiting Moon activates her Venus(beauty)/Saturn(jealousy) opposition, all of which show me that her mother was responsible for the murder itself, and that her father assisted in the clumsy cover-up. In this sense, both parents are guilty of her murder. [iv]

The First Concourse-A Supposition

A Theory of Relevance: Perfect murder, perfect town is a challenge to one's inability to comprehend the essence factor of truth as a least common denominator to any situation thought to be improbable. And the improbability of perfection is sometimes given to vagueness subject to eminent ambiguity. There is no such thing as a perfect crime, whether it be murder or otherwise. Any criminal situation or element of contrariness, (to the law establishment that is) always falls short of perfection. Which is to say, it is impossible for the criminal element to cover all of his tracks to the detriment of human discovery. This also include the murderers who killed little JonBenet Ramsey in the youthfulness of her innocence. If criminal perfection were possible, it would undoubtedly escape the awareness of God, to remotely imagine such a precept, the writer feels very well might be grounds for spiritual contempt.

A perfect town, if such were ever the case, serves only to infatuate the minds limited finiteness to apprehend the truth. And the latter is evidenced in the failure of all parties concerned to apprehend those who are responsible for the tragic demise of this innocent little child. Boulder Colorado, just happens to be the place situated in one of the greatest murder mysteries to come to pass in this time frame augmenting the advent of the 21st Century. Though, it may appear that Boulder Colorado, seen in the eyes of others, has perfected that town's inability to capture those responsible for JonBenet's death, the town is by no means wholly responsive to the criminal apprehension of the culprits liable in this case. If the case were so, the killers of this darling little girl would have been apprehended a long time ago, but as it stands now, such is not the case. The writer would be remiss, should there be any form of discrimination or covert innuendoes on the part of the people and the law to find and apprehend the guilty party or parties.

It is felt for this reason, the criminal mind or the criminal element always makes at least one mistake. In the case of the JonBenet tragedy, the criminal element involved in this senseless murder, has made one fatal mistake, peradventure there be three mistakes they should have been consciously aware of:

(1) They overlooked the overwhelming impact/bogus intent of the ransom note.
(2) The text-the manner in which the ransom note was written speaks to Patsy Ramsey.
(3) She was a remarkable young lady: Her personality preceded her in death.

(1) They overlooked the overwhelming impact/false intent of the ransom note: the most important piece of evidence in the case. In the space of a very little time, the ransom note will tell who the criminals are without the slightest of doubt. Its going to take a little time and a lot of effort on the part of the author to get to the bottom of the death of innocence, but rest assured, the truth of this murder mystery will come to pass.

The Ransom note will shed so much light on the child's killers until a little child will believe this report, and they, too, will find the parents culpable for the travesty of innocence. All that the writer would ask, is, that the reader comprehend this report with an open and not a closed mind.

The author has gone through the ransom note with a fine tooth comb, and will go through the ransom note again with a fine tooth comb until the truth is revealed in point blank clarity those who are responsible for the death and the travesty of innocence. Not only that, the author will prove time and time again the incredible fallacy of this bogus ransom note. The writer will also bring the reader to an undeniable point of conclusion proving without a doubt the Ramseys, John and Patsy Ramsey, are the sole respondents contributing to this horrible despicable death of an innocence child, their daughter, JonBenet Ramsey.

(2) The text-the Manner in which the ransom note was written speaks to Patsy Ramsey. After listening to her voice and her personal demeanor on various interviews, it was not hard for the author to relate her voice to the hand writing in a verbal sense contained in the ransom. The personality of Patsy Ramsey in her hand writing was all over that ransom note in every respect and in easily discernable thought detail capturing her very mind set. Especially when she used her husband's name in the context of John. Patsy Ramsey, in the tv interviews, and various news reports, the author was able to see, never once called her husband honey or darling, always John, the same use of the word John is captured in the ransom note, "don't try to grow a brain, John." The expression and the use of the name John in the ransom note conveyed a very close relationship with the person in question without a doubt. Who knew John Ramsey better than his wife, Patsy Ramsey.

There are several points of interest that needs be taken into consideration concerning an individuals handwriting. Handwriting captures the nature of an individual's true person. For example, if one wanted to know something about a person or an individuals personality, one have but to read a little of that persons handwriting to create a self image captured in a certain thought pattern. Which is to say, no two people think or write alike.

There is something distinctive in the way communicative skills in hand writing hooks up with a person's true personality. Most of the time, a person talks the way he or she writes, or writes the way he or she talks. Oftentimes, there is a direct correlation in ones handwriting and the verbal manner in which a person relates to his or her environment in the verbal sense.

Or more simply put, a person writes like in most instances, he or she talks, and talks like he or she writes. Now the ransom note found in the Ramseys home may have been written by several persons, and more in the feminine sense, even if it was dictated, the note would have to convey the thought perception of the person doing the dictating.

And/or if the note was mechanically written, the same thought pattern would prevail. Now of course, the latter statement is based on some form of acquaintance with both the individual's handwriting and obviously listening to the same individual speak, or speech equivalency. Had the criminal element not written a ransom note, they may have escaped the possibility of capture. Now, some say the ransom note was perhaps written by several different people is all the more evident that the death of JonBonet was planned and orchestrated by someone very close to her.

A Transcribe Version of the Ransom Note: Page 1.

Listen carefully! We are a group of individuals that represent a small foreign fraction. We do respect your business but not the country that it serves. At this time...we have your daughter in our possession. She is safe and unharmed and if you want her to see 1997, you must follow our request to the letter.

You will withdraw $118, 000.00 from your account. $100,000 will be in $100 bills and the remaining $18,000 in $20 bills. Make sure that you bring an adequate size attache to the bank. When you get home you will put the money in a brown paper bag. I will call you between 8 and 10 a.m. tomorrow to instruct you on delivery. The delivery will be exhausting so I advise you to be rested. If we monitor you getting the money early, we might call you early to arrange an earlier delivery of the money and hence a earlier pick up of your daughter.

A Transcribe Version of the Ransom Note: Page 2.

Any deviation of my instructions will result in the immediate execution of your daughter. You will also be denied of her remains for proper burial. The two gentlemen watching over your daughter do not particularly like you, so I advise you not to provoke them. Speaking to anyone about your situation, such as Police, F.B.I., etc., will result in your daughter being beheaded. If we catch you talking to a stray dog, she dies. If you alert bank authorities, she dies. If the money is in any way marked or tampered with, she dies. We will scan for electronic devices, and if any are found, she dies. You can try to deceive us but be warned that we are familiar with Law enforcement countermeasures and tactics. You stand a 99% chance of killing your daughter if you try to out smart us. Follow our instructions

A Transcribe Version of the Ransom Note: Page 3.

and you stand a 100% chance of getting her back. You and your family are under constant scrutiny as well as the authorities. Don't try to grow a brain John. You are not the only fat cat around..so don't think that killing will be difficult. Use the good southern common sense of your. It is up to you now John!

Victory!
S.B.T.C.

The Credibility, Believability of JonBenet: Amounts to the public's perception of JonBenet's ability to speak and relate to the circumstances surrounding her young life, relative to those things she approved or disapproved of. One of the motives, if not the primary motive, that perpetrated her death, was vested in her ability to convey herself in an audible sense. The criminal element in this instance failed to comprehend the thought pattern of those who could instantly see that JonBenet's personality was of the sort which easily made her a standout in the eyes of the public.

The perceptive mind set of this young child credits her with a personality which would make things she say very believable. The writers overall view of JonBenet's personality depicted in the various news clips of her leads one to believe that this young child was incapable of lying or fabricating a lie primarily because she looked so innocent. Therefore the believability of anything she had to say only adds to her innocence, and, secondly, the believability of JonBenet in serious contemplation is because she looked and acted very mature for a six-year-old.

Motive Behind Her Death: The motive for the death of JonBenet is contingent upon several scenarios, of the which are presuppositions in context: **(1) The Believability of Accusations:** It is suspect by the writer's intuition that one of the motives for young JonBenet's death is given to the believability of her testimony against her parents in whom she was apparently getting ready to spill the beans on. This young child was engaging in behavior of a sexual nature, of the which she apparently did not like or she was becoming fed up with.

Therefore, she must have alerted her parents to that fact; and it is a point blank fact that the child was molested, whether or not by her parents or someone else, the bottom line point of interest is, someone had sexual encounter or encounters with JonBenet against her will. And the only people to whom a finger can be pointed, are and were her parents.

The proof is evidenced in the vaginal area, because the nature of her innocence had been compromised. JonBenet Ramsey spent a great deal of time with her parents from the apparent show of participation in various pageantries and other programs that seem to be of particular interest to the parents more so than JonBenet. From the various costumes this little child wore, so provocative in appearance, is apparent to the author that she needed assistance from her parents to put them on, opening Pandora's box to various degrees of sexual infatuations that lead to child molestation. Some of the costumes JonBenet wore had to be with the help of her mother and her father.

(2) The Possible Pedophile Nature of Her Parents: The way the parents paraded this young child around in skimpy clad bathing suits, even for a six year old, proved to be to the parents lack of genuine concern for their daughter and her youthful innocence. Which may have lead to JonBenet's parents sexual infatuation toward her in so much that it would be cause for alarm in her physique, coming to pass as a direct result of child molestation and the possible pedophile nature of her parents. A preconceived psychological overview of parental behavior when a child becomes a status symbol (with sexual overtones) at the tender age of six years old, oftentimes is the cause for the development of a pedophile nature in parents who were before innocent.

Most people are unaware that one of the most powerful forces in existence is sex and sexuality. Sex and sexuality has no age barrier, and is not given to race, color, or national origin. It does not discriminate, although some might beg the differ. It has no preset premise of conduct. It does not care who, what or how it infects ones personality. Sex and sexuality is not concerned with how it is placated on in society, therefore sex and sexuality (given to a misunderstanding or lack of knowledge) can be the cause for many dysfunctional physical and psychological behaviors in people of all ages. Parents in relationship to their children are not at all exempt.

The thing that most people should understand in regards to one of the most powerful forces known to exist which is sex and sexuality is no play toy. Sexuality of any type should be handled and experienced with extreme utmost caution. Otherwise, the repercussions can be detrimental in every aspect of human behavior-mind, body, and spirit. Parents, of all people, need to exercise restraint and caution in the social, moral, and spiritual upbringing of a child. The reason stands to be, the caution flag in the family of the Ramseys should have gone up a long time before JonBenet's death.

Because medical examinations showed the child was sexually molested, not by an intruder, but by someone who was constantly in the home of JonBenet. And because autopsy reports were incomplete, suggestive of the parents, it is then reasonably fair to assume that John and Patsy Ramsey are most likely the culprits contributing to JonBenet's sexual molestation. Now, because the ransom note, the intruder theory and the kidnapping contains no credible accusations at all, but primarily meant to be a deceptive point of interest, non-reflective of the Ramseys involvement in their daughters death, serves only as an elusion to mislead the authorities.

The hurry up burial of the child (avoiding complete medical examinations) also suggest that she was perhaps molested more than once, but not in the same night or at the same time, but indeed on varying occasions. There were only two people close enough to JonBenet, to have committed such heinous acts of sexual molestation, those two people were her mother and her father!

Reasons of Deception: If the Ramseys, John and Patsy, are not guilty of child molestation, but are indeed innocent of any wrong doings, why didn't they allow a complete thorough medical examination of the child's body to continue until all who were concerned were satisfied to the fullest extent? A complete thorough medical examination, had John and Patsy Ramsey insisted, (not finding fault with them) would have also exonerated John and Patsy Ramsey from any false incrimination. Here again, this was not the case, nor a point of inference. But there is one point of inference totally undeniable by any sense of the truth, the child was indeed sexually assaulted and molested, how many times? Only John and Patsy Ramsey can answer that question.

One more motive for her death, there is a strong pretense that they killed her to keep her from talking and perhaps some day revealing the truth behind the pedophile-demoralizing behavior of her parents. In some instances, as has been said before, when parents becomes sexually involved with their children, there is a strong tendency later on down the road, the parents can become dominated and controlled by their own child. The other side of the coin is this, the Ramseys were certainly not going to allow this to happen by any extent of reality.

Traditional parents in this sense are the ones who spend a great deal of time relating to their children as they enter into the corridors of growth and hormonal development, constantly aware of incontinency and the steadfast necessity of self control. Non traditional parents allow themselves to be caught in the vice of promiscuousness not having or processing self control or incontinence over their emotional and sexual desires. If parents are not careful when exposing a child in the manner of Jon Benet, unwarranted self indulgence can lead to pedophile behavior.

There is a very thin line between sexual emotions of a parent and those of a child, when the constant element of close encounters are a common occurrence. From the apparent look of things, the parents assumed the responsibility of dressing and undressing Jon Benet during her various engagements. It is also apparent that they dressed the young child so that her appearance was not only appealing to the young child's audience, but she was so dressed by her parents so that her appearance was especially appealing to John and Patsy Ramsey, too. Had they not preserved those moments of their child's sensuous youthful unfolding, the public would not know that they made such a display of their daughter's appearance. To a pedophile, she appeared to be an afternoon delight. They made her look like a young woman when she was only six years old. So appealing was JonBonet's appearance to her parents that love turned to lust, lust to infatuation, infatuation to sexual arousement, sexual arousement to sexual molestation, sexual molestation to the travesty of innocence.

The Point of No Return: Long before the Ramseys allowed their nature to get carried away, unlike little JonBonet, they had numerous opportunities to seek help, when the first aroused inkling for their daughter came to bare on their consciousness. They had a choice whether or not to seek help. And in their failure to seek help, they became actively indulged in their sexual fantasies with JonBenet until they had allowed themselves to reach a point of no return.

The decision to seek help is not an easy one to arrive at. But when one gives thought to how much a loved one means to him or her, the adult individual, the decision to avoid sexual contact via an incestuous relationship is not so difficult at all. Incontinency then becomes a way of self control and the joy of being able to do that brings joy to the whole soul of an individual, especially years down the road the feeling of sexual avoidance and incest really kicks in, however latent it might appear. Avoiding the point of no return in the long run, can be a very rewarding state of mind and freedom from the emotional trauma that comes with incest, and, most assuredly, when the foul nature of this behavior is associated with pedophile sexuality.

A Testimonial In Truth Sincerity: Some parents at some point and time in the raising of their children, especially single parent families, had to come face to face with reality, and the sexual attraction for a son or daughter. The case of incestuous behavior only applies to those who would allow their sexual nature to overpower them and keep them from rational mental awareness given to the failure to avoid sexual misbehavior. By no means is this statement an accusation against the innocent. But the reality of the whole situation of incest is to come to grips with it and keep a positive mind structure that as a parent or guardian faced with the temptation or the latency of incest, whether it concerns the young or an older relative, the bottom line, point of interest is this, get help immediately. Talking about these fallacies of one's sexual nature with others does a lot to help avoid the possibility of engaging in an incestuous relationship with a loved one.

Let me, the writer, being the first to say, I have also been victimized by the satanic forces of darkness and the latent temptation of incest. My daughter fifteen yeas old at the time. To allow something of this nature to take place between a love one and myself was simply a no-no. Dysfunctional sexuality had been the downfall of many people who started out trying to do the right thing, but fall short of the mark because of a weak spirit of will power. The author was not about to let this happen to himself or his family and certainly not to his only daughter, even though our lives were intertwined into a closely knit two person family unit.

Temptation's Temptation: Being a born-again believer in Jesus Christ, I was warned by the Holy Spirit to abstain from the sexual temptation of a loved one, from incest, and from any form of incestuous behavior. This latter statement of fact is somewhat irrational for non-believers or non-Christians to understand. Let the author be the first to say that Christians are not above the temptation of the sexual impulse. For this reason, a Christian should always pray for deliverance from the evil aspects of satanic indulgence. And, this is what the author sought, spiritual guidance in the avoidance of a traumatizing situation such as the one the author had encountered. "Surely, if the author can avoid allowing a disheartening situation to come to pass, surely anyone else can do it too."

This warning from God prompted me to seek help, in order that my only child would not be victimized by an incestuous demeanor. I knew I needed help but my subconscious (sinful thoughts/nature) was telling me to indulge in my sexual fantasies and not worry about the devastating effects it would have on this only child in the aftermath. Though I am not in the least given to the nature of pedophilia, or the sexual attraction for a love of close kin, nevertheless, incest is incest, young or old. And one must do all that is in his or her power to avoid any confrontation with this form of iniquity and wickedness.

I am the type of person when something is bothering me to a point of anxiety and mental frustration, I get whatever it is within my person that's causing the disturbance out in the open, or I get it out of me. And I had no shame in telling someone or anyone, something was weighing heavily on my conscience. I believe I told several persons about the incestuous nature of attraction I was developing for my daughter. Most of them referred me to my Pastor, who at the time was the late Reverend Dr. J. Ray Butler. I spoke with him about this strange sexual urge developing in my nature toward my only child. His advice was a decision I alone had to make. Either I would allow this thing of incest to take place, or I was going to rely on faith that I had in God to overcome the whole situation which had befallen me. In his office that very same day, I made up my mind that I would not allow my sinful sexual nature of temptation to violate that of my only offspring. From that day to this day, I have been a free man, so help me God! "The preceding statement is the truth, the whole truth and nothing but the truth so help me God!"

Child Beauty Pageants Foster Sexual Abuse
New York Times
Friday, October 19, 2007

To the Editor:

The culture of children's beauty pageants that Frank Rich exposes in Jan. 18 column is the tip of the iceberg in the exploitation of children for adult needs.

In the United States and worldwide, the sexual exploitation of children in prostitution has escalated for more than a decade. Fear of H.I.V. infection is one factor. (Customers think that children are less likely to infect them, though the opposite is the case.)

A more pernicious factor is the explosive growth in child pornography that feeds the demand for children as sexual objects. Also feeding into this demand is the glamour of beauty contests in which children are made up to look like women.

In the past, this market for children was fueled mostly by pedophiles. Now, grassroots workers and brothel managers report widespread requests for children. In this country, affluent men from the suburbs head for the poorer parts of cities or to sex tourist destinations, where they look for children to molest for money.

Sexualizing children breeds exploitation. Mr. Rich has helped expose the sinister implications of the pageant culture, but the exploitation is more brutal for the children who are sexually exploited. That too must be exposed. ⱽ

The Ramseys had a chance to do the same thing, they refused to seek help, and in not doing so, they allowed their inner nature to overcome their outer nature, and the end result is, one little child is dead, and they are doing everything in their power to avoid the liability of their misbehavior, through the violent act of murdering their daughter. They allowed the force of their sexual nature and their aberrant sexuality to overcome their lesser desire to seek help which would have spared the life of little JonBonet and the difficulty in trying to avoid the guilt associated with the murder of innocence.

They probably had conscious and sincere thoughts to refrain from what they saw as pedophilous attraction toward their daughter, but here again, they had allowed themselves to come to the point of no return in their acts of molestation. And it was not so much that they were powerless against the forces of sex and sensuality to do anything about it; they apparently had become to enjoy what they were doing to this little child.

The point of no return is now become the point which could and will eventually bring the anvil of justice down upon their own heads. And because of their incontinency and lack of self control, young JonBonet Ramsey had to die!

The Fallacy of the Ransom Note: The Ramseys knew they needed help, but they allowed themselves to become powerless against themselves to do anything about it. And now, finally at last, their whole world of covert secrecy, corruption and murder is finally falling apart at the seams. Before this moment in time, everything in the way of evidence associated with the Ramseys has been steeped in presupposition and theory. But no longer is theory and presuppositions falling short of facts, they are now become facts which can be proven. Because the ransom note has been proven without the slightest doubt to be bogus and not worth the paper it was written on; and the fact that when the ransom note was found that morning by the mother; the child was already dead. What purpose would a fictitious ransom serve at this point in time?

The ransom note immediately became a worthless-useless piece of paper-a decoy of sorts to mislead the authorities and take their minds off of the Ramseys. Even the courts have gone along with the Ramseys, the ransom note, and belief that an intruder is responsible for the death of JonBenet. One would almost expect the sympathetic approach to John and Patsy if nothing but for the sake of their loss. JonBenet will never get justice in Boulder, Colorado for more than obvious reasons. The Ramseys have many friends there who would come to their rescue at a moment's notice. In Boulder, Colorado that's just the way it is, no matter what anyone thinks or says about it, and that's the whole truth without exceptions.

The Fallacy of the Kidnap Theory: When the body of this little darling princess was so mysteriously found by her father, the ransom note and everything contained therein became a big puff of smoke and not to mention one of the biggest lies ever told relating to the death of innocence. And because the child was not kidnapped, and the fact that she never left the confines of her home, the kidnap theory was nothing but a false apparition of the Ramsey's demented mentality in a failed attempt to remove the guilt and the truth they were so desperately trying to hide.

And again, the fact that she, JonBenet never left the confines of her home; and because of the proven fact that no one else other than the parents were the immediate persons in the house at the time of death, every ounce of guilt in every aspect of reality now, without the slightest of doubt, and undeniably, without speculation whatsoever, points directly to John and Patsy Ramsey.

Don't forget, it was the Ramseys who put the first lie out that JonBenet had been kidnapped, via the ransom note. And now, the ransom note has been totally discredited. Because the dead child was found in her home and was not remotely subjected to any attempt of a kidnap threat. The hard point of inference in regards to the ransom note in conjunction with any so-called kidnapping, is that very few people paid attention to the fact that the child was not remotely subjected to being taken from the residence. Which means in stark contrast and unreservedly, the Ramseys lied and fabricated this entire murder incident.

If no other point of interest is clearly stated, or seen, then know this for sure, JonBenet Ramsey was never victimized by a kidnapping, or anything close to a kidnapping. On this conjecture along and the wrongnesses that have preceded them, one would ask this question. What other lies have they told?

The Fallacy of the Intruder Theory: No one humanly possible can prove that the intruder theory existed, but, it can be proven that the intruder didn't exist according to the information contained in the ransom appertaining to the young child's death. *"We are a group, the two men who have your daughter,* together are nothing but a carefully concocted lie, which desperately tries to get the public to believe, people of the ransom note broke into the Ramsey home and committed the travesty of innocence.

The latter is also in association with the falsely contrived/information situated in the ransom note. Nothing in the ransom, not even the slightest intent of purpose has come to pass. What does that say for the truth factor? The truth and the real contents of the ransom note never existed, and was never intended to come to pass in any sense of its application, not then, not now, not at any time-before or after the death of JonBenet. *Listen to this, there was never two men who have your daughter, there was never a real bonifide request for a ransom, no one ever showed up to receive the money, or for that matter sent a return call to the Ramseys; why? The reason being none of these innuendoes existed, except on paper owned by Patsy Ramsey. There was never a real threat on JonBenet's life by someone outside of her home. The same cannot be said for someone inside the home. And the real threat on JonBenet's life came from someone inside the Ramsey home relative to the immediate family.*

There was never any need to not call the police, according to the ransom note, because there was nothing real about the Ramseys little display of convincing theatrics. When one considers all these little false theatrics (a shoe here, a bat there) contained in the ransom note, associated with superb acting abilities, what does that say for all the little false innuendoes of evidence found here and there in and around the crime scene. Question!

The ransom note, in conjunction with the intruder theory was nothing but a bunch of untruths and falsehoods, the Ramseys meticulously and fascinatingly put together; what does that say for the Ramseys? It says, "they lied about everything!"

After these works of the author are finished and set to publication, they, the Ramseys will not have a leg to stand on so help us God. The almighty Anvil of justice will have finally fallen on the culprits of the most heinous murder of innocence this century.

(3) She Knew Too Much
JonBenet Ramsey An Exceptional Child
Nation Knew JonBenet Ramsey Only In Death
Updated 8/17/2006 6:57 AM ET:

She was a remarkable young lady: BOULDER, Colo. (AP) — Most Americans knew JonBenet Ramsey only in death — as the blonde-haired brown eyed *little girl in the ruffled pink cowgirl outfit, bouncing across the stage with a million-dollar smile.* Beaming with all the excitement a little angel could muster up.

"I want to be a cowboy sweetheart," she sang, with a white hat atop her moussed, golden curls. In her death, she became America's sweetheart without a doubt. *The performance captured on video was*

played around the world after the 6-year-old beauty pageant competitor was found strangled and beaten on Dec. 26, 1996. The images persisted on TV talk shows for years afterward, helping feed theories about her killer. The tragic death of this little angel will live on in the hearts and minds of people of good will for many years to come. Hopefully her unwarranted death will cause those parents who find pleasure in making little beauty queens of the likes of JonBenet rethink such endeavors.

On Wednesday, authorities in Thailand arrested a man suspected in her slaying. The district attorney disclosed no details, but the Ramsey family's attorney in Atlanta said the suspect was a schoolteacher who once lived in nearby Conyers, Ga. The family attorney, Lin Wood, refused to say if the Ramseys knew him. John Ramsey had hoped this man was the killer of his daughter, but deep down in the remote recesses of his heart, he knew that could never be so for more than obvious reasons.

JonBenet was born in Atlanta on Aug. 6, 1990, to John Bennett Ramsey, a successful business executive, and his second wife, Patsy, a onetime Miss West Virginia. The family lived in the suburb of Dunwoody for several years before moving to Colorado in 1991. The couple moved back to Atlanta after their daughter's slaying. Why? Their guilt got the best of them; the result of their blood stained hands from killing the travesty of innocence!

JonBenet was named after her father, with the name pronounced in a French-inspired manner as "zhawn-ben-AY," and spent most of her life in the liberal mountain town of Boulder. JonBenet made the honor roll at her elementary school the month before she died, and attended a local Episcopal church. Family and friends described her as an inquisitive, giving child who loved Shirley Temple movies. JonBenet loved life period. Her love for life vividly expressed in her personality, made it all the more resonant.

In the last year of her life, JonBenet followed her mother's footsteps into beauty pageants. After her death, the world took a closer look at the children's beauty pageant circuit, where youngsters parade in makeup *and elaborate hairstyles, sometimes when they are barely out of dia-pers.* It is also sad indeed that these circumstances had to be the result of a picturesque little child before something was done about it,

She learned how to walk, gesture and perform, and collected a wardrobe of elaborate costumes, including that of a Las Vegas showgirl and a cowgirl. Although JonBenet loved to perform, family and friends said the competitions did not rule her life. At the age of six years old, this young beauty queen played a positive role in her destiny, and the road of life she would travel so inspiringly. Her talent went way beyond her years.

In her last months, JonBenet charmed judges into awarding her numerous beauty pageant titles, including Little Miss Colorado, America's Royale Miss and National Tiny Miss Beauty. As they traveled to competitions, mother and daughter would sing their favorite song, a tune from "Gypsy," a musical and movie about a mother obsessed with making her daughter a star. Little did the world know that this star of beauty would not live to participate in another pageant, no more forever. Her life would be cut short by an evil vindictive element of evil. It is a belief concept of the writer her senseless death will soon be vindicated by the soon apprehension of those who were responsible for her death, "and that's the truth, the whole truth, and nothing but the truth-so help us God!"

"Wherever we go, whatever we do, we're gonna get through it together," they would sing, *a minister told mourners at JonBenet's funeral. JonBenet was buried in Marietta, Ga., next to the grave of her half sister, Elizabeth Ramsey, 22, who died in a car crash in Ohio in 1992. In the coffin, she was dressed in a beauty pageant dress and tiara, with a stuffed toy animal in her arms.* [vi] "Sleep on little princess, those of us who believe just as you did, will see you in glory, by and by, when the morning comes."

JonBenet Ramsey was not only an exceptional child, she was also a unique child. Though she was only six years old, she had the mind and the mentality of a person much older than her years.

She was indeed an almost full grown person in a little child's body. And because of her phenomenal abilities and talent, her life would be snuffed out and extinguished before she would reach the age of seven.

JonBenet Ramsey Simply Knew Too Much: Somehow or somewhere in the concourse of time, the truth of this whole issue will come to pass. The underlying scenario of the death of JonBonet Ramsey is an overwhelming view of speculation and the possible fact that she was not willing to go along with the program any longer. She had become fed up with the immoral things that were going on within her little environment. Apparently, she was missing out on the most important aspect of her young life, her childhood.

One of the more important aspects of her life was that this little child didn't appear to have many friends. Whether or not this had anything to do with her participation in beauty pageants what have you, the fact remains that she didn't have many friends and, in most instances, parents who are as close to their children as was John and Patsy Ramsey, their children tend to have few real and close friends or associates. The author thinks this is because children have a great tendency to run off at the mouth, revealing things they should keep secret. That, coupled with the fact that she knew too much about the aberrant nature of her parents, she became a detriment to their social status in the community, should any word get out that the Ramseys were constantly mo-lesting their little playmate.

JonBonet's death was not a coincident or an accident, this little child died for a reason not given to everyday occurrences, she simply knew too much about her parents and what was going on in her life. In short gesture, she had the goods on John and Patsy Ramsey, her parents. For this reason and this reason alone, she was premeditatedly marked for death. And, oh another thing, parents do not kill their children for wetting the bed, neither by accident or other wise. Wetting in bed is just another childhood

habit in some children that has to be over-come by careful attention and awareness.

According to John and Patsy Ramsey, JonBenet had to go, she
had to die for reasons unbecoming of a child of her intellect.
There was great fear in the heart of her parents that one day this
little girl would grow up and spill the beans on them about how
they had molested her for years. And there is another fact to this
matter, if they did not shut her up for good, knowing what she
knew about her parents pedophile nature, they would become
prisoners to the will of their own daughter John and Patsy were
not about to allow this to happen. For this reason this young
child's death became a premeditated, preplanned state of execution and the snuffing out of this life by means of a false conspiracy
to take away her life.

Anyone with any degree of common sense should know that the
killing of innocence was not an overnight thing. It is virtually impossible to plan so far a criminal situation such as the travesty of
innocence in just one night. For this reason the writer believes
that all the false evidence associated with this child's death was
part of long term planning, months, maybe even a year or so.
The death of JBR was a situation conjured up in the minds of
John and Patsy long before her death ever took place. She was a
beautiful young child who had been, once again, marked for
death, simply because, "she knew too much!"

Their Social Status Greatly Undermined: The state of the
Ramseys status in the community meant more than the life of
this darling little child. And so, they carefully planned the death
of JonBenet to protect the standing of their social status among
the elite in Boulder, Colorado and else where around the nation.
And the writer thinks that in order for the death of innocence to
go on this long without being requited/unsolved, had to be a situation that took a long time to plan. So therefore, the planning
of the death of JBR was not, and the writer repeats, the death of
JBR was not an over night thing, her death was months in planning.

There is a memory bank hidden in the deep recesses of a child's thought process that will not allow situations of traumatic inferences to be forgotten. Young minds have a great tendency to remember in stalk vividness, unpleasant situations of the past. And in a young child's mind, the past, if it is a bad experience, may never go away. This saying goes double for girls, who may carry scars of past experiences throughout their entire adult lives. That saying, if it doesn't come out in the wash, it will surely come out in the rinse, probably petrified any remote futuristic plans they had for their daughter's continued participation in a fairy tale world of pedophile immorality.

The truth about little JonBonet's relationship with her parents was grounds for future prevention of *a tell it all* scenario. The child was being molested by her parents, and the case of point and interest is this, sooner or later JonBonet was going to let the cat out of the bag; and eventually spill the beans on her parents. This was also cause for great alarm by means of futuristic intimidation. The Ramseys simply could not allow this to happen, their elite standing in the community would be forever tarnished, *I loved that child with the whole of my heart and soul,* but that child for lack of better words knew to much, John and Patsy Ramsey would wrestle with this demeaning situation of resolve, time and time again.

The child, JonBenet Ramsey, had not in her little finite mind, the slightest idea that her parents were secretly, covertly, and by means of premeditated forethought, planning her death, perhaps more to the morbid grotesque inclinations of Patsy Ramsey. Knowing too much about her parents pedophile behavior, was liken unto a disaster getting ready to happen. In the performance of her participation in programs of pageantry, from the beginning, she probably never gave a second thought to any foul play in her person by her parents which included sexual and child molestation by the very people she had come to love and trust.

In the course of time, she would eventually come face to face with reality and the fact that her little world of innocence would be victimized by demeaned acts of child abuse which was not in the least her great expectation. Apparently, she was going to expose her parents to some reliable source that would believe her report, and if she told her story, the world would believe her, the thought of such were grounds that frightened her parents to death. Could this have been one of the reasons this young beauty queen had to die? Think about it!

She Did Not Want To Play Anymore: Most children have a low tolerance for the extremes when it comes to sexual indulgence with parents and adults. Not only that, but the irreparable harm imparted upon their mental skies as a result of sexual encounters with her parents, would forever become an indelible imprint on her life. Her estranged emotions would eventually become a concerted effort to separate herself from the uneventful and unwarranted circumstances involving sexual promiscuousness. Now, on the other hand, another reasonable assumption is this, JonBenet did not appear to be emotionally traumatized by sexual promiscuousness with her parents which is all together a horse of a different color. She appeared to be very skilled in hiding her true feelings, her acting and performing abilities showed a promising rising young movie actress. She was indeed a child prodigy, and that was well known by all those whom she came in contact with.

But the bottom line could also be, *she did not want to play anymore.* Her frail little body, was beginning to show and feel the unpleasant battle scars of a life no little child of her age should have to encounter. The puffiness of the bags under her beautiful eyes was evidence that she was not getting the necessary rest and sleep so important to her youthful invigoration and vitality. The little child appeared extremely tired, even though she managed to muster up a faint but deeply perplexed smile as her small hands and her bent elbows gave support to the perfectly childlike features of her beautiful rounded facial expression; perhaps one more reason she did not want to play anymore.

The writer would call it a false impression of what was really going on in her life; but only if walls could talk and door knobs were cameras, they would perhaps paint an awful picture of a little child's life that was filled with unwarranted and unwanted sexual indulgences. It is no doubt JonBenet was being sexually abused, a partial autopsy proved that to a great degree, but the bottom line scenario and a *fact* is this, JonBenet Ramsey had been sexually molested before her death. Perhaps not in the immediacy of her death, but perhaps days or even weeks before she was so brutally murdered in her own household. And again, a thorough autopsy would have proved that this little girl had been sexually molested for a prolonged period of time.

The autopsy was incomplete.............Why? And if the autopsy was allowed or given to completion, the exact time of death would have been determined which would more than likely greatly disprove the ransom note; this did not take place........ Why? Knowing the exact time of her death and the time the ransom note was found would prove beyond a reasonable doubt that JonBenet Ramsey was dead hours before the ransom note was found by her mother. What good is a ransom note if the child was already dead.

One cannot help but think she was also coerced and made to perform oral copulation on her father probably from every position imaginable, and then to have her little vagina stretched beyond reproach, is ample reason for any child her age to want to disengage from any relationship with her parents, by not wanting to play anymore. Too add insult to injury, she may have also performed the same (oral copulation) with her mother, who somehow appears to be very hard to please, *and I loved that child with the whole of my heart,* a lie if one was ever told. If this was the case and point, why is the little girl dead?

The deviant nature of pedophiles do not exercise a statute of limitation when it comes to their sexual attraction for children. A child to them is just like having sex with a grown person, any and everything goes. Oral sex is no exception. The writer is talking about what he knows and not what he heard and that's a fact one can take it to the bank. The writer was four years old when he encountered child molestation. It was an awful degrading experience no child should have to come against or come upon. Grown people out of the mind set of normality given to the deviant nature are capable of doing unconsciousable things to children; the Ramseys are not above this demeaning reproach in abnormal deviant behavior. The author's take on this subject matter is this, one simply does not kill the things or the ones they love. It is hate that kills along with overwhelming jealousy and not the latter, love that is. It is a depraved sexual individual who would take it upon themselves to destroy the peace and the sovereign tranquility of a little child.

To the author, Patsy's expression of, *that child,* is not a sincere expression of a mother's love for her daughter. If anything, if one were to look very closely at her statement, one might find reason for contempt and not love. Now, if she had said, I loved my daughter with all my heart and soul, perhaps would have been more convincing than the other apparently negative approach. Or perhaps a few tears here and an expression of remorse there, probably would have been a convincing thought of regret. Add to this statement given by Patsy Ramsey on national television, the fact that the woman expressed herself in a way which showed little or no emotion at all toward the reality of what had taken place, and the fact that her little child was dead. No tears, no remorsefulness, just a morbid statement, *and I loved that child with the whole of my heart.* Sometimes it is hard to hide one's true emotional feelings toward someone you hate, no matter how hard one tries. Patsy Ramsey hated her daughter, and she hated her enough to the point of almost denying her. And, the latter statement of course is solely from the author's perspective viewpoint.

The same lie *(and I loved that child with the whole of my heart)* in the first interview almost choked John Ramsey to death. It is to the writer a point blank fact and a foregone conclusion, Pat Ramsey hated JonBenet, perhaps, for more reasons than one. Love does not take a child through the changes JonBenet was going through, perhaps the whole picture show (the world of youthful glamour) was turning into something she did not relish at all.

Patsy's World: A Fantasy or Guilt: Having been a former beauty contestant, Patsy Ramsey was caught up in a make believe world of fantasy and repression which gave to her the impression that her world appeared to be closing in on her. She adored the fantasy but hated the fact that her little child was made to be a part of their immoral pedophile behavior. Which may also hide mysterious but dark apparitions of her past. In and on rare occasions, the mystique of past experiences have a colloquial informal way of repeating dark moments in the situational scheme of things in later adult life.

They (dark moments) may also be viewed as repeating themselves in the concourse of time associated with human behavior experienced along the road of life down through the years. Which is also to say, there is something in Patsy Ramsey's past that haunts her almost every moment of her life that would eventually be to the detriment of her little child. It was Patsy Ramsey's dark and benighted world that probably started the whole charade in the first place. Even the dark sinister expressions on John Ramsey's face, is given evidence that he may be covering up for his wife's demonistic behavior acknowledged in the whole scenario as being Patsy's world.

The author also feels that these abnormal behaviors are in part associated with Patsy Ramsey's ovarian cancer which she knew would, at some point in time, cut her life short. She also knew the ovarian cancer was terminal. In time, Patsy Ramsey would become her own worst enemy. And, perhaps also knowing that her daughter preceded her in death gave her some or maybe a bit of relief. Because she never attempted to shed a tear no way no how in any of the interviews she participated in, she at least could have held a handkerchief in her hand to show a little remorse/sympathy, or to hide a tear or two. Neither one of them, her or her husband, ever showed any remote degree of remorse towards the death of their daughter, JonBenet Why? "The answer is there wasn't any!"

On the other hand, this little child was mature enough to see the demon spirit in her mother's aberrant and deviant behavior. And because JonBenet did not want to play anymore, her life was weighed in the balance.

And because Patsy Ramsey refused to get help for her condition, little JonBenet Ramsey has become the outlet for her frustrations and her inability to cope with problematic situations of her past, her present, her future. Now, perhaps a long stretch of the imagination may be this, she simply did not want to leave her daughter behind with John Ramsey.

John Ramsey knew his wife was deeply disturbed, but perhaps love blinded him; therefore, he is just as guilty in the death of his daughter as is his wife. Her guilt precedes her in every circumstance of her life. Trying to hide it is about as bad as trying to make a bad picture show go away, it's just not possible.

Food for thought: The expression of a bad experience in her past (shown clearly on her face) blankets all the external exponents (facial expressions and her approach to speaking) of Patsy Ramsey's deeply disturbed nature. She appears to be in a trance, endowed by her inability to break away from a world of make believe to enter into the reality of the situation she is now faced with. Their daughter is dead, and no one has come forth to say, we saw some tears in their eyes not too long ago. Again, it might be that she and they don't have any!

And, there is also something deeply disturbing and grotesque about Patsy Ramsey, which is evidenced by the trauma bludgeoning of her six year old daughter, which Jon Benet witnessed with her own eyes before her life went from her; another reason, the writer would strongly suggest Jon Benet Ramsey did not want to play anymore. Her bonds, the taped mouth, secured hands were more than evidence of self denial and a non participatory demeanor to engage in further discretionary behavior toward continued sexual intercourse with her parents. The latter statement is a pre-supposition and not intended as an accusation.

God's Eternal Judgment and Patsy's Ovarian Cancer: There is an old familiar cliché going around in some circles of philosophical thought which says, one can fool some of the people some of the time, but you cannot fool God none of the time. During the early stages of Patricia Ramsey's ovarian cancer, the writer truly believed that her cancer was temporarily cured, based solely on the faith factor and the fervent prayers of the righteous. And the writer also believes that Patsy Ramsey was a person of faith. Real unwavering faith can move mountains out of your way. Patsy Ramsey, with help from others, put that real faith to work and for years, her cancer was in remission. Her life is a magnificent testimony that faith in God and prayer can make the seemingly impossible a reality in motion.

How ironic it seems that her cancer went into remission for almost ten years, only to raise it's ugly head as many years later! Question: why did Patsy's cancer after the death of JBR reoccur in such a violent way to end her life so suddenly, especially being a woman of faith? The answer is found in the realm of the Holy Spirit who sees all things, and who knoweth all things and from whom nothing is hid. And sometimes, God in His omnipotency/omniscient-all seeing eyes are in every place beholding the good and the bad/evil, reveals the truth of situational things and issues of life through his anointed prophet messengers.

Patsy Ramsey's life came to an abrupt end because her faith in God turned into a lie. She had the ability to hide the truth from society but she was not able to hide the truth from God and His Christ. Her life was cut short for the same reasons she cut short the life of JonBenet. God saw and, He is aware of everything, that went on in the Ramsey home that night His darling little angel was so brutally murdered by the same person in question.

It is absolutely impossible to hide the truth from God, though some might mistakenly believe that they can. Patsy Ramsey soon found out through the death of her lovely little daughter who died at the hands of her mother, her cancer came back again to haunt her to the point of death, her punishment for taking the life of innocence.

The dreadful sin of Patsy Ramsey in the death of JBR is endowed in the truth of divine preeminence which says in essence, your sins will soon find you out. Which is also a culmination of the truth, "you shall reap what you sow." Sow bad seed and bad seed will come back to you, sometimes in a worse way. Sow good seed and good seed will come back to you. And, in some instances, one's recompense/reward is not long in coming.

Patricia's ovarian cancer took a deadly turn for the worse as a result of her sins catching up with her. Even though she had faith, and even though one's sins will eventually find you out, the truth and the lack thereof, or attempting to hide the truth can sometimes be fatal. In the situation concerning the wife of John Ramsey, her death became her closest bedfellow.

Her personal relationship with her Lord came to a tragic end via her death, more than likely because she could not hide the error of her wickedness from Him. Needless to say, God knows what went on in that house, and he knows who killed this young child, and he knows for what reasons her life was so tragically taken, and to His prophets, He has revealed the truth.

Patsy's sins in the sight of God would not go unrequited, nor would they go unforgiving. The death of her daughter and the role she played in her daughter's death is one of the primary reasons her sins caught up with her. Another reason her sins caught up with her is because she tried so diligently to hide the truth and the fact that she killed her little girl in such a cold blooded manner that even God was irritated and angered by the hideous way she destroyed the life of her flesh and blood, JBR.

Does this mean that John Ramsey will go free? John Ramsey, because his role he played in the killing of innocence, will also have to pay to the piper. And by no means is he out of the woods. JonBenet's father is just as guilty of her death as is her mother. He may not have had a gun in his hand, but is just as guilty by helping to pull the trigger/weapon of destruction as did his wife. Sooner or later he will have to tell the truth to save his own neck, as the evidence against him is mounting up on every turn of the page of this book. If not guilty by fault, then he is most assuredly guilty by association.

When all the necessary evidence is gathered together against him and his deceased wife, he too, will join his wife in that world of darkness wherein the light of day will never again shine for either of them. Eternal darkness and eternal damnation as result of their evil assault on this lovely young beauty queen will come as no stranger and no surprise, because darkness is once again become their strange but familiar bedfellows.

And of course, the author is speaking of he and his wife Patsy Ramsey, who is already experiencing the darkness associated with the painful throes of eternal damnation. Soon and very soon he will be joining his wife who has gone on before him to receive her reward for the error of her ways. Oh, what a relief it will be, when the world has knowledge of their proven guilt, when it learns that these two persons killed their little princess, "who now must pay to the piper."

JonBenet's Death Premeditated: The believability and the credibility of JonBenet is become a premeditated act on her life. It stands to be a truth, the only persons on earth who wanted to see this young child dead were indeed her parents. They wanted her dead because she had the goods on her parents, they decided that there was only one course of action to keep them from being exposed by their daughter, that was too preplan and orchestrate her death to the degree of alien intrusion into the state of their privacy and the confidentiality of their home.

It is believed that the death and the premeditated murder of JonBenet could not be carried out in one night, all the evidence had to be carefully placed and set to the attention of an apparent intruder; this takes time and careful orchestration. No kidnaper/intruder in his or her right mind would implement so careful a scheme, and then turn around, kill the child, without accomplishing the means for which was the intended purpose in the first place.....ransom money.

How ironic is also the fact that John Ramsey found the child's body, and Patsy Ramsey found the ransom note! And still there was no real incriminating evidence that intruders had been in the home. Was this a coincidence? I would hate to think so. But what it is, is perhaps a classic case of premeditated murder, if there ever was a classic threat on human life. It was so carefully planned and orchestrated even to this day, the guilty party has not been apprehended.

Food For Thought-She Probably Witnessed Her Own Death A Supposition: A tragedy of tragedies, this young child was made to witness her own death. The same is evidenced in the fact that JonBenet was bound and gagged so that her voice would not cause an unwarranted disturbance or unwarranted attention, which also left the young girl in a defenseless but precarious situation. It is also apparent that she was not asleep when her death occurred by reason that she was bound and gagged. JonBenet more than likely had to be awake at the time of her demise also, because perhaps her parents were trying very hard to reason with her, or she was adamantly refusing to cooperate with them. Somehow it is sincerely felt, this six year old did not want to play the game anymore, and simply refused to grant her parents permission to entertain their pedophile behavior.

Although little JonBenet was already marked for death by a premeditated plot to take her life, John and Patsy Ramsey felt it their moral duty to try to reason with their daughter this one last time. One dead, deceased child is evidence that they were unsuccessful in their efforts.

Now the other side of the coin is this, there was no reasoning at all. This little child simply had to die, without question. JonBenet had become a threat to the Ramsey success status in the community, should anyone were to find out that they were molesting their little girl, a supposition of course. But just the same a probable cause, relative to the coin has many faces. "Only John Ramsey knows the whole truth!" Let's hope he doesn't die in the process of getting at the truth.

Patsy Ramsey either began the writing of the ransom note or she was putting the final touches on it. How shocking is the fact that all indications of JonBenet's tragic death seems to point to her mother and not so much her father, and by no means is the latter statement a testament of the father's innocence, no not in the least. Even though he may not have struck the blow that killed little JonBenet, John Ramsey is just as guilty as his wife in this young child's death.

Maternal and Paternal Affinity: Mothers usually have a strong affinity for their sons, fathers usually have a strong affinity and compassion for their daughters; which means John Ramsey had a decision to make between his love for his daughter and the love he had for his wife. John Ramsey probably would not have allowed his daughter's death to take place if he were not in part guilty himself of some form of wrong doing involving infidelity with his daughter. There are rare occasions wherein mothers have been known to not share the same affinity for a daughter as do the father. But for some strange reason, perhaps the latter was not so with Patsy Ramsey, even though it appeared that she and JonBenet shared a good relationship with each other.

This does not negate the fact that something, somewhere along the way, had gone terribly wrong. Maternal and paternal instincts don't always have to follow any prescribed order of affection toward their off springs, the latter is only suggestive to shed some light on the probability that Pat Ramsey is considered to be the primary culprit of her daughter's death. And it is for this reason, also suggestive, that Patsy Ramsey more than likely carried out the brutal attack on her daughter after or before she was bound and gagged. The author wants the reader to understand that this little child was brutally and heinously murdered in her own home by someone who was very close to her, no stranger or if there were intruders would kill such a young beautiful human being in such a way unless, they were mentally ill. If that was the case, a mentally ill person would have been caught by now; or unless there was someone who hated this child so bad that nothing short of death would have satisfied their consciousness. "The author wonders who could that be?"

The greatest oversight of those who conspired to kill little JonBenet is foresight and not hindsight, which is highly suggestive the entire scenario is congealed in the supposition that her death was planned and premeditated. It is a known supposition that everyone involved in the investigative aspect of JonBenet's death are looking at this young child's death in the hindsight scenario, or those contentious ideals that for the most part are contingent upon evidence gathered and thought of after the fact. Little thought has been given to the possibility that her death was planned and orchestrated long before her death occurred. The whole aftermath of her death seems to be an almost perfect act of criminal intent, many would be in agreement as to the mystique of her death, that it was a preplanned, premeditated plot on the young child's life.

She Was Not Kidnapped: The little girl had to die for obvious reasons, presumptuously relative to the fact that she knew to much on someone or she knew something very incriminating on those who were thought to be closest to her. They were the parents who appeared to be the constant visible specters within her very young environment. And it is highly believed that this young child died for a reason, which it is also highly believed that her death was not a haphazard circumstance, but again, a carefully orchestrated plot on her life. Those who killed little JonBenet wanted her dead for some reason not associated with an intent to kidnap her. A kidnapper (s) does not kill their victims without first making some form of verbal or physical contact with the victim's respondents in regards to compensation liability.

And, if the young child stayed on the premises where she dwelled, it is impossible to say that she was kidnapped. Is this an oversight on the part of those who conceived the ransom note? Or maybe, in their hurriedness to compose the ransom note, they forgot kidnap means to remove from one place to another without due consent. In order for the child to be kidnapped, she would have to have been taken away from her home to justifiably say that she was kidnapped by any standard of circumstance. JonBenet never left the confines of her home at no time, before or after her death. So therefore, it is impossible to say that she was kidnapped; she was taken from her bedroom, but not her home. This is also another fallacy of the fictitious but bogus ransom note.

The ransom note said taken your daughter, if the daughter was not taken off the premises or out of the house, she was not taken from the premises but only removed from her bedroom to another section of the house. Only a criminal mind of tremendous short sightedness would use the term kidnapped or taken your daughter, when they were yet still in the same house, on the same premises, which has now been proven to be a fallacy of intent, which is to say, nothing of the sort ever happened.

The author would be remiss if he did not ask this question again. Who is responsible for this humongous/stupendous lie of a so-called kidnap theory? No one in his or her right mind can remotely blame this great blunder on a "so-called intruder!" It would be a travesty of justice, not to mention a travesty of innocence. Obviously, to the author somebody does not know the difference between the word kidnap and a non kidnap situation.

The ransom note has to be considered a fallacy of intent, "and more than that, a premeditated smartly concocted lie!" If the ransom note is a lie, then, it stand to reason everything else is a lie also. The ransom note does not contain a shed of truth, and neither is there any real sense of sensibility, because later on that same day, the dead body of this little child was found by her father in the basement of their Boulder, Colorado home. To the author, it is no misunderstanding that someone in the Ramsey home wants the public to believe that an outside show of force entered into the home and killed JonBenet, again the author simply refuses to believe a lie.

The point of contention that the ransom note was found after the fact, greatly hindered the response time of the criminal element to seek a rebuttal does not indicate foul play from an outside intruder; but increases speculation that the intruder (s) were indeed inside the home of JonBenet Ramsey. A ransom note from within the premises of the home does not make much sense coming from an intended intruder having custody of the child outside of the home, (the two men who have your daughter) again, it doesn't sound real, the entire scenario is senseless and without merit.

JonBenet Ramsey was a victim of a despicable hate crime not basic to an outside intruder. The writer would be willing to lay his soul on the line to say that this little girl had no enemies who hated her so much that they would kill her, saving those who were closest to her, for reasons explained and yet to be explained. Question: If John Ramsey and financial compensation were the object of the ransom note, why kill the little child and let the real intent of the conspiracy to get back at John Ramsey go unimpeded. One would have to believe that the object of the ransom note was not about John Ramsey, financial compensation, or even JonBenet, the real object of the ransom note was primarily a deterrent to give the media, the public and the police department something else to think about, to assuage the fact that the Ramseys themselves were responsible for the death of innocence. So far, the Ramseys have been able to fool and mislead not just America, but the entire world.

No kidnaper in his or her right mind would come to the home of an intended victim, especially a young child, kill the child in her own home, without ever having made known or made clear their devious intent. The name of the game is money, to kill the child without having received any financial compensation defeats the whole purpose of the intent in the first place. Even with the criminal element in society, there is often a code of ethics, and what happened that wintry night in Boulder, Colorado is not one of them.

If the criminal element was in the house, the most logical explanation to secure the means of financial intent was to have taken into their custody one of the parents too! But this did not happen. To take this young child as means of a bargaining chip does not make too much sense; especially when as easily as they took the child, they could have taken one of the parents also. Here again, this was not the case. And the prospects of an intruder (s) entering the premises of the Ramseys, undetected **and** unsubstantiated by any remote degree of truth, is highly illogical. All the more reason to believe that JonBenet's death was a planned and a premeditated very carefully orchestrated assault on her life. Perhaps for the sole reason, she was unwilling to cooperate with her captors (perhaps those of her household) for reasons explained and yet to be explained.

Don't Call the Police: Is perhaps the most illogical statement that can be entered onto a ransom note by those of true criminal intent; unless the whole purpose of the ransom note was an intent to kill the child in the first place. Therefore, the ransom note, the latter statement, was without regard to monetary compensation. Ultimately, the child was marked for death by some source or entity who found the child to be so repulsive that it wasn't about money at all, because the child is dead and no money of any amount has exchanged hands. It was about the travesty of innocence, the death of a child who appeared to be a hindrance to someone in the Ramsey household.

Another irony is, at or by the time they discovered the ransom note, the child was already dead. What good then was the ransom note? Apparently, the note in and of itself was an intended deterrent from the truth, or the note was an altercation to infuse a lie to evade the truth. And the truth is, in the absence of an intruder, someone in the immediate Ramsey home killed young JonBenet.

Police compromization of the crime scene: It appears to be apparent that law enforcement deliberately allowed a compromising scenario of the crime scene for whatever reasons known only to them and the Ramseys. Trained law enforcement officials in most cases exercise restraint in an investigation wherein death has occurred, and apparently the officer could reasonably speculate that the body was lifeless, but allowed the child to be moved anyway....Why? Which would mean that the officer assisting in the crime scene was partial to the Ramseys for whatever might be gained from it.....$. One of the first things a police officer is trained to do in the investigation of a crime scene, especially a murder scene, is not to contaminate or allow anyone to contaminate the crime scene. This did not happen.........Why? Most law enforcement officials would have checked the child's pulse to verify if there was a heart beat, no heart beat or pulse would mean that the child was dead....meaning it was not necessary to move her, but this did not happen.....Why?

Some Time During the Middle of the Night: A great deal of the blame for this foul up should be placed on willful intent by the officer, who, along with John Ramsey, discovered the body. On a CNN interview with the Ramseys, during the week of April 23, 2000, John Ramsey made the statement that *sometime during the middle of the night* JonBenet was murdered. This is not just pure speculation on the part of John Ramsey, why didn't he say sometime during the night his daughter was killed; the statement itself was said with conviction. Is it because he had some idea about the exact time and nature of his daughter's death? Here again, if such was the case, the latter statement means that the intruders, those responsible for the ransom note, killed the child long before the ransom note was planted where it was first noticed by Patsy Ramsey. It also means that the killers themselves did not allow any time at all for a response to their monetary request; why? The answer is because the child was already dead. Then, the ransom note was just a decoy to make it seem like intruders were in the house. The only people to enter the house, prior to JonBenet's death, were John and Patsy Ramsey and young Burke.

Removing the body: A truly loving parent would not have moved the child's body from where it was found for fear of exacerbating any further internal or external harm to the child; and it was apparently obvious that the child suffered blunt force trauma to the head. Then, why would they take a chance on moving the child, causing even more harm if she was still alive? Was it a deliberate intent on the part of John Ramsey, the officer, who assisted him to destroy evidence and contaminate the crime scene? John Ramsey, and the officer, and others who found JonBenet had to have known in their hearts the extent of the trauma inflicted upon her body. Speculation would suggest that the little child was already dead.

And, by moving the little girl's body would ultimately eliminate any degree of parental provocation and incrimination because the crime scene was now so contaminated the Ramseys would escape any murder indictments and accusations that they were responsible for the death of JBR. Which also suggest that the whole charade was a foregone conclusion of premeditated murder and contamination of the crime scene. The Ramseys made it a point of effort to call every one they could in an effort to deliberately contaminate the crime scene. In most instances, when a family encounters a missing child, they usually call the police and then after the police have completed their investigation, which might take the entire day, they call friends and relatives.

John Ramsey knew if he removed the child's body, contaminating the crime scene, it would help to exonerate him and his wife of any involvement in Jon Benet's death; so far, the plan, the purpose of intent, has worked to their favor; and this is why the young child was buried in such a hurry, insisted by the Ramseys.

Limited Autopsy Report: Further autopsies and medical examinations would more than likely proved that the Ramseys had some part or something to do with the demise of their beautiful young daughter. Because JonBenet's civil rights had been infringed upon and violated, the Boulder, Colorado police department and the District Attorney should not have allowed the child to be funeralized until a complete autopsy and examination of her body to the satisfaction of the DA had been thoroughly carried out; here again, this did not happen...Why? A full-complete autopsy report would have at least pointed a finger at the real culprits, or perhaps the real culprits were the ones who were responsible for an incomplete autopsy examination for fear of guilty reprisals?

Food for thought; the Ramseys did not want a complete autopsy investigation of their daughter's death, this is evidenced by the quick burial.....Why? Was the Boulder, Colorado police department involved in the hurry up burial of little JonBenet Ramsey? Too many things were going in the Ramsey's favor at the time of their daughter's death, and shortly thereafter. They had almost total and complete cooperation from the local authorities, including the District Attorney's office......Why? Some would go as far as to say it was because of ....$$$; after all, they are wealthy people!

Most parents, upon the brutal discovery of their daughter's death, and her lifeless body, would want a complete and thorough autopsy investigation, provided they had no comprehension as to how their loved one died in the first place. Knowing how a loved one died is a horse of a different color; even so, if it meant delaying burial arrangements to find out the truth, this, the Ramseys simply refused to do.....Why? When the family moved to Atlanta, in one interview, they said they were not going back to Boulder, Colorado, the writer think this may be a sign of internal guilt more so than fear of living with their shame. Most parents, who harbored a sincere affection for a lost or murdered loved one, would more than likely remain on the premises of the crime scene-even their home, in hope of finding any degree of evidence that would lead to the killers of their little girl. Of course, that is, if they had nothing to do with her death from the initial standpoint; they should have nothing to be ashamed of and equally as well, nothing to hide.

Patsy Ramsey made a statement on public television that they knew that there was a least two people involved in the murder of JonBenet; the killer, and the person the killer confided in. But what she forgot to mention or include in her thesis was that there were three people involved in the ransom note, the writer of the ransom given to the first person, and the two men who have your daughter, given to the second and third persons associated with the ransom demand.

The Ramseys chose not to return to Boulder probably because they did not want to relive their own guilt. Patsy Ramsey was the killer, and the person she confided in was her husband. So, in a truer sense when she spoke of two people, (the killer and the person the killer confided in,) she was right. She was speaking of herself and her husband.

Remorsefulness And The Truth: The Ramseys never expressed in any way shape, or form a deep profound remorse for the death of their daughter, even when Patsy said that she loved that child "with the whole of my heart and soul," something very poignant was missing, (she really meant she hated that child with all her heart and soul) and it had nothing to do with love, or sincere remorsefulness. True remorse has a spiritual overtone which oftentimes helps to convey the sincere thoughts of regret when a loved one is entangled in a consoling situation. Patsy Ramsey tried to go there, by saying *God will find you out*, but somehow the gesture on her part was ineffective; and if her statement, meant to be remorseful, conveyed anything at all, it conveyed an element of serious implication that they were responsible for the death of JonBenet Ramsey.

To add insult to injury, they have together written a book to try and justify their non involvement in the death of their daughter in "The Death of Innocence." This is not remorse. What it does amount to is self vindication. If they are not guilty of anything, why are they trying so hard to convince the world that they were not responsible for their daughter's death. The time they spent on writing a book, it appears to some, they should have spent on trying to find the killer (s) of their daughter, instead of trying earnestly to vindicate themselves.

There is something innate in the truth of a situation thought to be detrimental to the outcome thereof. When the truth is told, the truth cannot change, the truth will always be consistent, and the truth will live or exist forever because the truth itself is eternal. But a lie will die, or a lie will change to fit the situation. Nonetheless, a lie will change, die or go away, and in some instances, after a period of time, a lie is hard to remember. The difficulty with a lie is that a lie also has to be remembered as opposed to the truth, which one can forget and, ten years later, the truth will be the same, not so with a lie. The Ramseys have not been able to be consistent in their story telling, for oftentimes in certain interviews they cannot remember some of the former things they said.....how ironic! No one should have trouble remembering the truth, if in fact it was the truth.

A lie devoid of substance: It might take some time to go away, but a lie will eventually die. Why? Because it has no substance to continue in reality. This is why the Ramseys were unable to respond properly to some of the things they have said regarding their daughter's horrific death. And on rare occasions there may be times when a lie will not go away or die, especially when the truth is in dispute. The truth here is this, the death of JonBenet Ramsey will not go away because the truth is not being told, primarily because the truth is caught up in a lie or some form of a dysfunctional act of respondency.

For the past several years the death of JonBenet Ramsey has saturated the airways the world over with alarming infidelity which is the failure by society to bring forth the truth concerning this travesty of innocence. And when the truth is told, then and only then will the memory and the life of this child rest in peace.

Supposition-No Criminal Evidence: Now, if the intruder (s) were still in the house at the time the ransom note was found and the police had not yet been alerted, it meant that the child was still alive. And, if the intruders were still in the house if this was the case, John or Patsy Ramsey, upon finding the ransom note, should have heard or seen someone on their premises or in their house. This, too, was not the case. If the intruders killed the child after the ransom note was found, within the time frame in which the note was found, then there should have been an enormous amount of blood where the child's body was found, or an enormous amount of blood wherever the child was killed. She did suffer trauma to the head, but no report of blood was mentioned when the child was found by her father and others...Why?

Due to the extenuating circumstances, there was never an intruder (s) in the house at any time. One reason is that the Ramseys did not go to bed that night which was evidenced by the fact that they had on the same clothes the day before, one report stated on the Today Show. The same means that they had little or no sleep during the night of JonBenet's death. Could you sleep, if you had murdered and bludgeoned your little daughter to death? Any other evident alluding to an intruder had to be planted or preplanned. Here again, the whole scenario perpetuates the premeditated behavior of criminal intent not by an alien source, but by those who were closest to Jon Benet..........John and Patsy Ramsey, her mother and her father. They were up all night, it was impossible to sleep, JBR was dead, and the finishing touches had to be set to the ransom note. Sleep was the furthest thing from their minds.

(3) The Ingenuity of Automation Technology: Now the truth concerning the death of JBR., is centered in the ransom note and those responsible for its contents. It is a fact and a bygone point of conclusion that the culprits who murdered little JonBenet Ramsey are also the ones who wrote the ransom note and placed it where it could be easily noticed. Little did they know that the ransom note itself in conjunction with 21st century technology can literally prove who the killers were who took the innocent life of Jon Benet Ramsey without the slightest of doubt or ambiguity.

This same technology will prove that the Ramseys wrote, and are responsible for, the ransom note. Which also means that they did in fact without remorse take the innocent life of JonBenet. But before automation technology of this sort is revealed, the writer would like to paint a clear and audible picture of the Ramseys and the error of their ways which will in turn convict them of the gruesome murder of their little daughter. And of course, the outcome of this grotesque scenario is based on the ransom note and those who wrote it.

Computer Technology: The innovative uniqueness of the most sophisticated piece of machinery in existence is the key to solving the problem as to the writer of the ransom note. The computer in conjunction with a new program called Speech Analysis and Voice Recognition used in many software voice speaking networks is a new innovation in speech-voice and writing recognition. Speech Analysis and Voice Recognition software works with most word processors in almost all personal computers. There are many speech recognition software programs on the market today, and all of them work on virtually the same principle, which is to allow one to speak to the computer word thoughts in the form of dictation, instead of typing the same thoughts of text into the word processor.

The amazing factors about this new technology is the computer's ability to replicate speech and text accuracy by way of voice commands. Voice commands are an effort by the internal networking of the computer to relate the voice to the person via verbal dictation. In this way the computer becomes almost one of a-kind to the person it is working with, up close and very personal. Once a relationship between the PC and the individual is established based on personal interaction, the computer then develops an intimate relationship with the person of the text by understanding the overall nature of that particular person through text or one's writing habits. In other words, the computer takes written word thoughts, (the nature of individual behavior by way of text in a written format), compares it to a person's voice, then puts the two together to come up with one true, distinct personality. The end results to this scenario is now the computer is able to recognize that particular voice and translate it (voice analysis and speech recognition) into written text on the PC monitor. The computer also has the ability to distinguish between the personality of one voice from the personality of another voice, because no two people have the same personality and just as no two people have the same finger prints, no two people have the same voice, when it comes to speech recognition and voice analysis.

The computer has the unique ability to analyze various written text and match it to a person's voice, relative to an individual's personality. The text does not really have to be the person or individual's own hand writing, what the computer does is analyze the person's or individual's thought patterns and matches those thought patterns to an individual's personal handwriting. The end results are the computer digitizing the overall personality of an individual through that individual's thoughts in written text. In most speech and voice recognition programs, the computer wants to know not only how a person thinks, from a sample of written text, but the computer wants also to match written thoughts with an individual's voice. Really, what it boils down to is this, the computer simply analyzes written speech to determine for the most part, the personality of the individual using the speech recognition program. Once the computer has an understanding of an individual's personality, then the computer can relate to that person in performing speech recognition on the PC monitor. **In other words, the computer takes a sample of a person's writing technique and matches it to that person's voice and comes up with a personalized computerized specimen of that individual's voice personality. Once this is done, the computer can then take voice dictation and write it into the word processor.**

The computer understands that a person's personality is inherently innate in an individual's handwriting, which, in most instances, is an exact duplication of that individual's overall personality. It's like this, we write what we are, and we are what we write; for instance, people write like they think and they also think like they write. There are occasions when a person's voice in conversion can be determined easily when a note or a letter is read which was written by the same person. Voice expressions through E-mail can also be easily detected without reading the name of the sender. It is called voice recognition and speech analysis.

A person's personality traits are also evidenced in the way she or he compose word sentencing for constructive speech presentations. And, a person who speaks well, in most instances, writes just as well, intelligent speaking and intelligent writing go hand in hand, or are synonymous to each other. By analyzing both, *the writing technique,* by analyzing thought patterns through *speech recognition,* the computer combines the two into one distinct personality relative to one's ability to write and speak. The computer is able to not only recognize the personality of handwriting, the computer can also recognize the voice and equate it with the person captured in its memory banks.

John and Patsy Ramsey made their fortunes working with computers which allowed them to become accustomed to innovative PC technology. But the writer believes that they never gave themselves to the remotest thought, or never in their wildest dreams, that one day, the computer would find them guilty of murdering their little daughter. Not for one moment did they comprehend that the most sophisticated technology known to exist, of which they were so accustomed to, could spoil their hopes for what could have been an almost perfect crime. Neither did they consider Providence playing a vital role in uncovering their sinister scheme to hide their guilt. And neither did they consider nor comprehend that it would be the ransom note that would take them down the corridors of doom and gloom-straight to the bar of justice.

The Ransom Note: that Patsy Ramsey found in her house will prove who the killers are by means of computer analysis and speech recognition. It is the writer's strong opinion that the Ramseys are the authors of the ransom note in its three page context. Because the computer is capable of analyzing the thought process contained in the ransom note, it can also equate the ransom note to the person/persons who wrote it by means of speech recognition. What the latter statement means is simply this, the computer upon analyzing the text of the ransom note, and comparing it to the voice and the speech of both Ramseys, it is highly probable that the computer will match one of or both of their voice-nature/personalities to the ransom note. Should either one of their voices be charged to the ransom note, it means one or both of them were responsible for the death of their daughter, JonBenet Ramsey. Whoever wrote the ransom note (John or Patsy Ramsey)were without a doubt the killers of innocence. Because new evidence had risen in this case regarding the ransom note, in so much that it has not been proven to any worthwhile degree that the Ramsey's home was intruded upon, leaves John and Patsy Ramsey holding the title of guilt by association and guilt by reality. They are the only ones of which it can be proven without the slightest of doubt who were in the house the night JonBenet was so brutally murdered. The ransom note could not have possibly been written by anyone else but the Ramseys-Patsy especially, and again, she was just that smart of a woman.

Technology In The Courthouse: The inevitable question facing courtroom drama in the present vernacular is, can technology be used as evidence against those suspected of a criminal offense? To the contrary of many who think not, the writer must beg the difference, primarily because in the commitment of serious criminal intent, anything that can be used to apprehend and convict the guilty party (s) should in fact utilize every means of catching the wrong doers, who by their own self will have violated the law. Hidden cameras serve as an integral part in criminal surveillance, and can be used in a court of law to convict the criminal element charged with a violation of the law.

Forensic Technology: It is believed that technology in its futuristic, the here and the now state of the art fixation in humanity, will be utilized unceasingly to assist law enforcement agencies to apprehend and convict those elements in society who are of the contrary. It is assumed with great assurance that what society has now in criminal detection devices is only the tip of the iceberg, the best as one would say, is yet to come.

Lie Detectors: Lie detectors are an exception to the rule for this reason, lie detectors can be manipulated by human emotions which may or may not be a true source of character evaluation. As a result of the latter statement in context, it is believed by most law enforcement institutions, lie detectors are not a reliable source of evidence to be utilized in criminal prosecutions. Lie detectors in some instances are only about 65% accurate, which is in part why some institutions of law consider lie detectors a non dependable source of prosecution, and may not be used in most courts of law. In the future, more advanced means and resources elevating the standards of lie detectors are on the horizons of inventions that very well might put them in competition with the new kid on the block, the personal computer.

The Personal Computer: is liken unto *the new kid on the block*, witty, intelligent, and is almost unlimited in its variant abilities to comprehend and differentiate anything, from mathematical equations to solving problems of today thought impossible. The *new kid on the block* has become to be an invaluable tool in every aspect of human endeavors with all the potential of becoming a "how did society manage to do without it" scenario. And from the apparent looks of things, the computer is without a doubt, here to stay.

Question: Can or should the computer be used in a court of law to convict those who commit crimes of a serous nature? The writer's personal view point is Yes. Computers involved in criminal prosecution relative to informative data and information are almost 100% accurate with a margin of error given to be a plus or minus 0. If computers are inaccurate more than likely it is because of inaccurate data has been fed to it, or a virus of some sort has compromised the program dialogue. It has been said, computers don't make mistakes, people do. And it can also be said, computers can be used for *good or evil.*

Here again, the writer would be remiss if some thought was not given to the Ramseys, who may have used the computer to orchestrate, plot and carry out their fiendish plan to kill their daughter, reason being, the crime itself has almost been fool proof. Richard Milhouse Nixon did it, and got clean away with it too. When the first usable computer chip was invented during the time of President Dwight David Eisenhower, Richard Nixon was there to examine and make use of it. He used the computer, because he committed almost a perfect act of criminal intent, was given a full pardon, and never served one day in jail.

The Orange Juice may have gotten some assistance from the use of the computer, in the death of Nicole Simpson and Ron Goldman. Who can say the possibility of such was not probable or is not a valid case of point. The latter statements are based on theory and supposition.

Guilty Or Not Guilty: The Ramseys are well deserving of an opportunity to understand the consequences of technology proving that they did indeed write and compose the ransom note. But another point of interest here is thought by the writer to be fitting and proper which suggest to the Ramseys the possible outcome of computer analysis of the ransom note may in fact prove that they are and were the author of the same. The primary point of interest, the writer wishes to express, is not whether or not the Ramseys are guilty, but the primary point of interest should be predicated on the seriousness of the crime they committed.

Whoever killed this innocent little child is also worthy of the death penalty, and that by the quickest means possible. If the Ramseys are innocent, it is felt that computer analysis of the ransom note will undoubtedly prove it beyond reasonable suspicions or accusations. Now on the other hand the opposite point of interest may apply, which says that they are guilty in the first degree.

In the event the death of JonBenet Ramsey was a callous premeditated act of vengeance on her life; and the Ramseys are found wholly responsible, should this be the case, the writer feels the Ramseys should be allowed to plea bargain in exchange for life without the possibility of parole. The latter statement of conviction applies only if they plead guilty to the heinous death of their little daughter, Jon Benet Ramsey before the computer is allowed to analyze the ransom note to bring about an indictment against them.

The Second Concourse-A Supposition

Hate And Jealousy Killed JonBenet Ramsey: John Ramsey made three statements on national media television during several interviews that undeniably points to the Ramseys as the principal culprits of JonBenet's death. The potential impact of his documented statements in relationship to his daughter's murder, he may not have realized those same damaging statements could possibly bring about an indictment against him and his wife respectively:

1. The Crime Was Committed During the Middle of the Night.
2. The Murder of JonBenet Was Premeditated.
3. The Culprits Were Either Jealous of Him or They Hated Him.

1. The Crime Was Committed During the Middle of the Night: This question comes to mind based on the statement John Ramsey conveyed on national media television; why did he not say, some time during the night instead of during the middle of the night the young child must have been murdered, unquote. Did he really mean what he was saying or was he just speculating on the approximate time of the murder? The writer doesn't think so. There are some things that are just not worth speculating on, unless one is absolutely sure of what he's talking about, and apparently the father of the dead child knew what he was talking about. John Ramsey knew exactly what time JonBenet was killed because he was present in the house when it happened. Speculation would also have to presuppose that he was somewhere else in the house during the time the incident took place. At that time of the night more than likely John Ramsey was in his own bedroom, which ultimately means that the killer was in the bedroom of little JonBenet.

Now, if this was indeed the case situation, the little girl was more than likely killed in her sleep, then bound and gagged as though an intruder entered the house indiscriminately and took the young child's life. And obviously no sounds of distress were heard by either John Ramsey or the other child who was sound asleep in his bedroom. Which also means that sleep for the other child (Burke Ramsey) could have been induced, so that he would not wake up during the night and the time JonBenet, his sister, was murdered. Or the other side of the coin is there was never any indication that there was a visible or audible disturbance in the home at any time during the night or during the time the young child was murdered. Or, at lease a disturbance great enough to awaken Burke Ramsey, if he was indeed asleep at the time his sister was killed. And yet, still unaware of what was going on in the home.

And apparently, there was never an outcry for help on the part of the slain child which gives more credence to the fact that she was probably killed in her sleep.

Question: Why kill JonBenet and not Burke Ramsey, he was sound asleep in his bed? If there were any intruders in the house (the writer think not) obviously they were not interested in Burke Ramsey whom they could have also extracted a ransom sum. But the question remains, why JonBenet and not Burke Ramsey, her brother? Burke Ramsey was not marked for death, only his sister JBR. If the case was so, as it was not, they or whoever would have killed him also. But, as fate would have it, this, too, was not the case. Another reason Burke Ramsey did not fall in harm's way was because there were no intruders in the home at anytime during and after the time the young girl was murdered.

Now if the ransom note itself mentions at lease three persons, and if at least three persons were in the house, someone should have heard or seen something wrong or heard abnormal goings on in the house that night; especially since the Ramseys did not get any sleep the morning of. They should have heard or seen something not common to their regular routine. None of these things took place by any stretch of the imagination. The author truly believes that everything that went on in the Ramsey home the night of the murder of innocence was nothing more than a big lie if ever one was told. The sad part of it all, was that it was also a very convincing lie other than the actual death of innocence.

No Trace of Blood: Now if intruders were in the home of the Ramseys and the little child was also bludgeoned to death, why was there not any trace of blood found. A wound of the caliber the child suffered would have left some blood somewhere in the house, but no blood was found. And if the intruders killed the young child, they would not have stopped to clean up blood; so therefore some reasonable amount of blood should have be found, either where the child was killed in her bedroom or in the basement where the child was found.

Food for thought, if blood was found under the child's fingernails, then some trace evidence of blood should have been found either near or on her bed, or somewhere in the basement where the young child was found. This presents a strange coincidence of circumstance, or maybe the investigation and those who were stationed at the crime scene managed to over look the blood factor. A mistake which could have been purposely avoided, since the crime scene was already contaminated. Blood under the JBR's fingernails and no where else makes an argument certain to be strange bedfellows.

Killed In Her Sleep: JonBenet Ramsey sustained a terrific blow to the right side of her head which signifies that the child was more than likely killed in her sleep, *(the Ramseys said in various interviews when they got home from visiting friends, they immediately put JonBenet to bed)* strangled, then bound and gagged to give the appearance of an intruder. Scratches and other abuses on her body were placed there as a decoy by the person who killed her, even the foreign blood under the fingernails. If the child died in her bed then her hands must have touched something, a sheet, a pillow or even her night clothes. Still there should have been trace amounts of blood found at or near the crime scene. Nothing to this effect has come to the knowledge of the author, or maybe it was just an oversight, not yet come to pass.

Another reason why kill JonBenet and not Burke Ramsey, JonBenet Ramsey was picked out to be picked on, is simply to say, she was marked for death by someone in her own family. This little girl from all outward appearances seems to be a very outspoken young lady, expressive of her own opinions in sincereness of her own personal intellect. In other words, JBR. had no difficulty in saying what she felt, or what was on her mind. And apparently, Patsy Ramsey had some problems with that. Which does not negate the fact that someone in the Ramsey household, more than likely Patsy Ramsey, wanted to see JonBenet dead so bad that she would stop at nothing to see that this little child, who was not the object of her affection, brutally murdered. "Could the ovarian cancer and the fact that Patsy Ramsey knew in her heart that she was going to die, have had anything to do with her negative feelings towards her little daughter?" The author would allow the reader to answer that question.

And it appears that around the middle of the night, Burke was so sound asleep, evidently somewhere in the deep recesses of la la land, it would have taken a bulldozer to wake him up. Or the culprit (s) exercised extreme caution as to not wake her brother up or cause a disturbance to the same. And, it was not until the next morning Burke Ramsey found out that his little sister had been murdered. Burke Ramsey was not a problem child, it was his sister who appeared to be the object of havoc in the Ramsey household given to her mothers growing disdain and her increasing dislike towards her daughter.

It is, therefore, highly suggestive that the Ramsey's son was not the object of a death wish, nor was he the object of concern in any way, shape, form, or fashion. His sister was the one, somebody (more than likely her mother) in that house wanted to see dead. What started out as love and compassion between a mother and her daughter, evidenced by all the pageantry, who alive would think JBR's life could end up in a premeditated death wish.

What a coincidence! JonBenet's Half Brother and Sister Away: John Andrew Ramsey, the son of John Ramsey and his first wife, was with his sister, Melinda Ramsey Long, in Atlanta when his half sister JonBenet was found dead. He is not considered a suspect. In the aftermath of JonBenet's death, which also appears not to be a random selected premeditated act on the life of this little child, was it a coincidence that her two other older siblings just happened to be out of town the night of her death? One would have to give some serious thought to the remote possibility that their being away from the Ramsey home the night their sister was murdered could have been a planned, premeditated circumstance of occurrence.

Here's a question for thought, did Patsy Ramsey have anything to do with the fact that these two siblings just happened to be out of town the night their sister was murdered? If Patsy Ramsey had anything to do whatsoever in suggesting John Andrew Ramsey and Melinda Ramsey take a spur of the moment trip to Atlanta, during the time period of JonBenet's death, then it is highly likely that Patsy Ramsey is guilty of pre-orchestrating the death of this six-year old beauty queen, perhaps without the knowledge of either John Ramsey or his older two children.

If any remote degree of evidence surfaces that suggests Patsy Ramsey was party to the other two siblings being out of town, "Patsy Ramsey is guilty of premeditated murder." And by no means is the writer saying that the other two siblings were in any way party to the death of innocence, not in the least, but only to honestly give conscious thought to the irony of a strange coincidental situation.

The parallels of reality in this instance are so closely congealed until its frightening when given to thought possibilities. But there is one point of certainty associated with the other two siblings being away at that particular time, it was certainly on the drawing board of a pre-planned situation. In other words, it was not just a happenstance or part of a secondary scheme that they just happened to be away on the night tragedy stalked the Ramsey household. How ironic or how coincidental that these two situations (the travesty of innocence and the older two siblings out of town) would run parallel to each other, which appeared to be almost perfect timing for the murder of innocence.

Question: The fact that someone in the Ramsey home wanted little JonBenet dead, the next inquisition of thought is, what did this child do that was so bad that Patsy Ramsey, her mother, wanted her dead? Wetting in bed is not a choice reason, or a misdemeanor strong enough to justify a parent's anger so devastating in nature that it would warrant the death of innocence.

The writer believes that JonBenet's behavior relative to one or both of her parents was so outlandish until the mind of one of her parents, namely her mother, was so mesmerized that it would apparently warrant her immediate death. The bottom line to this entire incident-scenario is, one of the parents hated this child so much that the death of JonBenet was the only medium of satisfactory contentment. Another point of inference is this, Patsy Ramsey was a very jealous woman when it came to John Ramsey.

The tabloids printed one week several years ago, how Patsy Ramsey had become angry and very overly jealous about John Ramsey when she heard that there was a possibility he was seeing another woman. She was so outraged until she immediately stormed out of the beauty salon in an attempt to catch him red handed. This action of response on behalf of Patsy Ramsey proved that she was a highly temperamental person and guilty of extreme jealousy.

Her highly temperamental attitude/behavior via her jealousy is certainly apparent when it came to her husband, John Ramsey. The same observatory analogy is more than enough reason to believe that her own daughter came between her and John Ramsey on more than one occasion. Patsy Ramsey also knew that the two were sharing an incestuous relationship (of the which in and at sundry times she may have participated in) because the autopsy report stated that the child had been sexually molested, over and above the instrument used to rupture her vagina.

If the intruder theory never existed except on worthless paper, with Burke out of the picture by virtue of precept and elimination, the only other person close to having a sexual relationship with JBR had to have been her daddy. If a person didn't know any better, one might be inclined to believe that Patsy Ramsey had a legitimate right to be jealous, but not to the point of taking another person's life.

As the plot thickens, the only logical culprit infuriated enough to want to see the young child dead has to be her mother. Now, what did JonBenet Ramsey do to her mother that was so bad in nature until her mother's greatest desire was to see this child in a lifeless state of total demise? Or one would ask, what was the nature of JonBenet's error of intent that was so atrocious, one of her parents (precisely her mother) was so provoked as to carefully orchestrate the death of an innocent child?

With Burke Ramsey out of the picture and the apparent scheme of things, it appears that the parents are the only likely suspects of the which one of them wanted the young child dead. It is the author's belief that only Patsy Ramsey wanted her daughter dead for more reasons than one which the author, intends to discuss later in the third part analogy of John Ramsey's media interview.

There is another scenario the writer thinks could have a direct bearing on the murder situation, which is intended for the third part point of interest relative to John Ramsey's un-coerced on air public statements. In this third part point of interest, the writer intends to prove, without the slightest of doubt, that the killer of little JonBenet Ramsey was someone connected to her in a sense that can only be given to her mother or her father, the two people who were closest to her, and in whom she placed a lot of trust.

Here again, John Ramsey stated that it was during the middle of the night, someone entered JonBenet's room and took her life. Which also means he may have been in his bedroom, but he was not sleep, but rather he was wide awake, or else he could not have made an assertive statement to the fact appertaining to the approximate time of death, or the approximate time the crime took place. Now, if John Ramsey could make such an assertive statement, then he must have some knowledge that there were not any intruders in the home or he would have known it before he made this accusatory remark that would eventually incriminate him and his wife.

Question: Why would he say on national television that *the crime was committed during the middle of the night,* meaning around midnight or there about, if he was not sure of himself? Perhaps, he had not given this statement a second thought; because if the child died sometime during the middle of the night, or the crime was committed sometime during the middle of the night, *then what good is the ransom note when it was found after the fact?* At this point, the author does not believe that John Ramsey was speculating on the time of death, he was indeed telling the truth, because he knew the exact time his daughter was killed by her mother and himself.

John Ramsey and his wife knew in their hearts the ransom note was placed where it was found by Patsy to simply hide their guilt, if for no other reason than that. Again, John Ramsey made a blanketed statement that JonBenet was killed sometime during the middle of the night. If he knew this, and it came out of his mouth on national television, then he also knew that when his wife found the ransom note, JonBenet was already dead, "or else why make such a derogatory statement?"

Question: Why would intruders enter the house, kill the child, leave a ransom, and then exit the home without leaving a remote trace of evidence that they had been there? This would certainly mean that there were no intruders in the home at anytime at all, before or after the incident took place according to the so-called ransom note; and especially since the Ramseys knew the child was already dead. Therefore, the ransom note could only be used as a alibi to hide the apparent truth as to what really went on in the home of the Ramseys the night JonBenet was so brutally accosted.

The Time of Death Crucial: The time factor is very crucial to the crime scene for more reasons than one. First of all the time factor in association with a complete autopsy helps to determine the approximate to the exact time of death, which tells the truth as to whether or not intruders were actually in the resident. No concrete evidence was ever presented as proof an intruder had indeed violated the sanctity of the Ramsey home.

In this instance without proof of an intruder, all is lost, because a complete and thorough autopsy on the young child's body was not made available. Secondly, the time factor relative to death would have to purport to both parents being aware of each other's presence in their bedroom, if John Ramsey was alone at any time in their bedroom, at or around midnight, then, where was his wife?

And finally, the time factor ultimately takes into account if an intruder (s) was in the house, the execution of a so called kidnapping had to be timed precisely as to not alert the Ramseys that someone other than the family was in the residence. And by the way, the word kidnapped was never mentioned in the ransom note, all that was said *at this time, we have your daughter in our possession.* Even with the latter statement in mind, here again, it is highly impossible to say the child was kidnapped because she never left her home as the public was lead to believe by the ransom note.

A highly illogical statement of dumb-founded rationale close to stupidity says that the so called abductors took the child away from her home, killed her and brought her back and placed her in the basement is without any remote degree of sense, stupidity but not a lot of sense. And the time factor would have to enter play also, commencing from the time the Ramseys came home from visitation, to the time the ransom note was noticed. There was not enough time to take the child from her home, write a ransom, kill her and then bring her back to her home, placing her in an obscure room in the basement. The theoretics here does not make a great deal of sense.

There simply was not enough time to do all that the ransom note implies, if the child was kidnapped and killed outside of her home, brought back and placed in the basement, the logic here does not make much sense and is not valid in any way, shape or form. Which means, the ransom note was not well constructed in a proof positive manner, ultimately meaning, the child never left her home, and most of all, it means that the ransom note was fictitious and bogus to the point of reality via the fact the ransom note never existed as a statement placed in the home by an intruder.

Fact: Fallacy of the intruder theory along with a fictitious and bogus ransom note points exclusively to John or Patsy Ramsey as its brainchild, because they were the only two people in the home that night capable of putting together a deceptive but fake ransom note. Therefore, one would have to assume the ransom note is nothing more than a lie to cover up the Ramsey's apparent murder of their daughter JonBenet, and to get the public to presuppose or believe intruders had violated the Ramsey sanctuary. *Fact:* Nothing contained in the ransom note makes any worthwhile sense, as was stipulated by the Ramsey's hired private investigator; but what the ransom note does say, with an alarming degree of sensibility, is that an amateur mind composed and thought of it; more than likely the mother of the child.

Professional Diplomacy: Professionals engaged in this kind of wrongdoings, (especially kidnapping) either stick with the plural such as we, and our, or if it is a single individual, I is the constant reference source. (*I will call you between 8 and 10 am tomorrow; I advise you to be rested*, first page of the ransom note) Professionals do not skip around its subject usage, especially when a valid point of interest is intended. The professional wants to be absolutely clear of the intent of purpose, and the numerical impact of those involved in the kidnapping. An error on the part of the person writing the ransom, not a big error but an error just the same given to an amateur.

Precise Timing: A planned kidnapping requires precise timing, and in most instances does not exceed an hour in duration. It is always a get in and a get out situation, this certainly was not the case if the intruders waited around to write a three page ransom note. And the ransom note was found to be written on material or paper that was found in the resident which means that the criminal element has to take time to write the ransom note on the immediate premises. The real criminal element is not that stupid, cumbersome perhaps with the weight of guilt, but not stupid.

And finally, if the correct time of the child's death had been officially established, which it wasn't, and the Ramseys found the ransom note early that morning, and they found no intruders in the house, and later notified the authority, and also later that day found the dead body of JonBenet in the basement, all evidence points to one profound fact: Around midnight in conjunction with the ransom note, it would have been proven (by the results of a complete autopsy) *that the ransom note was of non effect because when the Ramseys discovered the ransom note, the child was already dead.*

The ransom note served no real profound purpose except a deterrent to hide what really went on in the Ramsey home the night before. So why would a real intruder leave the ransom note, if the object of their real intent was dead already? It should be a known fact now in light of the latter that the Ramseys were lying all along, simply to protect their own rear ends. On this pretext alone, the Ramseys were able to deceive a great many people, however, they were not able to fool all the people, especially the writer.

The writer feels the ransom note was a means of distraction primarily to hide the fact that the Ramseys were totally responsible for the death of JBR. Here again, the logic of the ransom note does not make much sense especially after the fact. Death occurred sometime relative to the middle of the night, according to John Ramsey's media report. And frankly, the author has no real reason to disprove him, or dispute the fact that it was during the middle of the night young JonBenet Ramsey was so brutally murdered in her own home, in her own bedroom, in her own bed!

If there were intruders in the house, then they did not go by the rules, they did not give the Ramseys time to respond to the ransom note. And why would the Ramseys call the police when the ransom note specifically said, "do not call the police or your daughter dies?" Why did the Ramseys not give themselves time to respond to the ransom note? Had they waited until about noon of the same day, or after they had made contact with the so-called kidnapers, they would have justified themselves as not being criminally connected with their daughter's death. How so, one might ask? Contact with the so-called abductors-kidnapers would have proved that the ransom note was a valid artifact of criminal intent. But they called the police, why? Was it because they knew little JonBenet was already dead, and by their hands?

The writer can only surmise that the ransom note was meant to be a scapegoat to assuage or conciliate public sentiment to ease the burden of their guilt. John Ramsey may not have assisted in the death of his daughter. There is ample reason to believe he loved his daughter unconditionally, but now he is just as guilty as his wife. He has now become an accessory to the crime. Perhaps it was after the fact that the child's grotesque killing was brought to his attention. And it was during the middle of the night and not during the night that this little child was brutally murdered. And again, this is why he appeared to be rather adamant in his statement of the crime taking place sometime during the middle of the night. Therefore again, when the ransom note was found early that morning, both of them knew the child was already dead, from the time of the child's death to the time of Patsy's death, they were superb in the acting skills. But for the grace, they almost persuaded the author to believe that they were innocent.

And when he learned of his daughter's death is probably more reason to accentuate the time factor and the crime being close to midnight rather than during the night, which would not be an exact account as to when the criminal act took place, but the time factor helps to determine the proximity of JonBenet's death. Now to say that he had previous knowledge of his daughter's planned homicide, would be a statement of incorrectness.

The Coin Has Many Faces-No Previous Knowledge: The author truly believes that John Ramsey had no previous knowledge or any remote idea that his daughter would never again see the light of day, or another Christmas day. Had he any remote idea that JonBenet's life was in danger, he would have taken preventive countermeasures to protect his darling little girl. And as fate would have it, he was completely kept in the dark by the instrument and the culprit (s) of his daughter's death. But here again, he had not the slightest idea, that during the middle of the night JonBenet would breathe her last breath. Therefore, it is highly conceptual that John Ramsey's statement of his daughter's middle of the night bludgeoning and her apparent strangulation took place some time during the middle of the night, or sometime shortly after or sometime shortly before midnight.

John Ramsey appears to be man who finds it hard to tell a lie, and hold a straight face; although the same cannot be said of Patsy Ramsey. When he said that he did not kill his daughter, he was in fact telling the truth, he did not kill his daughter, neither did he play a physical role in the killing of young JonBenet Ramsey.

Now, the involvement in a cover-up is a horse entirely of a different persuasion.

The writer truly believes that when John Ramsey learned of his daughter's dilemma, the child was already dead. Even though Mr. Ramsey was a non participant in his daughter's murder, he never said he did not know who did it, or he was not aware of who did it to the author's knowledge. Perhaps the question was asked of him, did he have any knowledge of who may have wanted to kill his daughter, but here again, the writer cannot truly pontificate on the accuracy of such a statement. It is believed that the circumstances surrounding the little child's death after the fact, John Ramsey is well aware of, and he has a great deal of knowledge as to who killed his beloved little JonBenet. If he was not asked this question in its exact context, he still hasn't made a false statement, or allowed himself to be entangled in a lie or perjured himself relative to his personal involvement in the immediate death of his daughter. And again, it is believed that he was well aware of who did it, because he could have been in knowledge of the fact that JonBenet's body was dragged to, and he was also aware of the one who took the young child's body and placed in the basement, where later that same day he and the authorities found her; which takes the reader back to the original statement, the crime was committed during the middle of the night, as was so stated by John Ramsey on national television.

The latter statement, taken into account by John Ramsey, in and of itself is not a false statement; it was around the middle of the night or thereabouts JonBenet Ramsey died. And with that, not by the hands of an intruder, but indeed by someone who was already in the house, and by someone who had a thorough background knowledge of the entire floor plan of the Ramsey's home. Could it be John and Patsy Ramsey?

The reader is allowed three guesses, scratch the son, scratch the other children who were in Atlanta, and now the reader has only one guess left, who might that be? Well, if the reader doesn't know by now, the people having the exact knowledge of the floor plans were the people left in the house shortly before and after midnight. The only people known to be in the home of the Ramseys before and after midnight were the Ramseys themselves and little dead JonBenet, the not so soon to be forgotten flower child of the new millennium.

The Murder of JonBenet Was Premeditated: This is a statement the father himself made concerning the death of his daughter seen on the Larry King Show and the NBC Today Show during one of their live interviews. John Ramsey knew that the death of his daughter was not an accident, that it has to have been a preplanned event of undeniable circumstances of ill wills and mutual discords occurring between his daughter and his wife.

John Ramsey had some remote idea that the relationship between his wife and his daughter was strained to level one in perhaps the first degree which is a very serious conflict of interest between a mother and her daughter, but he gave it little thought. When he learned of his daughter's death, shortly after she was murdered by his wife, he knew then, that she had been planning the incident for several days or perhaps several weeks. And from the looks of things, his failure to interact on behalf of both of them, would extract an awesome price. But he came up a day late, and several dollars short, as the old saying goes. Now, he will have to carry this torch of guilt for the rest of his life.

The only reason John Ramsey could make such a statement is because he had exact and precise knowledge of the killer of his daughter. Shortly before reality set in, and John Ramsey saw his dead little girl, lying lifeless in her bed or on the floor in the basement, he knew then that his wife had been planning his daughter's death all along. All the materials used to tie the child up, the instrument used to bludgeon her to death did not jump up all of a sudden. Reality told him, Patsy Ramsey had labored quite some time to fulfill the grotesque murder of JBR. **And the partially completed** ransom note was further evidence that Patricia Ramsey had concocted a fiendish plan to take the life of little JonBenet. The completed ransom note in its original context was undoubtedly the work of his mentally deranged wife.

Materials Used in the Child's strangulation: Proves without the remotest bit of doubt that JonBenet's death was a premeditated event of calculated circumstances. Circumstantial evidence proves that the materials used in the young child's death were not purchased the night she was murdered. So therefore, those items has to be premeditatedly bought before the night of her death. Most of the materials used in JBR's death were previously purchased by Patsy Ramsey several days earlier.

The thing that is a coincidence is how did a so-called intruder (s) manage in the darkness of night to find all the materials necessary to kill the child and write the ransom note without having fore knowledge of where everything was? "It was virtually impossible for the latter to be a happenstance, somebody knew exactly what he or she was doing, and not to mention the same entity/entities has a fairly good knowledge of the internal layout of the Ramsey home. "Here again, this could not be a coincidence by any stretch of the imagination!

Looking from a point of foresight and not hindsight, and the preparatory thought of Patsy Ramsey "once again proving that this little child was marked for death from the moment the material was purchased." Was it a coincidence that the intruders happened to use this same material to kill the child? Heaven forbid that such would be a valid case and point; the same material that was earlier purchased by Patsy Ramsey. The use of the materials purchased by JBR's mother several days earlier is so far from being a coincident until it is "the truth, the whole truth, and nothing but the truth, so help us God."

Intruders Mentioned: In an earlier statement, the word intruders was mentioned. This was done for several reasons. 1. Because the ransom note spoke of at least two culprits, three to be exact, the two men who have your daughter and the writer of the ransom note. If one would pay close attention to the ransom note itself, one would have to agree that more than one person/intruder was so-called involved in the kidnapping of JBR.

It is therefore impossible according to the ransom note to say that an intruder and not intruders were supposedly responsible for the death of JonBenet Ramsey. **2.** And to also prove a fact that the ransom note had to be strategically placed as to be readily found by the Ramseys the following morning, with snow outside on the ground, and the intruders were so-called no longer in the house, there was no positive evidence that the note was placed where it was with no evidence of an outside intruder /outsider (s) placing it there.

3. The ransom note proved undoubtedly to be invalid for more reasons than one. There was no invasion of the Ramsey's home by anyone outside of the immediate family. This cannot be substantiated by any creditable circumstance or evidence. There is no other recourse but to believe that the culprits of JonBenet's death came from within the house itself by someone who had to also be a resident there, who also had prior knowledge of the home's floor plan.

John Ramsey finding the body of his deceased daughter was no happenstance, he knew exactly where her body was in the basement, because he had prior knowledge of who placed it there, immediately after Patsy Ramsey had strangled her to death. Patsy Ramsey, in her state of illness could not carry the child, so after killing JBR, she dragged her lifeless body to the basement and placed her in the secluded area of which she later made John Ramsey aware of.

The doctor's report said that the child had been sexually molested, if therefore there were no intruder/intruders in the house the night of her death, and the fact that Patsy Ramsey is dead, and Burke Ramsey having been cleared of any involvement in the his sister's death, leaves John Ramsey as the primary living culprit of child molestation. This is one of the reasons he had hoped for the conviction of John Mark Karr.

Now former detective Lou Smit hired by the Ramseys to investigate the child's death via the intruder theory, boldly made the statement that an intruder instead intruders had invaded the home of the Ramseys and boldly took the life of their little six-year-old. Detective Smit and his intruder theory does not coincide with the ransom note in lieu of the fact that at lease three so-called persons invaded the sanctity of the Ramseys home on the night that their daughter was so tragically murdered.

Why was there a failure to follow the instructions of the ransom note?
Bogus-Fictitious Ransom Note: A Transcribe Version of the Ransom Note: Page 1.

Mr. Ramsey,
Listen carefully! We are a group of individuals that represent a small foreign fraction. We do respect your business but not the country that it serves. At this time...we have your daughter in our possession. She is safe and unharmed and if you want her to see 1997, you must follow our instructions to the letter.

You will withdraw $118, 000.00 from your account. $100,000 will be in $100 bills and the remaining $18,000 in $20 bills. Make sure that you bring an adequate size attache to the bank. When you get home you will put the money in a brown paper bag. I will call you between 8 and 10 am tomorrow to instruct you on delivery. The delivery will be exhausting so I advise you to be rested. If we monitor you getting the money early, we might call you early to arrange an earlier delivery of the money and hence a earlier pick up of your daughter.

A Transcribe Version of the Ransom Note: Page 2.
Any deviation of my instructions will result in the immediate execution of your daughter. You will also be denied of her remains for proper burial. The two gentlemen watching over your daughter do not particularly like you so I advise you not to provoke them. Speaking to anyone about your situation, such as Police, F.B.I., etc., will result in your daughter being beheaded. If we catch you talking to a stray dog, she dies. If you alert bank authorities, she dies. If the money is in any

way marked or tampered with, she dies. You will be scan for electronic devices, and if any are found, she dies. You can try to deceive us but be warned that we are familiar with Law enforcement countermeasures and tactics. You stand a 99% chance of killing your daughter if you try to out smart us.

A Transcribe Version of the Ransom Note: Page 3.

Follow our instructions and you stand a 100% chance of getting her back. You and your family are under constant scrutiny as well as the authorities. Don't try to grow a brain John. You are not the only fat cat around.. so don't think that killing will be difficult. Use the good southern common sense of yours. It is up to you now John!   Victory!
S.B.T.C.

And for anyone to believe the contents of this fictitious/bogus ransom note, has got to be rather dense, overwhelmingly short of brains, and lacking good common sense to see that the ransom note was full of holes and false illogical innuendoes:

The first page by the supposed child abductors said, *we respect your business, but we do not like the country that it serves,* is almost saying the culprits if they were real, are punishing the Ramsey family because they do not like the country his business serves. How ludicrous can you get? And then on page two, the same so called culprits of the ransom note said, *the two men watching your daughter do not particularly like you,* speaking of John Ramsey. Who in his or her right mind would call kidnapers gentlemen for one thing, but Patsy Ramsey. And it seems that the kidnapers appear to like John Ramsey with one breathe and a taste of dislike with the other.

None of it (the ransom note) makes any worthwhile sense. It is to the writer, the clear and not so concise amateurish mental temperament of Patsy Ramsey. Look at this, also on page two, the writer of the ransom note states that *two men are watching over your daughter do not particularly like you so I advise you not to provoke them.* Apparently there seems to be three persons of the evil intent in the picture now, the two men watching your daughter and the person who is writing the ransom note. It is virtually impossible for the person writing the ransom to include him or herself as one of the two men who have your daughter, a statement of highly unlikely reality.

In this instance the subject matter relative to the intruders is concerned for the most part with at least three persons, the two men, and the writer of the ransom note itself. The apparent air and the logic of the ransom note does not include the writer thereof as one of the two men who have your daughter, the logic simply does not co-agulate/come together into sensible logic.

Patsy Ramsey said emphatically at the first interview that she knew that there were at least two people who were involved in JBR's murder: the killer, and the person the killer confided in. But now there are three persons given to the murder incident, according to the ransom note; something she apparently overlooked, the two men and the writer of the ransom note, it appears that Patsy Ramsey, the suspected writer of the ransom note, forgot to include herself. But the truth is, there was never three people given to the bogus ransom note, only two people as she said initially, we know of at least two people, the killer and the person the killer confided in; meaning herself and her husband, the one who she confided in.

The logic (we know of at least two people) doesn't make much sense to say two men and later find out that three persons were mentioned in the ransom demands, she probably was so caught up in the lie, she forgot to include the third person in her interview. But just the same the writer interjects this statement of cause and effect, the killer was Patsy Ramsey and the person she confided in was her husband, who is now just as guilty of the murder of JBR by association and accessory to the fact as she is. And the author also believes that the ransom note is nothing more than a deterrent to alter the truth and the real people responsible for the killing of innocence. Those people would be the ones of her immediate family, John and Patsy Ramsey.

The Ransom Note Dissected And Psycho-Analyzed-Page One A: *At this time we have your daughter in our possession. She is safe and unharmed and if you want to see her in 1997, you must follow our instructions to the letter.* Now according to the ransom note and the approximate time it was written, it is obvious the child was supposedly not in the home, but somewhere outside of the home. Question, where does sense and sensibility fit in here?

Sense and sensibility is totally absent from reasonable logic in this latter statement written on the first page of the ransom note. Now what doesn't make sense is this; the so-called abductors or kidnapers have in their possession the daughter of John and Patsy Ramsey, which obviously conveys to the reader that they are not inside the residence of the Ramseys. If then the child is outside of the residence, in the hands of the abductors, and she was later on that same morning found dead in the basement, reasonable logic would suggest the abductors took her from the house given to the ransom note, killed her and brought her back into the residence of the Ramseys and placed her lifeless body in the basement. But, if the child was outside of the home, from the time the ransom note was found, how were the abductors of the child able to get her back in the house, place her in the basement without anyone seeing it? The house was full of people, someone would have had to see her kidnappers place her dead body in the basement, nothing remotely close to this circumstance took place to anyone's recollection, why?

Because nothing of the sort ever happened, the whole charade and the kidnapping, along with the ransom note, was nothing but a lie, if ever one was told. This action or behavior by so-called kidnapers given to the ransom note is highly improbable and non responsive to any degree of common sense or sensibility. Question; where is the logic behind this latter statement? Seeing that the statement in and of itself doesn't make sense in any remote degree; but what does make sense is that the ransom note is easily every bit the inflammatory temperament of Patsy Ramsey's illogical thinking.

Professional criminals are not that stupid to take unwarranted risks by coming back to the Ramsey home, if indeed the so-called kidnapers, abductors wrote the ransom note and were at all in the home of the Ramseys on the night in question. But so far, "no evidence has proven to any degree three persons were in that house, outside that house, on top of that house, around that house and least of all, under that house!"

The author speaks of three persons because the ransom note speaks of at least three people, the two men who supposedly had JBR in their captivity, and the person supposedly to be the writer of the ransom note. (*I will call you between 8 and 10 am tomorrow to instruct you on delivery.*) Now if three people were in the Ramseys home that Christmas night, some trace of their presence, other than the shoe, should have been found. It is virtually impossible for one person not to mention three persons to enter the home in the dead of winter with snow on the ground, wet sidewalks and not leave some kind of evidence given to intruders violating the privacy of the Ramsey's home. Its not possible. The police report said there was no signs of forced entry, no signs of an intruder, no foot prints in the snow, and apparently no truth to the ransom note and these are not suppositions in the least, but are indeed provable facts.

Even to this day, no evidence of an intruder (s) in or outside of the house presented any conclusive proof that alien persons had entered the home. Therefore, the ransom note has to be a not so carefully concocted lie, if nothing else. And the band played on.

According to the ransom note, three people are responsible for the so-called abduction of little JonBenet; entering the home and leaving the home at approximately the same time without any trace evidence makes it very hard to believe that there were intruders at all. Outside the home, snow was on the ground, still no trace evidence. The only other alternative to this murder incident is to establish without the slightest of doubt that intruders in the home of the Ramseys is again a point blank lie, primarily brought to pass to hide the fact that they themselves murdered JBR. And again, the ransom note is just as bogus as the evil intent they are trying to hide.

Therefore, the writer of the ransom note was either an amateur or lacked the sense to compose a ransom note not void of accusatory indiscretions and illogical statements. Or, John and Patsy Ramsey made a botched attempt to belay-put aside the blame of their daughter's death on themselves. But the author cautions the reader to this fact, it was not proven beyond reasonable doubt that there were intruders in the Ramsey home on the night-morning their daughter was so brutally murdered. And if the ransom note doesn't make much sense relative to the abductors of JBR, the only other avenue of guilt must lie with the decease's family, namely John and Patsy Ramsey with added emphasis of blame given to the mother of the dead child.

Page One B: *You will withdraw $118,000.00 from your bank account. $100,000 will be in $100 bills and the remaining $18,000 in $20 bills. Make sure that you bring an adequate size attaché to the bank.* Now make sure you bring an adequate size attaché to the bank sounds as though it is coming straight from the mind set and the temperament of Patsy Ramsey. If this statement was not part of the ransom, the author would have reason to believe the note itself had a little validity to it relative to the guilt of John and Patsy Ramsey. And if Patsy had left this statement out of the ransom demands, the author would have reason to also believe she was innocent of any wrong doings.

Who cares about what one puts the money in, so long as the money is withdrawn and given to the so-called abductors mentioned in the bogus ransom note given to the penmanship of Mrs. Patricia Ramsey. Kidnapers do not take time to advise the victims of a ransom note to the adequacy of a proper size attaché. They are only interested in getting the money through and by the least medium possible. And good common sense will tell a person to make sure one has proper means of transporting that amount of money.

The writer of the ransom note is undoubtedly a person of little intelligence not fully acquainted with this type of criminology, which means that the writer of the ransom note had to be connected to the murder scene, because here again, the logic of the ransom note does not make much sense. Real criminals are given to be very short in their demands, and very timely. The ransom note in and of itself had to much of a feminine sympathetic overtone to it, not common to a masculine approach to a ransom demand.

The fallibility of the ransom demand is like unto putting money in a bag with holes in it; and vainlessly trying to make sense out of nonsense. This ransom note in all of its sordid demands has Patsy Ramsey stamped all over it. The only thing that could be more precise than this, is for Patsy Ramsey, was she alive today, to come straight out and admit that she is the writer of the ransom note. Other than that, it doesn't take a rocket scientist to figure out that JonBenet's mother is the guilty party and the author of the mysterious note in question.

Page One C: *I will call you between 8 and 10 am tomorrow to instruct you on delivery.* Apparently, this kidnapping/abduction was not about money at all, the so-called abductors have kidnapped the child for the sole purpose of financial reward, and once the money is taken from the bank placed in a brown paper bag, the same day the murder incident took place, and now in the ransom note the writer of the same is saying, *I will call you on tomorrow to pick up the money* is very bad taste on the part of the criminal element, if such was the case. Why wait until tomorrow to get the money when the money can be picked up today.

Now, if I (the author) were associated with the kidnapers I would demand the money as soon as they could get it, even yesterday, if it were possible. And, if money was truly the name of the game, but apparently not, the note said the so-called abductors would call tomorrow, which also doesn't make too much sense.

And I will call you, should have been, we will call you, another mistake on the part of the writer of the ransom note. I in the singular format is not representative of the two other people who were supposedly part of the bogus ransom demand. Now it appears that Patsy Ramsey, the writer of the ransom note is making herself the sole benefactor of the ransom demand. This ransom note written by Patsy Ramsey has so many holes in it, it can easily be used for target practice by a person blind- folded. There is absolutely no clear or concise logic about or pertaining to the ransom note.

This is another mistake made on the part of the person writing the ransom note, who is none other than Patsy Ramsey, in her vain attempt to hide the fact that she murdered little JonBenet. In most instances wherein a great deal of money is to be extracted from the victims or their families, the criminal element would want the money as quickly as they can get it. And, if the criminal element could get the money today, certainly they would not want to wait until tomorrow, unless it was not about money at all. Most criminal elements know that the longer you wait on a ransom demand, the greater your chances of getting caught.

This apparent bogus ransom note, the brainchild of Patsy Ramsey, says very little of her intelligence not given to a criminal mind, and the fact that the ransom note was never about money, no not in the least. The money, according to the ransom note, was reserved by the Ramsey's banker, but no one ever showed up to claim it. Why? Nothing in the way of the truth was ever associated with or related to the real validity of the ransom note's existence as a valid demand. In a plain simple state of gesture, there was no truth to the ransom note from the time it was found by Patsy Ramsey the morning of, or to this present day and time.

No one responded to the ransom demand because the whole situation was nothing but a lie, conjured up in the hellacious mind of JonBenet's mother. If a vain attempt was made to get the ransom demand, it would have said that there was at least some validity to the note itself. And again, there was absolutely no response by anyone at any time to the money requested for JBR's safe return or her life.

No one remotely at any time called the Ramsey home in response to the ransom demand, no one tried to contact John or Patsy with further details as to the ransom demand, and no one showed up at the Ramsey's home discreetly or indiscreetly relative to the ransom demand. Everything about the ransom demand was a carefully concocted lie of massive covert deception that had even the United States Federal Bureau of Investigation fooled. "How in the world could two people of the nature of John and Patsy Ramsey make literal ass rags of one of the most vital segments of U.S. government, is beyond the author's wildest imagination! But, they did it!" And the same is also a very serious flaw by any technical standards intended to distract any implication of her and her husband having anything to do with JonBenet's tragic death. The author almost gets goose bumps all over just from the possibility of the Ramseys having so much clot and believability, "but they have it!"

Page One D: *The delivery will be exhausting so I advise you to be rested.* Another point of interest alluding a bogus ransom note is an overt act of sentimental compassion. Criminals who extort money may at times exercise a little compassion, but not in the overt way so demonstrated on the first page of the ransom note. *The delivery will be exhausting so I advise you to be rested,* is a joke in itself. How can any parent rest when their daughter is in the hands of a supposedly bad criminal element, threatening at any given moment to kill the child. Is the public stupid or is the writer of the ransom note stupid? Rest would undoubtedly be the furthest thing from the mind of parents whose daughter could be killed at any moment in the twinkling of an eye.

On page two, the child's so called captors makes very clear their intentions should the family fail to follow explicit instructions: *Any deviation from my instructions will result in the immediate execution of your daughter. You will also be denied her remains for proper burial. The two gentlemen watching over your daughter do not par-*

ticularly like you so I advise you not to provoke them. Speaking to anyone about your situation such as the police, F.B.I., etc, will result in your daughter being beheaded. If we catch you talking to a stray dog, she dies. If you alert the bank authorities, she dies. If the money is in any way tampered with, she dies. You will be scanned for electric devices and if any are found, she dies.

Now what parent in his or her right mind would be able to rest under these circumstances? Every moment the threat of death is constantly focusing on the parents abducted child. How in the world can a parent think about sleep or rest, when the next day might very well be the last day of life for their so-called kidnapped child, as the ransom note would put it.

The author sincerely hates to say what he is about to say, only a fool would believe any degree of truth relative to this ransom note, and certainly if John and Patsy Ramsey do not believe it, then they are certainly fools, too, to think that any reasonably rational thinking person would believe it also. There are still a lot of us who do not believe the gullible meandering lies and false pretenses of the killers of innocence.

Only a mind not given to the criminal intent would make such a statement of provocative absurdity. Very seldom men think in this fashion, for the most part a man could give a damn how you feel, just as long as you get the money to them. But the highly sentimental nature of a woman would think differently, granted all due respect. And, this ransom note is the highly sentimental nature of Patsy Ramsey in every regard. Not only that, but it is highly suggestive that one of the three so-called abductors of little JonBenet relative to the supposed kidnapping is a woman, the writer of the so-called ransom note.

The highly sentimental nature of the ransom note is very conducive to feminine behavior, again with all due respect as not to offend anyone. Professional criminals given to the evil intent do not act in this manner, it is just not good criminal behavior. And the author would like to remind the reader that everything done and said so far, is conjunctive to the premeditated murder of JBR, in light of the bogus-fictitious ransom note.

And to add insult to injury, the so-called ransom note further stipulated: *But be warned that we are familiar with law enforcement countermeasures and tactics. You stand a 99% chance of killing your daughter if you try to out smart us.* Mother of reason, please give us a break! Under these circumstances along with the almost unbearable stress, sleep/rest would be the furthest thing from one's mind. Could it be that the woman who wrote the ransom note (namely Pat Ramsey) was just toying with personal feelings by trying to exude a little not so well welcome degree of sympathetic compassion, speaking to the statement in the ransom note: *I advise you to be rested?* Can you believe the nerves of some people?

More insult and injury comes to pass when the lady writing the ransom note sends out more threatening gestures by saying: *You stand a 99% chance of killing your daughter if you try to out smart us.* Under these sordid conditions contained in the ransom note, who can remotely think about rest, especially the whole transaction could have been carried out in the same day, thus alleviating any further prolonged custody of the so-called kidnapped victim, and the stress it has inflicted on the parents of the so-called kidnap victim.

Either the lady who is responsible for the ransom note is extremely naive or she is suffering from hypothermia of the membrane with an acute sense of compassion and coldness at the same time. Hell, will somebody please give the lady an Oscar in the category of deranged stupidity, she deserves it! Better yet, give the lady a medal, and a chest to pin it on! Man, talking about little-lord fauntleroy! This ransom note is not just a joke, it is a very poorly concocted lie, an ill conceived conjured up deterrent by the Ramseys to assuage any beliefs that they had anything to do with the death and the murder of JBR!

Compassion related to rest, something only a woman could conceive, given to hypothermal coldness-showing little regard for the feelings of the parents of the so-called kidnapped child; which is duly a false premonition of an occurrence which never took place. But only in the minds of the parents of little JonBenet Ramsey, the ones who took her innocent life and are using a bogus ransom note to hide the preplanned-premeditated guilt of murder in the first degree.

The Guilt Complex: The third page of the ransom note proves the bogusness of the Ramseys misguided, malignant intentions to use the three page letter as means of escape from the accusatory implications regarding the horrific murder of their daughter: *You and your family are under constant scrutiny as well as the authorities. Don't try to grow a brain John. You are not the only fat cat around so don't think that killing will be difficult. Don't under estimate us John. Use that good southern common sense of yours. It is up to you now John!*

How ironic, all of a sudden John has become the object of the ransom note's affection, or the object of Patsy Ramsey's hate. Patsy Ramsey's hate for her husband is to be soon revealed by the author congealed in her jealousy towards her daughter. Now, she has him up against a rock and a hard place because he, too, had been molesting their daughter. It appears that she is sending a clear and concise warning to him, "Don't under estimate us John." What she is really saying is, "John don't under estimate her." She has the goods on him.

The message she is sending via the bogus ransom note appears to have a tri-fold effect; but it also conveys to the author that John is very aware of the murder incident, and he knows who the killer is. And, it is believed that the ransom note is given to the personal feeling of Patsy Ramsey in regards to her husband, and the point of interest intended as a ransom demand. The killer is his wife, and she is warning him don't try to grow a brain that would expose her as the murderer of their young daughter. And she is also saying don't under estimate her or her ability to involve him in the murder scene. She adds to the second statement a personal note of inference *use that good southern common sense of yours.* Is to the author a statement so personal in its context that only a person in close contact with John Ramsey could make such a remark. And, who knows John Ramsey better than his wife, who uses his name in such a close personal way?

Finally, *It is up to you now John!* She is saying whatever the outcome of the murder incident, it is left up to him. He can either go along with the program or he can expose her as the killer of JBR, which would mean he would also have to expose himself. At the same time the would be ransom note is also conveying a message to the family from the abductors who supposedly have taken young JonBenet as a bargaining chip in a so-called kidnapping. In the various interviews of the Ramsey family, Patsy Ramsey oftentimes used John in the first part personal aspect of his name, and the way she called his name.....John, sounds just like the way she used his name in the ransom note, *it's up to you now John.* For anyone to think that Patsy Ramsey is not the writer of the ransom note in light of this analysis is more than likely very partial to the family.

The truth relative to the contents of the bogus-fictitious ransom note is an undeniable statement of *fact* in conjunction with the mother's premeditated scheme to kill the young child, and the fact that no one has proven beyond the shadow of a doubt that intruders were indeed in the home of the Ramseys during the night of JBR's death, especially if the ransom note makes mention of at least three persons. Question: How then is it remotely possible for three people to enter the home and not leave one piece of positive evidence that they had been there?

The only logical conclusion to this statement is that there were never any intruders in the home at all. But on the other hand, there is positive proof that there were four people given to the Ramsey family that were in the house during the time JonBenet was so brutally murdered: JonBenet, the victim, Burke Ramsey, who was so sound asleep he may have been sedated, and then there is John and Patsy Ramsey.

No one else was in that house that particular night, if such was the case, (given to at least three persons) then it would have been virtually impossible to hide every and all means of trace evidence. Snow on the ground outside, some form of foot prints or trace evidence should have been found inside the house, but none was found. Here again, there was no trace evidence because there was no one else in the house except the immediate Ramsey family.

The Motive Revealed: The Ramseys fabricated this lie (intruders in the home) to avoid criminal prosecution for the death of JonBenet. The fallacy of the ransom note and no apparent true concrete evidence of intruders in the home of the Ramsey the night JonBenet was killed is proof positive evidence that John and Patsy Ramsey are the guilty parties because, there is simply no one else to blame with any degree of sensibility. Now, Patsy Ramsey has said in reference to the killers of her daughter: *God knows who you are and we will find you.* Never was said a more poignant statement, for by the grace of God, we have found you (John and Patsy Ramsey) to be the killers of innocence!

The Father's Error: John Ramsey appears to be a good natured person, but apparently he takes some things and some situations for granted. Living in the same home with his wife and his daughter, and knowing that they together shared a very common and close bond, by all intensive forethought, should have known that something was not completely cohesive in the relationship between his wife and his daughter. Being naive is no excuse for not taking evasive countermeasures when he knew something was not exactly the same between the two of them. And perhaps his wife spoke to him on any number of occasions, but he refused to heed the warning signs that were springing up all around him; and it appears he wasn't about to give up having sex with his young daughter, to cater to the whims of his over zealous, jealous wife.

His ignorance would eventually cause him to pay a heavy price for the error of his neglect, especially when he found out his wife had murdered his daughter. And, by this time, it was too late to do anything about the unpleasant situation, his daughter was dead.

The bottom line state of intimacy amidst the three of them was at some point in time destined to come to a climatic and cataclysmic end, and would be the cause for a major rift and conflict of interest between the three of them. The volcano had erupted and apparently there was nothing on God's green earth he could do to stop it. The breach of trust and confident was at this point beyond fixing.

Men oftentimes choose to be naive about certain situations in the home when mother and daughter are the center of confusion. Other men take a dim view of conflicts of interest especially when women in the household are at odds with each other. The author believes that John Ramsey was well aware of what was going on between his wife and his daughter, primarily because he was having sex with both of them, but more so with JonBenet, because of Patsy Ramseys terminal ovarian cancer illness.

Sometimes the haughtiness of masculine behavior encounters the greed level, which is to say, John Ramsey did not want to give up neither one of his ladies. He wanted both of them and he wanted to remain in a pleasant comfortable family setting. But as fate would have it, he could not have his cake and eat it too. And in a small but non bodacious way, he is somewhat responsible for his daughter's death. In fact, he just might be the very reason why JonBenet is dead. Pedophiles, in their obsessive deviant nature, find it hard to avoid the very thing their nature is calling for.

Sexual Promiscuousness: Now, not to be redundant, one does not have to be totally ignorant or naive to understand that John Ramsey was having sexual intercourse with both his wife and his daughter. Which became the cause of a terrible misunderstanding between the three of them, especially Patsy Ramsey.

Apparently, both of them (John and Patsy Ramsey) were pedophiles who enjoyed having sex with little children, in this instance their daughter, JBR. The author would presuppose that such behavior had been going on probably at the start of JonBenet's pageantry exposure, because of the provocative clothing she wore. She appeared to be a pedophile's afternoon delight, with all due remorse.

The autopsy on the body of JonBenet clearly showed that someone had been having sex with her. It is also a clear fact that her vagina was ruptured and torn severely not by an intruder, but more than likely by her daddy, to hide the fact that he was having sex with her. The thing that started the whole charade of death in the first place. Mothers do not kill their daughters for wetting the bed, but mothers in some instances will kill their daughters for having sex with their husbands, though cases of this nature are very rare, but the possibilities are still there. Most of the time, it will occur out of jealousy more so than hate, not negating the fact that hate will oftentimes play serious role in a dysfunctional household like the Ramseys.

Three Invalid Points of Interest: Sensory skepticism about an intruder or intruders in the home can now be ruled out, because there is no positive proof someone else other than the Ramseys were in the house that night. Here is the bottom line truth about **the intruder theory,** no one be it an intruder or intruders invaded the home of the Ramseys at any time ever during the entire murder scheme and the travesty of innocence, and that is now a proven indisputable fact.

No one anywhere or at any time with any degree of proof has proven or is able to say that the Ramsey home had been invaded by a foreign or alien source. Not then, nor ever, was there anyone other than the family in that home that night. Because the intruder theory, and its well worth repeating, existed only on paper and only in the minds of John and Patsy Ramsey.

This statement in and of itself is not, I repeat, is not a supposition or a presupposition anymore. Because, for the first time during this murder investigation, facts have surfaced that positively refutes any so-called intruder theory. There is real solid evidence that refutes **the bogus ransom note**, and real tangible evidence that refutes the fake and fictitious kidnap theory. And, there is real concrete evidence that denies the kidnap theory ever existed. All three of these situations of intense scrutiny are factually non-existent in the sense that persons other than the Ramseys were behind it all.

The thing that the writer is trying to get the public to understand is, these three items are now invalid. Nothing associated with the **ransom note theory** came to pass in any remote way, especially since the body of the dead child was found in her own home. And certainly there was no remote attempt at kidnaping the child. The ransom note theory went through the roof into the atmosphere of nothingness and lies. The Ramseys were so sure of themselves they thought no one would ever find out about their little murderous secret. How sad of them. So, therefore the ransom note had to be the working of the culprits who killed the young child and left her lifeless body in the basement cellar of her home.

Nothing associated with the intruder theory ever came to pass in the proof positive. If the ransom note had been proven invalid and a lie, then the intruder theory must be invalid and a lie also, because it was supposedly to be the intruder who wrote the ransom note. Question: How can a so-called intruder write a ransom note if the so-called intruder never existed?

The intruder theory cannot be validated by anyone associated with the detective division, the police department, the FBI, or any eye witnesses, only speculations which cannot be proven. Any evidence that says an intruder was in the home was placed there by the persons who killed JBR. And, only three other persons were ever in that house during and immediately after this child was so hideously murdered! The mother, the father and her brother, the brother is crossed out for obvious reasons, which leaves the mother and the father as the culprits of the death of innocence.

Nothing associated with the **kidnap theory** ever came to pass in the proof positive that would suggest in any way that this child was ever taken from the confines of her home before or after her dead body was discovered. All these items are now facts and no longer given to suppositions. "These items didn't make much sense then, and they certainly don's make much sense now!"

One dead child minus one ransom note, one dead child minus one intruder theory, one dead child minus one kidnap theory equals one humongous lie. It brings all who are concerned about this child's death closer to the truth and the culprits who are responsible.

The author believes in order to get to the truth of this whole issue out in the open, the truth of the matter concerning the kidnap theory, the ransom note, and the intruder theory, must be clearly and indisputably understood to be non-existent from all points of view. Once this is done and the public realizes that it is so, then and only then can the truth behind the DNA associated with the child's fingernails and the spot of DNA on her panties can be sufficiently dealt with.

It is for this reason the author is and has been strongly stressing the importance of the fallacy associated with the DNA. The DNA found on JonBenet's body-her panties, is the only thing that's keeping John Ramsey out of jail and perhaps an unannounced date with the needle. The facts of the DNA will be dealt with later, keep reading.

Token items of an intruder were more than likely carefully placed where they could be easily found, and placed in strategic locations by none other than the Ramseys themselves; a shoe here, token blood under the fingernails, meticulously placed there, a foot print here, a shoe there, a situation carefully planned and premeditated. With these thoughts in mind and the fact that the child was sexually molested on more than one occasion, is in the proof positive that apparently the child had been engaging in previous sexual intercourse, evidenced by the inflammation in her vaginal area, no intruder/intruders, no kidnaping having taken place, obviously points to only to one person capable of penile penetration, that person is John Ramsey. These token items simply will not stand the test of time and chance. Not by a remote degree of factual circumstances.

JonBenet was more than likely drawn into sexual promiscuousness with her parents in light of her parents pedophile nature. The author would venture to say that this was something she did not relish, but young children are sometimes encouraged to do things against their will, especially if it is in the nature of pedophile behavior. Then, there are other times when a child is not so much disheartened by sexual encounters of this type, when they have the complete trust and confidence of the parent (s). And all reasonable assurances seem to indicate that little JonBenet had the complete trust and confidence of her parents.

This is evidenced by the fact that she made no concerted effort to expose either one of them; and the reason being, she had probably fallen in love with her father. Even though she probably cared a lot for her mother, the fact remains, she was more than likely in love with her father, and did not care if her mother knew it primarily because both of them were having sex with her, or both of them were using the young child as a fatal sexual attraction in some form or fashion even if it wasn't physical which is highly improbable in light of the damage done to the child's vagina. Children, especially little girls, show a greater affection for the fathers in some instances that if not given immediate careful attention, might lead to child abuse.

Apparently there was no alternative resolve to the issue at hand as seen in the mind of Patsy Ramsey, and it is more than likely the reason she began developing a strong disdain for JonBenet and the close relationship she was having with her father, especially the sexual part. JonBenet has now become the object of her evil intentions brought on by the constant sexual encounters she was engaging in with her father. Patsy Ramsey's anger probably was fueled by the fact that she was no longer an integral part of the once playful moments all three of them shared together.

So as it was, or so as it appeared to be, John was beginning to fine more pleasure in having sex with his daughter than he did with his wife. From all indications on the part of Patricia Ramsey, it appears that all other efforts to counter the situation apparently failed, and Patsy Ramsey had no other choice remaining to her but to plan an act of premeditated murder on the life of little JonBenet. John Ramsey could never be so close to the truth when he said the murder of JonBenet was premeditated. And at the same time, the author is very confident that he had the knowledge of who did it, none other than the person of his wife and soul mate. She had become so infuriated and so enraged at her daughter, JonBenet, that all sense of rationale and thoughts of good common sense took leave of her. Question: Did it have anything to do with her earlier diagnosis of ovarian cancer?

It is a foregone fact of conclusion that the young child was engaging or had engaged in perhaps a brief period of prolonged sexual intercourse given to the partial autopsy report. And that's no joke! But there is one thing for sure which cannot be denied or unsubstantiated which is *a valid fact*: the child had been sexually molested; whether prolonged molestation or a random act, *it is again an undeniable fact*; JonBenet Ramsey's body at the time of her death indicted some form of sexual intercourse, and that's no lie!

3. The Culprits Were Either Jealous of Him or They Hated Him: This statement by John Ramsey is eluding to the fact that the writer of the ransom note either was jealous of him or the writer of the ransom note hated him. From all indications exacted from the crime scene it appears that the writer of the ransom was given to both jealousy and hate. One must understand that jealousy for the most part is based on love. And where there is no love, there is no jealousy, for it is extremely hard to be jealous of something or someone you don't love.

Even the God of creation falls into this category for the Bible says that He is a Jealous God. And, out of His jealousy, Israel was almost destroyed, and this, too, is an undeniable fact. Love, through a candied example of religious piety, also has a destructive force behind it when the balance is not carefully weighed for and against in all intensive purposes. Which is to say, jealousy and hate can kill in a moment and in a heartbeat. God is an exception to the rule, but humanity is not. And, there is no apparent evidence that John Ramsey was engaged in any extra marital affair besides his immediate family.

So, if the writer of the ransom note supposedly given to the abduction of JBR was jealous of him, it must be said that apparently the writer of the ransom note was in love with him, too; which also gave way to hate and disdain at the same time because the truth is, someone else was disturbing a once picture perfect relationship in the Ramsey household, for jealousy and hate has its reasons to propagate malice of intent. Here again, the author wonders who could that person be? Based on the latter intent of purpose, the person who appears to be jealous of John Ramsey must be coming from the mind set of a woman. It is highly unlikely that a gay person would be responsible for the death of innocence.

And this same disdain for John Ramsey by the writer of the ransom note was enough to kill the child he loved very dearly. And this, too, is an *undeniable fact:* the little child is dead, buried and sleeping in her grave. Based on the fact that the little child is deceased says that it wasn't about money at all. Money was just an excuse to justify the death of innocence. What the whole situation really boils down to jealousy and hate multiplied to the power of the death stroke.

Human behavior and emotional trauma given to violent acts of culpable mental anxiety borders or perpetuates a very thin line between jealousy and hate. And, it is also evidenced in the ransom note that the writer had a personal grievance with the father of JonBenet. Question: The author wonders who could that be?

This is the last of the three incriminating statements given by the author made by John Ramsey during one of his and his wife's former interviews. Though not an exact quote, but just the same, the words came from his mouth on national television. The next thought or question is, why would he say that the culprits were either jealous of him or they hated him. Would it be because he had some idea as to why his daughter was murdered and knew who the culprit (s) was? The statement in itself was just not a blanket statement, or something he blabbered off the top of his head. Somehow it is felt he knew exactly what he was saying.

The ransom note did not give any clues as to whether or not the so-called abductors were either jealous or an intent of hate to the same. So then, the so-called ransom note should be ruled out at this point, nothing in the ransom note exemplified jealousy or hate. What else would cause John Ramsey to come to such a conclusion? If he was not speaking of the so-called abductors, then who was it that he had in mind. Could he speaking of Patsy Ramsey, his wife? She had all the reason in the world to be both jealous of him and hate him at the same time.

For one thing, he was having sexual relationships with their daughter, more than enough grounds to hate him. More than likely jealousy crept in when she felt his compassion growing more for their daughter than it was for her; in light of the fact that both of them were having sex with JonBenet, and the fact that JonBenet was probably showing more affection for her father than her mother, were even further grounds for hate, jealousy and animosity on the part of Patsy Ramsey. What else could have gone on between them that would aggravate Pat Ramsey so bad that she would want to see her daughter dead?

Sometimes there is a very thin line between love and hate, apparently the Ramseys and their daughter, little JonBenet, had come to a crossroad in their relationship that had to be rectified with all relevant expediency. And from the apparent look of things, John Ramsey appeared to be riding in the backseat of an emotional roller coaster that could run off the tracks at any time.

Apparently, he chose to ignore it. Maybe he had a problem deciding who was going to be the first lady, or he didn't have a choice at all because he loved both of them. It also appears that he had a great deal of trouble making up his mind, so Patsy Ramsey had no other choice but to step into the ring and give him a little assistance in the only way she knew how, JonBenet had to die!

And certainly this was not a case of mistaken identity, Patsy Ramsey had become fed up with this tri-fold relationship, especially when her own daughter appeared to be taking her man from her. Patsy Ramsey doesn't appear like the type of person that would indiscriminately jump into water, especially when she knew the water was hot. It took careful planning to carry out her fiendish deed to be rid of JonBenet.

In light of the apparent rift of confusion, jealousy and hate, this situation between the three of them was worse than an accident trying to find a place to happen; to say the least, this tri-fold relationship was boiling hot, and the steam from the heated temperaments was also hot enough to cause tempers to flare out of control, especially Patsy Ramsey. They needed help, and the sad part about it, they didn't even know it. Hate and jealousy, jealousy and hate is about to give way to darkness and death, and Mrs. Ramsey is sporting the Bon Appetite hunger for revenge.

Pedophile/Incest: Father/daughter sexual infatuations/attractions are not so common place behaviors in normal households, but the latter is not the same in many dysfunctional households. In a dysfunctional home, the same scenario may also apply to mother/son incestuous pedophilia behavior. In the situation with the Ramsey family, this type of dysfunctional behavior had gone on for quite some time without incident, primarily because the mutuality of sexual respondency between the three of them had not come to a point of disagreement and animosity.

Here again, in many households where incest is given to a father and a daughter, the mother sometimes sees the situation with one eye closed and one eye open, especially if she is involved in the incestuous affair. At other times, in families highly suggestive of dysfunctional sexuality, the mother might overlook a sexual affair of the father and the daughter if she is engaged in dysfunctional sexuality with her son.

Dysfunctional sexuality is not given to be the case in the Ramsey family concerning their son Burke Ramsey. Only with JonBenet is there such suspect of misbehavior in a dysfunctional sense. Wives do have a tendency to become over jealous at times when the eye of the father is more in sink with his daughter. This was perhaps the situation in the Ramsey family. It's like this, some women can deal with the situation, and some women have problems accepting the fact that the father is sleeping with the daughter. Patsy Ramsey, it is believed, did not have a problem with John Ramsey sleeping with his daughter.

Patsy Ramsey may have had a problem with this father-daughter situation based on three accounts: (1) John Ramsey and JonBenet were probably, more often than not, excluding Patsy from engaging in mutual sexual interplay, a vehement excuse given to great anger and an ill inflated ego on the part of the mother. (2) John Ramsey was probably paying more attention and engaging in sex more often with his daughter than he was with his wife. And sexual interplay with his daughter may have been more pleasurable than sexual interplay with his wife.

The author believes that this is the thing that started the whole ball of wax rolling to meet up eventually in a highly traumatized-emotional melting pot. (3) Patricia Ramsey did not want to lose her husband to her daughter, especially in the format of dysfunctional sexual behavior and pedophile child play of which it is believed that she was also a part of. It is also given to belief that this was the real source of her anger and animosity towards her daughter and the child's father. And, eventually, she would punish them both, JonBenet's death, and John Ramsey's unexposed guilt.

The True Motive Redefined: *The Child Was Caught In A Web;* JonBenet Ramsey was caught between a rock and a hard place, not fully understanding the degree of intimidation she had placed upon her mother as a result her relationship with her dad, and not willing to relinquish the affection she had for her father to appeal to her mother for the both of them. As a six year old beauty queen, she more than likely understood well what was going on and the fact that her mother's compassion for her was weaning with each passing day.

In the midst of it all, JonBenet did not want to let go of her dad, who had also become her lover. JBR appeared to be somewhat of an intelligent young girl, but maybe she had not fully comprehended the extent of danger and animosity developing between her and her mother which eventually placed them at odds with each other. And John Ramsey was probably off somewhere in the background, not having the remotest idea that his wife harbored in her emotions a total disdain for perhaps him and his daughter.

Mother-Daughter-Violent-Confrontation: Almost in every instance of dysfunctional family situations, there comes a time when all parties involved must come to grips with reality. And it does appear this family needed to give themselves over to a reality check. If something wasn't done to curb the ensuing disturbance, all hell would eventually break lose. It appears that Patsy Ramsey was at her ropes end, and a reality check was very necessary. But she chose to overlook it. Perhaps this is what the Ramsey family needed in light of the circumstances they were faced with. A good reality check of the situation would have avoided the death of innocence. But as fate and time would have it, mother and daughter would soon meet up at the crossroad of their mutual dilemma in a violent verbal confrontation, in light of the fact that all else had failed.

So now, she (Patsy Ramsey) must call her daughter into a private conversation to discuss the troubling situation now confronting the two of them. More than likely Patsy Ramsey conveyed to her young daughter regarding the impending circumstances and her relationship with her father in the sexual sense must come to an end immediately, for she could no longer endure the awesome pain of knowing her husband was beginning to feel more compassion for his daughter than he did for his wife.

The Straw That Broke The Camel's Back: Mother and daughter conversation may have sounded like this: JonBenet for some time now we have been sexually acquainting ourselves with each other, but in light of the situation and its detriment to this marriage, I am asking you to stop seeing your father in the manner in which you have been seeing him in the past. And it may be that this whole dysfunctional situation has gotten a little out of hand and it must stop because he loves me more than he loves you, and I am his wife. *Yes mother, you may be his wife, whether he loves you more than he loves me is a matter of debate. But this one thing I do know, and again, you are his wife, but he enjoys having sex with me.....mother! And yes mother, he has more fun with me than he ever did with you!*

In light of the latter horrific statement coming from JonBenet, Patsy Ramsey's response was probably given in this manner: You little Bitch, I'll teach to you to fool around with my husband. JonBenet, completely unaware of the impact the negative impulse of her offensive statement to her mother, not realizing at all the immutable fact that she had just signed her death certificate, she became a child marked for death.

Her death was now set into motion, and in the mind of Patsy Ramsey there was absolutely no turning back. JonBenet Ramsey would never live to see her next birthday. The irony of this statement by the author is somewhat similar to the statement made in the ransom note: *(At this time we have your daughter in our possession. She is safe and unharmed and if you want her to see 1997, you must follow our instructions to the letter. page one of the fictitious ransom note)*

In actuality, the child did not live to see her next birthday, what a coincident. Patsy Ramsey thinking to herself, can you imagine the nerve of that little bitch, speaking to me in such a manner, you little bitch, you'll regret you ever said that. Patsy Ramsey was not only jealous of her daughter's relationship with John Ramsey, she had now begun to hate her with a passion so strong it would warrant the death of this young child.

An Addendum to the Mother-Daughter Violent Confrontation

The writer also believes that the violent confrontation between Patsy Ramsey and her daughter was also the result of the mother's ovarian cancer going into remission. Remission of this deadly disease was an unexpected intermission in Patsy's previous diagnosis, and her unwillingness to allow the continued pedophile relationship of her daughter with her husband John Ramsey, to continue, was also the spark that ignited a violent change of heart/confrontation. Perhaps the cancer remission was because of the constant prayer vigil held in her behalf by her church family. With the ovarian cancer in remission, it was no longer apparent for the continued physical/sexual relationship her daughter was sharing with her father. The cancer now in remission, she could once again assume her duties as an active wife performing her marital bedroom duties.

In the mist of all of the latter was a big but! The big but, was an obvious fact that the child was not so willing to relinquish the relationship she was having with her father, John Ramsey."The writer believes that it was on this premise that Patsy Ramsey approached her daughter in such a violent way in the aftermath of her ovarian cancer diagnosis, slipping into remission. The ovarian cancer going into remission, and taking a turn for the better, was definitely a non-preconceived notion of happenstance, the Ramseys did not remotely anticipate.

This non-anticipatory event of circumstance, of course, threw a monkey wrench into the entire scheme of things, orchestrated and fostered into reality, a sad response by the mother to her daughter's unwillingness to cooperate with her. And, the fact that her husband was allowed to have sex with their daughter did not make the situation at hand any easier. In her mind, Patsy Ramsey was rehearsing these responsive but repulsive moments of thought over and over, again and again. Why could not her daughter accept the mother's plea to refrain from sexual encounter with her husband? It was at this very moment that Patsy Ramsey clearly understood that her six-year old daughter was six-years old in age only. Not only that, but the young child's mind set was that of a young lady many years her senior.

Had they known that the cancer would go into remission, there is a great probability that John Ramsey would not have suggested that they enter their daughter into competitive beauty pageants. As an alternative means to help assuage the fact, the hurt and the unbearable pain that his wife's cancer, was diagnosed to be terminal. And to add insult to injury, they never remotely conceived in their minds or their hearts that their lives would take such catastrophic change for the worst. Somehow, the author can imagine the Ramseys saying to themselves, if only the ovarian cancer had not gone into remission, perhaps, the entire scenario of the this heinous situation, would have been lost in the valley of the Dolls. But instead, a little child of enormous talent, who was gifted with the spirit of a well rounded personality even at the young age of six-years old, is long since buried in a grave in a cemetery in Atlanta Georgia. Silenced by the over zealous jealousy of a mother, whose vengeance would dispel an unparallel evil that would ruthlessly snuff out the life of this darling little child of God.

The wheels were spinning and the only satisfaction remotely given to appeasement was to ultimately see JonBenet Ramsey dead, dead, dead, and nothing else would satisfy Patricia Ramsey's quest for revenge, but the death of JBR. She would now plan and carefully orchestrate the murder and the death of her daughter, JonBenet Ramsey, as a callous act of intrusion by alien sources not given to the Ramsey household but indeed a carefully orchestrated intruder theory. JonBenet had crushed her feelings and to add insult to injury, she had never been so insulted in her life. And when she thought of her daughter, she could only think that she brought JonBenet into this world and now, the time had come to take her out.

This Patsy Ramsey would try to do with utmost care and caution. And there would be absolutely nothing that would change her mind, not hell, not high water, and not even the darkness of night, this child was marked for death, no if's, and's or buts; JonBenet Ramsey was a dead child walking. This little child, according to the mind set of Patsy Ramsey, had allowed her mockingbird brain to overload her alligator mouth. Her death was imminent, and just a matter of time.

All that Pat Ramsey could think about was that no child of hers was going to talk to her in that fashion and live to tell about it. As a mother, Patsy Ramsey could think of nothing more demeaning than your own child to speak to her mother as though she was the scum of the earth. The nerve of the little bitch, living in my house, wearing my clothes, and eating my food, and thinking that she can have sex with her father, my husband and show no respect at all for me. She will be in hell long before the devil gets the news that she's there.

And perhaps this was a promise Patsy Ramsey made to herself. And the obvious brutality of JonBenet's death, it is also apparent Patsy Ramsey meant everything she said. The young child died an awesome death, and the author feels compassion for JonBenet in the sense that no child should have to face death the way this little girl did in spite of anything she had done.

Death Threat-Death Wish Is Carried Out: One need not look but to the news media and find out that Patsy Ramsey held true to her sordid intentions, JonBenet Ramsey was found dead in her home on the morning of December 26, 1996; apparently, her mother had made good her threat on the life of her daughter. And the motive for the young child's death was, *she dared to love the wrong man!*

JonBenet Ramsey was more than likely killed in her bed or in her bedroom on or during the early morning hours of December 26,1996. Though there is no established time of her death, it is reportedly assumed the child was murdered sometime during the middle of the night as purported by her father. Patsy Ramsey, it appears, killed the child while she was asleep, evidenced by the heavy blow to the right side of her head, strangled the young girl to make sure death would become her, and then bound and gagged JBR to make it seem like an intruder had entered the home and killed the young child. And again, it is believed that blunt force trauma to the right side of the head more than likely brought instantaneous death to the child as she lay asleep in her bed. On this supposition, she probably never knew what hit her. And the ransom note would also play an integral part to incorporate and deceive the media and to cause the public to believe a lie.

The child's lifeless body was taken and placed in the basement by John Ramsey, or the child's lifeless body was dragged to the basement and placed there by Patsy Ramsey. When he was made aware of the fact that his wife had premeditatedly killed their young daughter, there was nothing he could do but accept the fact that his daughter had been murdered by his wife. After placing the child's lifeless body in the secluded area in the basement, the body stayed there until John Ramsey came later on the same day, pretentiously to retrieve it. For this reason, it is very ironic that he found the body of young JonBenet, and his wife found the ransom note, things were exactly as they had planned them in hope of avoiding criminal prosecution and a possible murder indictment charge in *The Killing Of JBR.*

John Ramsey probably would have reported the death of his daughter to the authorities, but his hands were tired, and his wife placed a gag order on his mouth. And he couldn't say anything or, for that matter, do anything because it would have been revealed that he was having sexual encounters with his daughter. So therefore, he was up against a rock and a hard place. Because his wife had the goods on him, he was powerless to do anything about the death of his daughter. Had he exposed his wife as the killer of JonBenet, she would in turn put his business and the fact that he was engaging in sexual interplay with his daughter in the street. And Patsy Ramsey surely was not going to tell on herself, because her pedophile nature would have been revealed also.

It is believed that there were times when both of them were having sex with JonBenet and that would be even more damaging to her personal persona. Patsy Ramsey, were she not so involved in child molestation, could have reported John Ramsey to the police, but she didn't. Why? Because she, too, could have been incriminated. She chose to play it safe, and made an offer to John Ramsey he couldn't refuse, *tell on me, I'll tell on you.*

Neither one of the parents wanted this ugly mess to get out into the public eye, so John Ramsey had no other alternative but to go along with the program and defend his wife's so-called innocence. And neither one of them remotely speculated that as fate would have it, one day the murderous plot against their daughter would be exposed to their evil unenviable detriment.

John Ramsey, A Victim of His Own Circumstance: John Ramsey never in his wildest dreams would have thought his life, his marital status, and his non-regrettable relationship with his young daughter would have made him the victim of his own circumstance. Or maybe the other side of the coin in a minute sense of ethics, is his way of getting back at his wife for the senseless murder of JonBenet, his deceased beloved daughter.

More nights than one, even to this very moment, he has contemplated that Christmas day and has given hours perhaps days to that horrific Christmas night, and wished that moment had never come to sanction itself in the corridors of true surrealism, a contradiction of sorts and the reality of not so common everyday circumstances. Or just maybe, sometimes when the guilt of ones conscience weighs heavy on the mind, it may inherit thoughts of perhaps it would have been better to have never been born than to be one of the primary culprits in a murder scheme that has touched hearts of people around the world.

The author would think, had John Ramsey not opened his mouth at all, even with the bogus ransom note, the chances are there would not have been any grounds or accusations of criminal intent strong enough to involve him in the murder plot against his daughter. And the implication of his wife as the murder suspect would have been very difficult. But as fate would again have it, he opened his mouth and convicted them both.

The fact of the earlier initial intent, still remains the same, there is no such thing as a perfect town or a perfect crime. Sooner or later the guilty party will have to face the bar of justice, and no one, free or bound, rich or poor is above the law. John Ramsey became the victim of his own circumstances:

1. The Crime Was Committed During the Middle of the Night.
2. The Murder of JonBenet Was Premeditated.
3. The Culprits Were Either Jealous of Him or They Hated Him.

With these three statements carefully weighed, John Ramsey's comments on national television clearly points to his wife as the killer of JonBenet. The evidence carefully weighed in the balance, and presented in the context of relative circumstance, speaks for itself. Patsy Ramsey maliciously killed her little daughter. And her husband John Ramsey assisted her in the failed attempt to cover up her murder.

And they also failed in their attempt to charge the child's murder on so-called intruders breaking into their home the night JonBenet Ramsey was so brutally killed in her own bedroom. The fact remains that JBR was murdered by none other than Patricia Ramsey, her very emotionally disturbed mother. And the lack of proof positive evidence must point to the fact that intruders in the home of the Ramseys is a fabricated statement of falsehood.

Intruder or intruders violating the home of the Ramseys is a lie, and the so-called ransom note is a lie, and JonBenet Ramsey having been kidnaped is a lie. None of these incidents have been proven beyond a reasonable doubt that they did in fact occur, but are only speculations and heresay. The only proof positive evidence pertaining to this incident is *(1) Fact:* the child is dead, and that is an indisputable fact; *(2) Fact:* the only other people in the house at the time of death was the immediate family, her mother, her father and her half brother, Burke Ramsey. *(3)Fact:* and no one can prove beyond reasonable suspicion and doubt that there were others in the home during the time JonBenet Ramsey was so brutally assaulted.

The reason why these innuendoes cannot be proven is because none of these things ever happened or became actual facts of circumstances. And the author thinks that because none of these circumstances ever took place, the burden of proof lies in the ballpark of John and Patsy Ramsey. All these false precepts, and pretentious lies, says very loud and clear, that the Ramseys are guilty beyond any reasonable doubt and suspicion of the heinous murder of JBR.

To all three of these fabricated lies and false innuendoes (false intruders, false ransom note, false kidnaping) there is no positive proof or evidence that either ever occurred before, during, or after the murder of JonBenet Ramsey. *(4) Fact:* it has not been proven (by either the party of the Ramseys or law enforcement) beyond reasonable suspicion and doubt that the Ramsey home was violated by unwanted guest (intruders), then the ransom note written on paper and materials found in the home, had to be written by someone who was already in the house.

Law enforcement must do one of four things: *(A)* Prove the intruder theory to be a valid situation of circumstance, which they have not done. *(B)* Law enforcement must prove the intruder theory false and not worth the paper it was written on which they have not done. If law enforcement cannot prove that intruders were in the home of the Ramseys, then the guilt lies in the ball park of the Ramseys, who must prove otherwise, which they have not done.

And if law enforcement can prove beyond reasonable suspicion and doubt that the Ramsey home was indeed victimized by intruders, then the Ramseys are not liable for the death of innocence. And if law enforcement cannot to any degree of culpability prove that there was no intrusion into the Ramsey home, then the Ramseys are guilty in the first degree of murder and the violation of their daughter's civil rights and the child's right to life.

The author reminds the reader again, no valid ransom note, no valid intruder theory, and finally no valid or other wise proven kidnap theory, (how could the child have been kidnapped when her body was found in the house in the basement by her dad?) means that the Ramseys were lying all along.

The negative facts/factors, here and now speaks for themselves. Which also testifies to the fact that the Ramseys were not only liars from jump street, they themselves fabricated this whole scenario of false innuendoes about the death of their daughter, JonBenet. No lie can live forever, sooner or later a lie will die because there in no truth or real substance for a lie to strive or live on. It may have taken some time but little by little their whole world of lies and false innuendoes is falling apart piece by little piece, revealing more and more of the truth each time. Like an axe man would go through the woods falling trees. "The author fines these lies and false innuendoes, an invalid ransom note, a false intruder theory, and a false kidnaping, good for nothing but dung!"

In conjunction with these findings, the Ramseys are immediately held to be the writers and the authors of the ransom note, and the writers of the ransom note stand accused of killing this young child. *(C)* Law enforcement must prove the ransom note to be fictitious, and was indeed written by someone in the Ramsey home by disproving the intruder theory. Disproving the intruder theory also proves the ransom note invalid. And not only is the ransom note invalid, it also disproves the intruder theory and the kidnap theory at the same time.

Since law enforcement is taking their own time to seek out more positive proof proving that John and Patsy Ramsey killed their daughter in cold blood. The author took the liberty to do it for them.

The proof of their error is now in the pudding. Only the DNA is left to be proven that it came from an independent source not associated with the direct crime scene or the DNA was part of the whole setup and the crime scene. And the fact that it (the DNA) was deliberately and meticulously placed on the body of JonBenet and upon her clothing, points directly at the culprits and the guilty party. *(D)* Law enforcement must also prove the ransom note to be a non valid alibi to validate John and Patsy Ramsey as given to the umbrella of suspicion. In other words, the Ramseys cannot use the ransom note to serve as an alibi for their non-involvement in JBR's death.

Not to sound redundant, for all intensive purposes, the ransom note does not in any way support the intruder theory, because it is virtually impossible for two or three people to enter into someone's home, kill a little child, place her lifeless body in a secluded place in the basement and then leave without leaving any worthwhile accusatory incriminating evidence. No way by any stretch of the imagination! It is just not possible given the non-incriminating circumstances relative to aliens surrounding the crime scene. And, it has been established that no proven artifacts which establishes in the proof positive evidence that intruders were indeed in the home the night the murder occurred have surfaced to prove otherwise.

Supposition: If the Ramseys were indicted on murder charges and the deadly assault on their daughter who died so violently on that cold winter night of December 26, 1996, then all the DA's office would have to do is prove that there were no intruders in the home of the Ramseys before or after the young child's death. This action alone would also invalidate the ransom note as well as invalidate the intruder theory and place the burden of guilt on the Ramseys themselves. Or the Ramseys themselves prove without a doubt their home was in fact compromised by intruders which they have not done to be a convincing artifact of truth. And it is also fair to say that the ransom note a non valid fictitious worthless piece of paper, was written only for those foolish enough to believe it.

Add to this scenario the *fact* that to date, the Ramseys have not proven (for their sake and for the sake of their daughter) that there were intruders in their home beyond reasonable suspicion, (And not just a shoe, or token blood stains under the fingernail, what have you, etc. And it is hard, almost to the point of impossible, to prove something that never took place, this the Ramseys are very well aware of. For if they could prove beyond reasonable suspicion and doubt that their home was indeed intruded upon, they would have done so by now, for nothing but to take their names from under the umbrella of suspicion. They cannot prove what is impossible to prove, because the intruder theory only existed in their minds, and the ransom note proves it.) Therefore, the Ramseys are guilty or their guilt remains with them for the most heinous crime of the new millennium.

If it can be proven beyond reasonable suspicion and doubt that intruders were indeed inside the Ramsey dwelling, then the Ramseys are innocent of any and all allegations that they had anything to do with their daughter's death. And the umbrella of suspicion should be removed from all criminal innuendoes towards any possible indictments; and the umbrella of suspicion, given to the Ramseys, should be declared null and void to the degree of complete closure.

But on the other hand, or the other side of the coin is this: There is only one logical conclusion which can remotely substantiate the death of innocence, the child was victimized by one or both of her parents. No one else was in the home saving little Burke Ramsey who was somewhere off in la la land. All the incriminating evidence points to her mother striking the death blow, and her father allowing himself to become involved in a cover-up. Perhaps his thoughts were on his daughter, or maybe the fear of his wife to the point he failed to consider the outcome of his criminal behavior. To be charged with incest, which amounts to rape of his daughter, is far better than being charged for murder, rape and incest! So now, both of them must pay to the piper.

What About the DNA? After JonBenet's father, John Ramsey, found her body in the family's basement on Dec. 26, 1996, police collected DNA from blood spots in her underwear and from under her fingernails. Investigators have said that some of the DNA was too degraded to use as evidence, but that some was of sufficient quality to submit to the FBI in 2003. The sample did not match any of the 1.5 million samples in the agency's database at the time, according to the Ramsey family attorney.

One of the last strong points to solving this murder mystery is centered in and around the DNA. Here are some newly discovered facts concerning the travesty of innocence that must refute the DNA theory associated with a so-called intruder theory: All real and illogical evidence pertaining to the death of JonBenet Ramsey are now proven by the author to be null and void and lacking real substance and truth to validate the Ramsey's assertion that an intruder broke into their home and brutally murdered little JonBenet Ramsey.

By now, it should be clearly understood via precept and elimination that the Ramsey home was never intruded upon by any outside show of force, responsible for the death of JBR. There is no real tangible evidence to prove someone else was in the home of the Ramseys the night this horrible incident took place. Here now are some established facts: The dead child was never kidnaped or taken from her home according to the fictitious ransom note. Because her body was found that same day in the basement by her father-John Ramsey.

If the child was never taken from her home in light of the failed and false intruder theory, if the child was never taken from her home in light of and relative to the fictitious ransom note, if the child was never taken from her home in light of the a non-valid kidnapping, this question of significant relativity comes to mind, if none of these things or innuendoes never took place, "**where did the DNA found on the child body and her clothing come from?** *And who could have possibly placed it there?*" *Certainly not Burke Ramsey!*

The only other people in the home were JBR's mother and father. Now, it doesn't take a rocket scientist to see that no one else but the Ramseys themselves could have placed the unidentified DNA where it could be so easily found on the child's clothing and her body for obvious reasons. Those obvious reasons were to circumvent any premonition that John and Patsy Ramsey hiding the guilt of the error of their death wish for their daughter and any future accusation they had any sexual contact with the travesty of innocence. Unproven and un-associated DNA would go a long way in proving their innocence.

JBR's Clothes Had To Be Changed: Question, where could the unidentifiable or un-associated DNA come from and how was it placed so meticulously on the child's body and clothing? The author believes that one thing is for sure, the planning and the careful placement of the DNA was not an overnight situation of accomplishment or circumstance. It took time and effort over a period of many circumstances to arrive at this point in the horrendous travesty of innocence that stale mates even the Federal Bureau of Investigation.

The author thinks that this DNA found on the child's body and her clothing came from a source not found in the United States, but secretly taken from a source that would not immediately incriminate the Ramseys. The meticulous placement of the blood DNA was accomplished with a syringe and or either an eye drop container, something the Ramseys could easily discard without attracting unwarranted attention. Two points of interest comes to mind at this moment: one point of interest is the clothing had to be changed at some point and time to effectuate the authorities inability to authenticate the DNA and who and where it came from.

In the author's estimation, the child's panties did not show any abnormal disturbance when her vagina was so badly ruptured or at least, it was not mentioned in any of the investigations relative to the child's sexual molestation. Which is to say again, the child's clothing had to be changed more than likely after she was so brutally murdered, or not too long after she was killed. These actions further substantiates the author's insinuation that this entire murder scenario of innocence had to be a preplanned premeditated act on the life of this darling little girl. The author would go as far as to say, it is virtually to almost impossible to plan and orchestrate a crime scene so articulate in its presentation over night.

Since there was no intrusion into the Ramsey home, they had to be the ones to change the child's clothing and place the unidentifiable DNA where it could be easily found and speculated upon by the authorities. This is probably one of the reasons Patsy Ramsey was not able to change clothes from the day before, and in all actuality, she did not have a chance to do so in light of what had taken place prior to discovering the ransom note. In all of their efforts to hide the fact that they are responsible for the death of innocence, the Ramseys almost committed a perfect crime in what had been surmised as a perfect town.

Somehow fate would not have it that way, because there is no such thing as a perfect crime in a perfect town, somehow the author feels the Ramseys, especially Patsy, knew this. Sooner or later they were going to get caught, even if she wasn't around to see it. In her efforts to hide what could have been the crime of the century, her innermost thoughts and feelings were eventually the truth surrounding the murder crime of the century, would have to be the unfolding of a mind set just as good or better than her attempt to create a murder mystery that would placate itself on the mind set of people the world over for many years to come. She would probably call it poetic justice that took its time in coming to pass.

The Coin Has Many Faces Patsy's Ovarian Cancer: The study also found that compared to healthy women, germ cell tumor survivors had significantly greater reproductive concerns and experienced less sexual pleasure and more sexual discomfort. However, the survivors were more likely to be in partnered, meaningful relationships.

"The finding should allow oncologist and therapists to better inform and counsel patients and their families about expectations in the preoperative period, during primary treatment and long term," says Gershenson. "Ultimately as a cancer community, we need to develop better interventions and pay much more attention to both the psycho-social and fertility issues of our patients."

To ovarian germ cell tumor patients, Gershenson stresses the importance of having their fertility-sparing surgery performed by a board-certified gynecological oncologist who understands the clinical behavior of these tumors and who is trained to optimize patients' probability of undergoing appropriate surgery and chemotherapy.

"Still in 2007, despite medical advances, too many of these patients are operated on by general obstetricians and gynecologists or general surgeons who do not make a proper diagnosis during surgery, or may not truly understand the biology of this disease. As a result, both ovaries and the uterus are removed, leaving a patient unnecessarily sterile."

Other study authors include: Anna M. Miller, D.N.S. and Stephen D. Williams, both of the Indiana University Cancer Center; Victoria L. Champion, DNS, Indiana University School of Nursing; Patrick O. Monahan, Ph.D and Qianqian Zhao, both of the Indiana School of Medicine and David Cella, Ph.D., Evanston Northwestern Healthcare. [7]

The Motive to Kill the Second Time Around

The Horrible Pain of Death: Patsy Ramsey died about 3:30 a.m. at her father's house with her husband by her side, lawyer Lin Wood said. She was diagnosed with cancer in 1993 but was cancer-free for nine years until a relapse three years ago. The unsolved killing of JonBenet in December 1996 put Patsy and John Ramsey, the girl's parents, in the spotlight. A grand jury investigation into the death of the child beauty pageant winner ended without charges in 1999.

The horrible and the excruciating thought of death can sometimes trigger in a person the evil thoughts of taking a loved one or love ones with you, whenever death sets itself upon ones eminent domain. This kind of mind set is 99.9% based on jealousy. Not only that, Patsy Paugh, appeared to be a woman used to having things go her way, in most instances. Her life now would take a 180-degree turn into another but opposite direction. She was indeed an obsessively jealous woman who apparently dreaded even a remote thought of dying and leaving those of whom she loved to live life without her, especially John Ramsey-her husband and JonBenet, her and John's darling little beauty queen.

Patsy Ramsey lived the kind of lifestyle very few people encounter and most people dream about. And to have to give all that up to enter into a world endowed in darkness is sometimes more than the rational mind can take. Patsy Ramsey and her husband John Ramsey had worked together and in that effort amassed a great fortune that centered around the multi-millionaire status. The fabulous home, the expensive clothes, for Patsy Ramsey all of this was coming to an end, because the terminal point of stage 4 ovarian cancer waa getting ready to deal the Ramseys a stacked deck, with no wild cards.

The lavish parties, entertaining guests whose social status were of the standard of the elite, the reknowness of being associated with some of the most outstanding people in the neighborhood, all of this and more was coming to a slow and eventual end, via the horrific pangs of death. How tragic most would say. Patsy Ramsey, in all of her years of life prior to learning of stage four ovarian cancer, never in her wildest dreams or in any remote degree of her imagination thought that she would die before her time. She did not live long enough to see her fiftieth birthday.

By now, (after she came to grips with her terminal medical situation) all kinds of irrational thoughts were invading the mind set of Patsy Ramsey, who some say, knew she was going to die of stage four ovarian cancer. Whenever ovarian cancer reaches this level, death is almost certain, in most instances, it's just a matter of time. But Patsy Ramsey was so blessed because of her faith, she would be spared the pains of death for almost ten years.

Ovarian Cancer Changes Everything: *The Coin Has Many Faces;* when Patricia Paugh Ramsey was diagnosed in 1963 with possibly terminal ovarian cancer, Patsy Ramsey and the entire Ramsey family had to come to grips with the painful reality of death. What was once a picture perfect family also had to come to grips with the fact that sooner or later, a wife and a mother would have to face death. Which would leave a huge void where there was once laughter and the joy of being some of the wealthiest people in the neighborhood, somehow would be depleted of one very admired person the person in the likes of Patsy Ramsey.

Cancer and Aids: There are few medical conditions that come to mind which can in essence scare the living hell out of most people, they are cancer and Acquired Immune Deficiency Syndrome or Aids. And, of course, Aids carries a more deadly impact than cancer because all cancers do not have to result in death, but on the other hand once full blown Aids develops, death is almost always certain. When a deadly form of cancer is come to pass medically, it is sometimes just as bad as full blown Aids. And then, there are some forms of cancer like stage 4 ovarian cancer that will make Aids seem like another day at the Doctor's office. For Patsy Ramsey, she was caught between a rock and a hard place, her condition was bad any way one would look at it.

In light of her recently diagnosed condition, without showing it outwardly, Patricia's world began to turn upside down. Finding something to do with the little time she felt she had left played on her consciousness like a plague of locust. She had to find something to do, and it had to be fast, quick and in a hurry, just like that, with no time to lose. Then John Ramsey came up with a miracle but brilliant idea, enter little JonBenet into beauty pageants. For this idea of relief, Patsy Ramsey could compliment John Ramsey for having a mind to think. This action (entering little JonBenet into local beauty pageants, for Patricia, it was the very thing the doctor called for) it also would become the straw that broke the camel's back.

To the author, "there is one thing worse than death itself, that is knowing in jest, that you do not have long to live and facing up to it." Patsy Ramsey had resigned herself to not only facing up to it, she had resigned herself to destroy two other people in the process, John Ramsey, her husband, and little JonBenet, her only daughter. She simply could not bare the thought of death and leaving behind the two people she cherished the most on this earth.

She, soon after learning of her condition, allowed the one side of her nature she did not want to come to pass take total control of her inner consciousness via the means of excessive jealousy. And the fact that her life would at some point in time take a turn for the worse and with it, her dreams of what could have been.

Burke Ramsey, her blood son, was much loved but not to the degree of jealousy she felt for John and JonBenet. The other two stepchildren did not matter at all from the apparent look of things. She would in essence carefully plan the death of JonBenet, and leave John Ramsey who would assist her to deal with his guilt for the rest of his life. This woman also knew that living with guilt can be worse than jail or a prison sentence. John Ramsey, after suggesting the idea of entering JonBenet into local beauty pageants, had not the remotest thought/idea of what his wife was up too.

The way she would torture JonBenet would be somewhat different from the way she would torture her husband, John Ramsey. She would leave him engulfed in mental anxiety, JonBenet, she would kill. She felt better if her daughter was with her in death than to be left alive with her father, whom she knew was sexually involved with her. But how strange and how bizarre this murder mystery, Mrs. Patricia Ramsey still loved and hated them both at the same time.

Patsy Ramsey was a master strategist, unlike anyone or woman of her time and life span. She almost planned a perfect murder; not only that, "she almost got away with it."

The Thought of Death and Jealousy Can Bring Out the Worst in a Person: The discovery of ovarian cancer and the strong possibility of death along with it, can bring out the best or the worse in most people. Nobody wants to die, especially those who are considered to be among the rich and famous. Though the Ramseys did not become a household name until the death of JonBenet, their daughter, just the same they were considered to be among the wealthy if not the famous. The rich and the famous sometimes forgets that into every life, every household, some rain must fall, and by no means are the Ramseys an exception.

Patsy Ramsey was far above being an exceptional woman, her idea of perfection bordered on immaculate and absolute. The author believes that it is for this reason no one has been able to solve this murder mystery behind the death of JonBenet Ramsey. Who would think in a remote sense, that Patsy Ramsey was a perfectionist of the first magnitude! Everything about this case surrounding the death of innocence is centered around a perfectionist mindset/attitude. How much so, one would ask? The author's response is ten years plus and climbing, and still the case has not been resolved or solved yet. To the author it says a lot about the individual (s) behind the travesty of innocence.

Which also says that Patricia Paugh Ramsey and her entire world bordered on a thin line between love and hate, good and evil. Perhaps, it was just a matter of time before the dark side of Mrs. Ramsey came to surface in the spotlight of one of the most hideous murders to take place in this new millennium, the travesty of innocence. The thought of terminal ovarian cancer brought to the surface the demon that lies in many people.

Someone once said there is good and bad in all of us, the only difference is, some people choose to allow the bad side to get the best of their good side especially in chaotic moments, when almost unbearable situations comes to grips with reality. The evitable thought of death so early in life did nothing to help the situation, if anything, worse.

The other side of Patsy Ramsey was sinister and evil. It was the side very few people could see, in light of the very jealous nature she possessed when it came to John Ramsey and the remote thought of imagining him with another woman other than herself. Even knowing that her life span was to be short lived, the agony and pain of death authored the demon rage in her.

In the back of her mind, another woman helping John spend his millions, was more than enough to conjure up the dark side of her nature. The evil/dark side of Patsy Ramsey began to set in motion the very moment the doctor told her of her cancerous but deadly condition.

Patricia Paugh Ramsey had a brilliant mind, not only that she was also a brilliant criminal thinker. She loved John Ramsey so much, she could not bare to think about dying and leaving perhaps the only man she had ever loved other than her father behind for other women to enjoy. "This according to the mind set of Patsy Ramsey was an absolute no-no!" The ovarian cancer, death, and another woman in the arms of John Ramsey was all that it took to set the spinning top in motion. She would eventually do everything in her power to see that John Ramsey's life would be living hell in her death.

If one would look very closely at the conditions surrounding the death of a beauty queen, one could see also related facts showing and proving without the slightest of doubt that this child's murder was definitely a preplanned premeditated event of circumstances. Which is associated with the dark deviant mind set of John Ramsey's deceased wife.

The Irony of It All: *"the truth-the whole truth and nothing but the truth lies in John Ramsey!"* In light of everything that has been said and done, John Ramsey is the only living person who knows the truth behind the death of his daughter and the facts now show he was an accomplice in that death. When the author is finished with this segment of the travesty of innocence, John Ramsey will be more than glad to tell the world what went on in that house the night JonBenet Ramsey was so brutally murdered by her own parents, and that's the God's heaven truth.

By now, it is no remote doubt in the mind of the author that somebody in the home of John and Patsy Ramsey is responsible for the death of innocence. There were no intruders, no other persons in the home capable of murdering JonBenet except the immediate parents, and this report will prove that both of them took part in the killing of innocence.

But first of all the author once again must tell the reader or remind the reader that the ransom note was nothing more than a piece of paper Patsy Ramsey used as a deceptive means to fool the public into thinking that this child was kidnaped, when in essence she never left the confines of her home for any reasons whatsoever. This makes the ransom note false and invalid. A great deal of the truth relative to JonBenet's murder investigation is centered around this non valid-super nonsense ransom note.

A Contradiction of Sorts: The ransom note in and of itself is dead in the water, not only the ransom note but the intruder theory is dead in the water, and also, everything the Ramseys thought to be a kidnaping is also dead in the water. By this, the author is eluding to the fact that the ransom note contradicts everything the Ramseys have said relative to the intruder theory, *"there's a killer out there on the loose,"* when in actuality, she was really speaking of herself and her husband, John Ramsey. The token evidentiary physical objects found in various places in the home does not prove to the slightest degree that the Ramsey home was invaded or compromised by an alien source.

Those token items of evidence eluding to an intruder, a little child could have done a better job than they did. The only thing these tokens objects of accusatory evidence proves is that someone very clever authored and put together this entire murder mystery.

The ransom note contradicts everything that Judge Carnes has said concerning the intruder theory in light of allowing the Ramseys to somewhat escape the umbrella of suspicion. And, the ransom note contradicts everything that was suggested that this young child was not molested by anyone other than her father and her mother. And, the ransom note is impossible to resurrect to a form of truth syntheses because there is no truth to or associated with it.

Now that the truth has surfaced in the fallacy of the note, an intruder, or a felonious kidnaping, it (the truth) will never change. In other words, the ransom note has no truth to it, it was a lie then, it is a lie now, and the ransom note will always remain a lie even unto the third and the last millennium, and that is once again, *"the truth, the whole truth, and nothing but the truth so help us God."* So then the ransom note also makes void the intruder theory, the felonious kidnap accusations.

The deceased Patsy Ramsey deserves an academy award (post-humorously) for her superb acting abilities; and her endowed abilities to deceive if it were possible, the elect of God. The same inept abilities sanctioned in a criminal, allows one to see why JonBenet was so talented. And, this statement of fact can be backed up with proof that makes the truth undeniable in every aspect of its relevance.

According to the ransom note the child was never kidnapped, and again, she was never taken from her home, from the time she was so brutally murdered until she was taken away after the report of the coroner, late the evening of the next day. Nothing about what went on after the murder makes much sense to the author.

The Fallacies of Reason: The author mentioned at the onset of this book, that there would be three things to consider which would ultimately prove the guilt of the Ramseys standing in the dire straights of one of the most heinous crimes of the century. That if one could prove beyond any doubt of circumstance regarding the ransom note, the intruder theory, and the kidnap theory, were fallacies of reason, the artifacts of culpability in the travesty of innocence do not make sense, or is non-valid. Then the killer/ killers of the travesty of innocence would certainly come to pass via this new found truth.

And the truth in conjunction with proving the fallacy of reason will eventually set free the imprisoned spirit of this lovely little darling child, whose life was cut short by a jealous mother and a pedophile father. And also, ultimately, find those responsible for the hideous crime and put them in jail. If it were left up to the author, I would vigorously seek the death penalty.

The fallibility of reason encompasses all the lies that were told to hide the truth regarding the fact that the parents and the parents alone are responsible for the death of JonBenet Ramsey. Not only were the lies pertaining to all three theories, a fallacy of reason, all three lies about the ransom note, the kidnap theory, and the intruder theory, given also to the fact that it cannot be proven someone other than the Ramseys violated their home in the death of innocence. And, the lack thereof (the truth) turned this entire murder situation into a game of tic-tac-toe in regards to John and Patsy Ramsey concerted effort to protect their guilt. And not allow the fallacy of reason to play major role in getting at the truth. The reason being they were well aware of the truth, and they knew exactly what went on in their home the night JonBenet was so brutally murdered.

One order of thought in the fallibility of reason or circumstance for all intensive purposes, asks the question, why did John Ramsey leave the home the morning of the child's death, to get a breathe of fresh air? Sometime early the morning of JonBenet's death, John Ramsey took a walk alone away from the house, the exact time spent on this walk alone is not known at this moment. But the question still looms over the death of innocence, and why would Mr. Ramsey leave his home the morning of his daughter's tragic murder?

One might speculate that perhaps he was discarding the bloody clothes from the crime scene that were never found. JonBenet, having had her skull cracked, should have produced some trace evidence of blood to some remote degree. But none was found. Somebody spic- n-spanned the entire crime scene, even the child's body, long before the ransom note was found the morning of.

The bed clothing she had on before she went to bed were not the same clothes she had on when her dead body was found. Did someone change her clothes, and was it the mission of John Ramsey to discard them the morning of? Remember the duct tape with the dog hair on it, it was not found in the home either. Why? John Ramsey could have easily taken these things of evidence and discarded them the morning of the child's tragic death. When he left the home to get a breathe of fresh air and to ponder the tragic events taking place in his home he could have thrown all this discarded evidence into a neighbor's trash can early that morning, the day of his daughter's death.

The same gestures in thought reminds the author of the O. J. Simpson trial in regards to Ron Goldman and O. J.'s wife Nicole, who were also brutally murdered, of which the murder weapon and possibly the bloody clothing of the killer was never found. Perhaps John Ramsey took this walk to do the same thing the author thinks O.J. did. John Ramsey took the young child's clothing and all other incriminating evidence out of the home the morning of the day the dead child's body was reluctantly found and discarded them in one of his neighbor's trash cans the day of the incident which also was possibly the day of trash collection.

Of course, the latter is pure speculation which only suggest what might or what could have happened. But one thing is for sure, John Ramsey left his home for a short time during the morning the ransom note was found at the foot of the steps leading to their upstairs bedroom. At this particular time, it is good to re-member that the little child was already dead, and when John Ramsey returned from his short walk, not long after, he went down to his basement and found the body of his deceased daughter, how ironic. At this particular moment, everything was going according to Patsy's plan.

In order for the author to prove beyond reasonable suspicion and doubt the appalling guilt of the Ramseys as the culprits in the death of innocence, the report of the fallacies of reason must be taken into serious concern by the reader and all who want and desire to see an end to one of the most tragic events to take place this side of the third millennium. Now is the time to make sense out of nonsense and to put aside all anomalies/difficulties of skep-ticism and false innuendoes and concentrate on evidence that now will prove John Ramsey and his deceased wife are the people truly responsible for the death of JonBenet.

There are pros and cons related to the travesty of innocence, people who stand with the Ramseys and people who stand against the Ramseys; but there should be a common goal or a commonality in all concerned about the death of this little child. That common goal, that common bond should be to get at and know without a doubt how JonBenet died. It is not so much about John or Patsy Ramsey as it is about getting at the bottom line of this entire murderous incident, which again is getting at the truth of what really happened in the Ramsey home the day of the brutal death of the Ramsey's little child prodigy.

A confession in the travesty of innocence will go a long way to solving this mystery of murder and mayhem. But by the same token, a confession by the person of interest, namely John Ramsey is not in a profound sense of things necessary, if he does not want to interact with the proper authorities, because all the evidence gathered by the author points to the father of the murdered child and her mother, who, of course, is decreased as the primary culprits in the little child's death.

Now the awesome task of the author is to prove and show to the public that a confession from John Ramsey will come to pass in light of the compiled evidence against him, and all the false innuendoes culminated in the ransom note, the false intruder theory, and the false kidnaping have proven he and his wife to be the guilty parties of interest. There is absolutely no one else close enough to this case, other than the Ramseys who come remotely close to being liable for the death of JonBenet.

"The truth of the whole matter via a confession-lies in John Ramsey." It has been said by great minds, if there's a will, there's a way. Now to get to the bottom of the travesty of innocence John Ramsey, the only other person who knows exactly what went on in the Ramsey home the morning of, must make a statement of confession publicly or make a confession to the proper authorities to know most assuredly and understand how this tragic death really occurred. John Ramsey and Burke Ramsey, the only two people who are still alive with any questionable concerns eluding to the death of innocence, with Burke Ramsey having been cleared of any association with the death of his sister, leaves his father, John Ramsey, holding the bag.

The truth relating to the death of innocence sets squarely in the area of this child's pedophile father. And, eventually, he will tell the truth because the FBI will make him an offer he can't refuse; either the FBI or the Boulder, Colorado police prosecution investigation department. With new information in hand, further highlighting JonBenet's death, prosecutorial teams will be able to legally place John Ramsey not only back under the umbrella of suspicion, he will also be caught between a rock and a hard place.

Ultimately, leaving him with no where to run and no where to hide. Especially, when all of the false evidence, relating to the ransom note, the kidnap theory, and the intruder theory have now been proven by this author to be lies and non-valid innuendoes of misconceptions and unproven ideologies about someone from the outside having been responsible for the death of innocence and its travesty. Further proving, beyond reasonable suspicion, the Ramseys (John and Patsy) did plan and did carefully execute the death of their darling little daughter.

The Consummate Fear of Death: In a life and death situation, most people, most of the time choose life, death almost always is not an option. The threat of and the thought of death, the least common denominator of all life, will to a great degree bring people to their senses. People ultimately realize that death does not play games, death is not bias or susceptible to coercion or enticement. Death does not care whether or not a person is black or white, green or purple. Death is absolutely color blind.

Death is not picky or choosy, death is not concerned for the most part with an individual's status in life; death does not care if one is rich or poor, and again in the ultimate state of thought, death hath no compassion for anyone, man, woman or child. If death placed Jesus, the Darling Lamb of God, on the cross at Calvary, *death will surely bring all of us to that one place* (wherein, one does not have to be concerned with paying property taxes) *a 2X6X8 foot hole in the ground.* If nothing else brings an individual to his or her senses, the fear of death will do just that.

When this new investigation is over with, John Ramsey will gladly choose life over death. Mr. Ramsey will have no where to run and no where to hide, finally justice will have come to those who have for so long avoided the travesty of innocence to bask for a moment in their delusions of innocence, when they were truly unable to hide from themselves and from their own guilt. Death may have caught up with Patsy Ramsey, but she too, is guilty, just the same.

And, perhaps the only reason she did not want to live up to her guilt and the death of JonBenet lies in the deep recesses of her psychic demoralizing demeanor. And the great expectancy of protecting her legacy, her husband, and her children from further embarrassment had the world found out she was the primary element in the travesty of innocence. She was not going to allow this to happen, not in a remote sense of the circumstance. This woman took the truth to the grave with her, and perhaps left instructions with her husband to keep his big mouth shut, talk as little as possible and "the world will never know the truth."

Even in death, Patsy Ramsey felt that she would have trouble resting in peace if the lives of her family and friends would be turned into a living hell, if they knew the truth about what really went on in that house the night JonBenet's life was so tragically taken. A lot of people both in and around her community thought very highly of her, to say or confess anything to the contrary would jeopardize her high esteemed reputation. This was certainly a no-no. So, she left this world without ever revealing to any degree whatsoever the truth regarding the death of innocence. Perhaps this is one of the reasons she did not make a death bed confession the day of her death.

She had most people thinking that, but it never happened, because Patsy Ramsey was a very articulate, very smart and a very shrewd woman. This is the way she planned it, and this is the way the premeditated circumstance of events eluding the travesty of innocence would go down. And she also did not want the world to know she was the one responsible for all the untimely and some timely course of events that centered around the death of her daughter at the hands of her deviancy.

John Ramsey will not tell the truth on his own, he must be made or forced to tell the truth about everything that went on in his home the night and the morning his daughter lost sight on the world. Every little detail, from the planning of the murder of innocence, to the day the little child was ever so carefully laid in the ground in Atlanta, Ga.

The author believes that Mr. Ramsey is well aware of every little minute detail of the crime scene, the tedious placement of all the incriminating evidence they had hoped would lead to an intruder killing their daughter, and how he assisted his wife in planning and carrying out the cover up after they had so brutally murdered the darling beauty queen. Getting John Ramsey to make a confession in regards to his role in the death of his daughter will not be an easy task, but the author believes that by the grace of God, it can be done.

Make Him An Offer He Can't Refuse: Most people believe that those who are responsible for the brutal slaying of this six-year old, should be brought to justice, tried in a court of law, convicted and sentenced to death by any means available. Death is almost too good for John Ramsey as punishment for the role he played in the death of innocence. After his conviction, the author thinks that he should be taken out to some remote desert place and "hanged by the neck until he is dead-dead-dead!" Even death by hanging, or death by lethal injection would appear to be too good for him.

This child suffered one of the most heinous forms of death of any little child to this point in time in the history of the world, to the author's recollection. Her little body beaten, brutalized, molested, strangled including a cracked skull, the author asks himself this question, why shouldn't death show to him, the same inconsiderate ineptness, he and his wife showed to the travesty of innocence?

Someone has said, down through the annuls of time, turn-around is fair play, what goes around comes around; in this life you reap what you sow, he who lives by the sword shall die by the sword, and finally, let there be an eye for an eye, a tooth for a tooth, and a head for a head, plain and simple as that. In short gesture, John Ramsey's punishment should fit the merciless slaughter of innocence he and his wife inflicted on JonBenet. The reward for the death of innocence should be a life for a life, that's the way the author see's it. "And, that's the way it should be!"

Forensic Molecular Biology In Association With DNA: Technology and forensic medicine in every spectrum of global research has achieved phenomenal heights in the advancement and discovery biological circumstances associated with the human body and those issues pertaining to causes of death. Forensic medicine is so advanced in its exactness until it baffles the mind as to what this science can do to reproduce the human enzymes associated with the destruction of biological cells and tissues so badly needed in the determination of death in certain human response stimuli.

The forensic science of biological medicines or forensic molecular biology can today determine not only the exact cause of death, forensic medicines applied to the biological sciences have become so profound in its applications of discovery, cause and precept, until it can establish the DNA and the cause of death in individuals who have been expired for several decades. Skeletal, facial, and body reproduction of biological tissues associated with organisms of the human body almost to exact replication to such a degree of realism, until it is very hard to differentiate between the exact and the not so exact replicas from a biological point of view.

Not only replication of human organisms be done to precise exactness, if there is a remote degree of forensic matter to be examined under a finite microscope, (precise study and examination) forensic medicines in association biological technology can pin-point any causal effect to the human body resulting in death, even if the human element has been expired for several decades. This type of forensic medicine is to the author way past amazing.

There is an entire new world opening up in the exhaustive/unlimited field of forensic sciences in association with the biological proponents of DNA research with the capability and the capacity to go further into the biological sphere of finding out the truth of criminal issues before this day and time were almost impossible to solve or bring this kind of informational science to a conclusive culmination of facts. An exciting **new Forensic Molecular Biology M.S. degree** involves an unprecedented collaboration and cooperation between the Department of Biological Sciences and the New York State Police Forensic Investigation Center situated adjacent to the university campus. **More information** about the program can be found in the University at Albany Graduate Bulletin or see an article from UAlbany Magazine

With the rapid development of advances in modern biology, and because of the precision of the science, courts are apportioning greater weight to physical DNA evidence. This has created a critical need for personnel with specialized training in the field of forensic molecular biology. Even at ground level, forensic technology has not yet begun to truly explore the fascinating infinite limits of this medical, biological, criminal phenomenon, both in its scientific molecular field of work and in its exponential out look into criminology ascertainment.

Foxnews.com
Pennsylvania Authorities Exhume Unidentified Pregnant Woman Slain in 1976 Tuesday, October 30, 2007

WEATHERLY, Pa. — Authorities on Tuesday exhumed the body of a pregnant woman whose dismembered remains were stuffed in suitcases and tossed off a bridge more than 30 years ago, hoping DNA and other new techniques will help identify her.

The victim, known only as "Beth Doe," was buried with her full-term fetus in a pauper's field in rural Carbon County. "We knew this is one of the things we wanted to do, to apply today's technology," said Cpl. Thomas McAndrew, a state police detective who took over the case two years ago.

The woman, who was in her late teens or early 20s, was strangled, shot and dismembered, her remains stuffed into three suitcases that were flung off a bridge along Interstate 80 near White Haven in December 1976. The killer was probably aiming for the Lehigh River, 300 feet below, but missed. Two of the suitcases broke open on impact.

Though the victim was estimated to have been dead less than 24 hours, police had few solid leads, and the case grew cold. "The baby was full term, a healthy female. If that would have happened today, we think we would have probably gotten a solid tip," said McAndrew. "But it was just a different era."

A forensic pathologist, two forensic dentists and a forensic anthropologist will examine the remains. A forensic artist is working on an updated sketch of the victim that police expect to release soon.

The woman's DNA will be run through a missing persons database, although McAndrew acknowledged that a match is "a total, total long shot at this point" because a maternal relative of the victim would have had to submit a sample to the database.

Police have also re-interviewed Kenneth Jumper, who was a teenager when he found the body. He remembered every detail, "like he just found her yesterday," said Cpl. Shawn Williams, McAndrew's partner.
http://www.foxnews.com/story02903,306440,00.html.

"The FBI In Lieu of An Indictment By Court Order Can Have the Remains Exhumed:" The untimely death of JonBenet Ramsey, a felony criminal offense, **new Forensic Molecular**

Biology gives to the complexity of this murder case a seemingly breathe of fresh air. With the involvement of the Federal Bureau of Investigation, more concrete evidence can be given to the exact time of death through new inroads in forensic medicine with respect to molecular biological DNA. By exhuming the remains of JonBenet and reexamining those remains using the most modern forensic technology to date, compiling new information that was overlooked during the first autopsy, certain other factors relating to this child's death is set to be further proven.

The author came across a documentary recently that conveys the very thoughts of the writer almost to the exact point of pretext. Here's a classic example of case and point relative to exhuming and reexamining the remains of JonBenet Ramsey:

Pathologist: Ex-cop's third wife was killed
Saturday, November 17,2007

NEW YORK (AP) — Amid the search for a former police officer's fourth wife, a renowned pathologist said Saturday he has examined a previous wife's exhumed remains and determined she was killed. Kathleen Savio's family says a pathologist ruled she did not drown but was beaten and placed in a bathtub.
Former New York City chief medical examiner Dr. Michael Baden said he analyzed Kathleen Savio's remains at the request of her relatives, who disagree with an earlier ruling that her death was an accident. He concluded she died after a struggle, and her body was placed in the bathtub where she was found.

"I'm convinced she was the victim of a murder. 'Who done it' is up to the police to resolve," Baden said in a telephone interview. Results of a separate, official autopsy will not be available for several days, authorities said.

A coroner's jury initially ruled that Savio's 2004 death was an accidental drowning. But now, with Drew Peterson's fourth wife missing for more than two weeks, authorities are re-examining he circumstances of Savio's death

Peterson, 53, who resigned this week as a Bolingbrook police sergeant, has not been named a suspect in Savio's death. But he is a suspect in the disappearance of his fourth and current wife, Stacy, who was last seen October 28,2007, and whose case authorities have called a possible homicide.

Peterson has an unlisted number. He has denied any involvement in either case and said he believes his 23-year-old wife left him for another man and is alive. Savio's body was exhumed this week at the request of Will County State's Attorney James Glasgow, who has said after examining evidence he believes her death was a homicide staged to look like an accident.

The state's attorney's office allowed Baden to use the county morgue for his work and a state's attorney's investigator attended the autopsy, spokesman Charles Pelkie said. Don't Miss

> Husband now suspect, authorities say
> Body of cop's third wife exhumed

The purplish color of bruises on Savio's body indicated she got them shortly before she died, Baden said. "It was consistent with a beating," he said. Baden said Fox News paid for his flight to Chicago so he could examine the remains Friday in suburban Will County with the family's consent. He insisted that he first give his opinions to Savio's family and let them decide whether he could then talk to the media, including Fox, he said.

Documents released by Savio's family indicate she believed, at least briefly, that he would kill her: "He pulled out his knife that he kept around his leg and brought it   to   my   neck," she wrote in a letter the family says was sent to prosecutors.

Pelkie said it remains unclear if that letter ever came to the office. Attorney Fred Morelli, who once represented Peterson, said he never heard the knife claims about his former client. "That's the first I've heard of that," Morelli said. "That's crazy. ... (Peterson) was a very pleasant, personable fellow. Other than that, I don't know."

Pathologist: Ex-cop's third wife was killed
Copyright 2007 The Associated Press. All rights reserved. This material may not be published, broadcast, rewritten, or redistributed.
http//www.cnn.com/2007/us/law/11/17/cop.wife.ap/index.ht

It is beginning to be a well known fact that modern forensic pathology has seemingly transcended the boundaries of time and space/the essence of molecular biology concepts to discovery of facts and truth that simply amazes the boundless concourse of sense and sensibility. Upon the conclusion of reexamination this forensic pathologist was able to find additional information concerning the death of Peterson's third wife was not a drowning accident as previously suspected. The new evidence in the case associated with the pathologist report clearly points to the fact that the woman was murdered and her death made to seem like it was an accident.

In light of what took place in this forensic investigation, which may prove to be the straw that broke the camel's back, the author feels that the remains of JonBenet Ramsey should be given the same due respect. Because of new and ever growing technology in the field of forensic science/pathology, the nation and the world may soon see closure to a case that's been long overdue by any stretch of the imagination. [8]

It's Time for the FBI to Take Over the JonBenet Case
Tuesday, December 26, 2006
By Jeffrey Scott Shapiro

It has been 10 years since John Ramsey found his 6-year old child, **JonBenet, dead in the basement of their Boulder home. Despite the fact that police conducted an exhaustive investigation, the case officially remains unsolved. Among the more notable police officers who investigated the Ramsey murder** was former detective Steve Thomas, a veteran police officer who had received over a hundred commendations. Thomas, who was logged in as having worked more overtime hours on the case than any other police officer, resigned nearly two years into the investigation and publicly announced that he believed JonBenet's mother, Patsy Ramsey, was responsible for the little girl's death.

Although authorities never officially commented on Thomas' argument, many law enforcement sources have confirmed that Thomas was merely revealing the conclusion of the Boulder Police Department's investigation. After former District Attorney Alex Hunter convened a grand jury to investigate the case further in 1998, the law enforcement community's suspicion of Patsy Ramsey increased, but Hunter decided not to file charges because he did not believe there was enough evidence to obtain a winning verdict.

Despite the fact that a panel of pediatric experts concluded that JonBenet was a victim of long-term sexual abuse, current District Attorney Mary Lacy publicly announced in 2003 that she believed the little girl was murdered by an intruder. Her theory stems from the fact that minuscule particles of foreign DNA were found in JonBenet's underpants—*DNA that renowned forensic expert Henry Lee believes is the result of contamination and totally unrelated to the crime.*[ix]

Lacy was so convinced an intruder committed the crime that she arrested an otherwise innocent man earlier this year and charged him with the murder. Only a few days after extraditing 41-year-old John Mark Karr from Thailand, forensic tests prompted Lacy to drop charges against the man, leaving the case cold once again.

The most revealing fact that came from the Karr debacle was that there were several details in his arrest warrant that didn't add up. Lacy's primary reason for arresting Karr was that he allegedly had inside knowledge of the case that only top investigators and the killer could know. But by the time the warrant was made public, it turned out that the "inside knowledge" had been widely published in local newspapers and supermarket tabloids.

As a result, Lacy quickly came under fire by a number of law enforcement officials and media commentators. Among the many officials who quietly expressed criticism were federal agents who have repeatedly advised Boulder investigators that they suspect Patsy Ramsey and do not subscribe to the "intruder theory." Their suspicions stem from years of analysis and comparison of Patsy's handwriting with the text and handwriting of the three-page ransom note found in the Ramsey home.

Although the Boulder Police Department and former DA Hunter did an effective job investigating JonBenet's murder, Lacy's blind faith that the crime was committed by an intruder now makes it virtually impossible for the case to move forward under her leadership. The FBI is in a position to assign highly skilled investigators who have spent decades specializing in child murders to JonBenet's case. Federal prosecutors who have the financial and legal backing of the United States government can effectively consider a long-term strategy that will not be impeded by local taxpayers or politicians.

The murder of JonBenet Ramsey remains one of the most heartbreaking and cruel child murders ever in America. She was known in her community as a warm, loving child who showed unique signs of talent, intelligence and even compassion. Her murder, like all child murders, is a tragedy that should not be forgotten.

On Tuesday morning, it was reported that Mary Lacy has requested another $40,000 to hire a new investigator to research the Ramsey case. Unfortunately, history has proven that she is not equipped to succeed. It's time for Lacy to relinquish control of the Ramsey case — along with her ego — and invite the federal government to take over. JonBenet deserves nothing short of the very best. It's time to turn this case over to the FBI. Jeffrey

Scott Shapiro (jshapiro@ufl.edu) is a reporter who has written about the JonBenét Ramsey case for several news outlets during the past 10 years.

Originally Published in the *Denver Post*-June 27, 2006, July 29, 2006 in Current Affairs | Permalink. *Jeffrey Scott Shapiro is an investigative reporter who has covered the JonBenet Ramsey case for a number of different media outlets for nearly 10 years.*
This article was taken off of the Internet on Tuesday, October 30, 2007.

The first autopsy missed a great deal of informational knowledge more than ten years ago that could have brought closure to this once baffling mystery involving the death of innocence. Because of the historical advancement in forensic technology and the phenomenal strides in forensic DNA at the criminal level, science can now determine exactly how this child was killed, the time factor, the number of times she was molested other than the night of the incident, whether or not she was having routine sexual encounters with a male figure, namely, her dad, reexamine the exact time factor related to the death.

One of the primary factors or one of the primary reasons for reexamining the remains of JonBenet Ramsey is to prove that she was having regular and routine sexual encounters with her dad to the amazing contribution of forensic biological DNA. It is not so much the biological thought of finding any DNA relative to John Ramsey, the child's father, what federal forensic experts will be seeking to find is how often was this child having sex with her father. This proof alone is enough evidence in and of itself to put John Ramsey to death or put in prison for the rest of his natural born life.

Since all the newly compiled evidence proven by the author denies the three primary factors of illusions not having any factual premises to validate someone outside of the home was responsible for this child's death. This statement is in regards to, the intruder theory, the kidnap theory, and the false report contained in the ransom note, leaves her father to be the only person close enough to the child to be having sex with her and her killer too! The latter would also prove beyond reasonable doubt that the father, John Ramsey also had something to do with her death, if nothing more than an accomplice, besides the molestation.

It is also very important and very necessary to re-examine the remains of Jon Benet (via the medium of forensic molecular biology in association with criminal intent) to get more information that will more positively prove to the public this child was routinely engaging sexual encounters. The author believes that one of the reasons this child had to die was because she was being both physically molested and sexually molested. These would be what the author believes were the primary reasons JonBenet had to die.

Even though the child's forensic biological DNA is approximately ten years/deceased, forensic DNA biologists can take what is left of the child's remains and reconstruct a reasonable facsimile, detailing exactly how often this child was molested and by re-examining the trauma to her vaginal area, determine how her enlarged vagina came to be so, even after the damage done to it, proving that she was sexually molested, before the time of her murder. And, the only male figure that had any involvement in this young child's life on a regular basis was her father, John Ramsey. Remember, it was John Ramsey who suggested to his wife (after finding out she had terminal ovarian cancer) that they start entering their little daughter into local and state wide beauty pageants.

The author believes that before this incident regarding the beauty pageant and the terminal cancer, the Ramseys were one happy go lucky family. This family to others in the community were a God send, everything they could ever hope for had been handed to them on a silver platter. And then, here comes the devil in the form of ovarian cancer, a ticking time bomb.

The ovarian cancer would raise its ugly head into the lives of the Ramseys, a very bitter pill they had to swallow, and by shear circumstance caused the Ramseys to be unavoidably trusted into a world of irrationality and bitter expectation. The report of Patsy Ramsey's terminal ovarian cancer would eventually turn their fairy tale world upside-down. And, in the aftermath, they all would suffer loss, misery and the bitter frustration of having to deal with death. The end result of this bitter pill of frustrated lives would eventually end up in death, lies, and invalid alibis.

Patsy's Revenge: within her ultimate self spirit, Patsy Ramsey would question her divine Creator, and ask the question, why did death have to come for her so early in life? She understood herself to be a Christian of impeccable character, she paid her vows to God and church, she tried to be a good neighbor in her upscale community; in all these things, Patsy Ramsey felt she deserved better and her only response to God was Why? Why me, and why now, at a time when life is at the apex of splendidness. John's work was paying off big-time. The cash expense account was at the highest it had been since they were married, and lavish parties and guest who were of the renown category gave splendor to their home. One of the finest homes in the community was owned by them. It was a period of time wherein they could really enjoy themselves and they were truly able to whole heartedly enjoy life and the amazing thing was this, they could truly "let the good times roll!" In the back of Patsy's mind, she knew for her, the gaiety of life would soon come to an end, so she began to question God, "Lord, why me?"

This gesture of thought in and of itself, began to set in motion acts of deviancy so heinous, that her jealousy towards her daughter and her husband would cause her to pre-plan a murderous scheme that would impel the both of them to engage in one of the most unsolve murder plots to date. Even the death of her once beloved daughter JonBenet, and ultimately the moral destruction of John Ramsey, prompting one to believe indeed, that there is truly a thin line between love and hate.

In her mind and in her heart, Patsy Ramsey would hold God liable and responsible for her incurable ovarian cancer. In the privacy of her own demeanor/mind, she would curse God to his face for allowing her life to be cut so mistakenly short! What little love she had for the worship experience she allowed darkness to take over, and eventually compelled her to plot and plan the death of innocence.

When one really with utmost care and patience consider what went on in the Ramsey home the night JonBenet was so brutally murdered, appears to be to the author, an un-imaginable situation of vengeance and hatred played out in premeditated murder and mayhem. For one to call the death of this child actress an accident, falls short of what the author calls good common sense, somewhat devoid of common sense ethics. Nothing remotely close to this child's death falls under the category of an accident trying to find a place to happen, "not so, not by a long shot!"

The ovarian cancer and beauty pageants would be the coup de gras, the death blow, to a family that would never again be the same. The cancer would eventually kill Patsy Ramsey, and her eventual plot on the lives of JonBenet and her husband would eventually kill them. Talking about scandalous behavior and uncompromising deviancy and death, Patsy Ramsey would set the wheels of death to motion, allowing her husband to become sexually involved with JonBenet their six year old beauty queen, knowing that at some point in time, she would reward both of them for their sexual deviancy. JonBenet would suffer death by her hand, John Ramsey at some point or other, would eventually be found out, and for his part in the scandalous murder plot be put to death or spend the rest of his life in jail for his unwarranted part and the role he played in the death of innocence. Patsy Ramsey knew she did not have long to live even if her cancer went into temporary remission.

When John Ramsey suggested entering their daughter in beauty pageants, he had no remote idea where/what it was going to lead to. In a small remote way, his mentioning of a beauty pageant also assisted his wife in making up her mind to get revenge because of her recently announced short life span and the doctor's unwelcome statement of possibly terminal ovarian cancer.

John Ramsey's Guilt Via Biological Forensic Pathology: The stake in the coffin for John Ramsey will come by way of forensic biological pathology and criminal investigation. When the technical aspects of this child's death in conjunction with specialized expert forensic examinations of the remains, further proving that the child was physically molested more times than can be counted. The proof of guilt will be in the pudding, convicting her father and holding him liable for sexual molestation and because this child is under age, he can also be charged with incest, and rape via having sex with a minor.

To add insult once again to injury the child's vagina was physically ruptured to hide the fact that John Ramsey was having sexual encounters with his deceased daughter. Would there be any other reason to cause this heinous injury to her body other than trying to hide the fact that her daddy was having sex with her?

To these charges add the participatory indulgence/assistance in the murder of a minor. And, of course her father is also guilty of the deliberate violation of this child's civil rights in conjunction with the violation of this child's right to life; and her individual right to divine existence. These are some serious charges that should be levied against her father with or without detailed forensic evidence.

Because of the complexity of this murder investigation, Supreme Court Justice Clarence Thomas should be called upon to authorize the remains of this young child to be exhumed and reexamined by federal unbiased biological forensic experts/scholars. The author believes without the slightest of doubt that this little beauty queen deserves to have the truth relating to her untimely death revealed in such a way as to allow the entire world to come to grips with those responsible for killing her.

The Supreme Court via the FBI has the authority to have JonBenet's body exhumed for several reasons, the child was murdered/killed in a state other than the state she was buried in. Because the crime is still an unsolved murder case, which constitutes a felony, the murder now crosses state lines of which the Federal Bureau of Investigation can be involved and by court order have the body exhumed, and reexamined by federal forensic scholars. Had the child's remains stayed in Boulder, Colorado, the chances of getting the remains exhumed may have experienced some/great difficulty. Because the severity of the crime committed, the FBI in conjunction with a Supreme Court order signed by a federal Supreme Court Judge, the family and John Ramsey have no jurisdiction or authority to hinder or deny such an order given and signed by a supreme court judge.

There is one thing undoubtedly the forensic scholars would have to say convincingly, no intruder can be held liable for this child death because the Ramsey home was not compromised by some outside source other than the Ramseys themselves, the report of the author proves that. The conclusion of all forensic evidence would have to culminate on this principle of fact, the child was murdered by someone within the home itself. Results from a new forensic examination of the child's remains after almost ten years can still reveal evidence that will prove the child's body never left the confines of the home, if the child's body went remotely outside of the home, some form of forensic evidence would speak to the fact.

Question: Did the Child's Body at Any Time Leave the Confines of Her Home?
Even forensic scholars in the expert ranks of biological pathology and DNA criminology, upon reexamination, would have to say, according evidence observed or recorded as related to the child's remains, the child never left her parent's home after her death, at any time for any reason. When a new team of forensic scholars prove with factual evidence, in conjunction with the exhumation of the remains, JonBenet was never removed or taken from her

home, this conclusion will automatically invalidate the ransom note, the intruder theory and the false report relative to non-factual pretense that the child was kidnaped. The invalidation of all three of these incidents will sanction further facts of interests, given to the premeditated/preplanned circumstances of events propagated by Patsy and John Ramsey to try and clear their names from being associated with the death/travesty of innocence.

The new forensic evidence (because JonBenet was never kidnaped) will say with verifiable proof that the home was never intruded upon by anyone other than someone in the immediate family. Reasonable assurance and logic of rationale would have to contend with a now established fact: the home was never broken into or compromised by an outsider. Therefore, it is well within reason to say, the child's death would have to be attributed to her mother and her father. Since JonBenet's mother is now deceased, the only other living culprit responsible for her death, a now punishable suspect, has to be her father.

The Father Is Guilty As He Should Be Charged: When the dust is settled and the air is somewhat cleared, the new results compiled by forensic scholarship, will make unmistakably resonant and valid. The new evidence taken from the reexamination of JonBenet's remains, expressive of these facts, she was brutally assaulted, brutally molested, and brutally murdered. Which is the truth, the whole truth, and nothing but the truth, so help us God.

The final conclusion of the new autopsy report based on expert forensic testimony and research of the little child's remains will make ever so clear the fact that JonBenet Ramsey was truly traumatized and brutalized by someone who knew her very well. Her killers knew her very well, they knew her well enough to be familiar with her room and where it was located in a three story home besides the basement. Her killers knew her well enough to articulately maneuver their way back and forth throughout the child's home that resembles a maze, almost. Her killers knew her well enough to change the child's clothes and where to properly discard them. Her killers knew her well enough to hide her deceased body in a well secluded part to the home, namely the basement.

The final conclusion of a new autopsy via forensic science in association with the child's remains and her DNA, and the interior conditions of the home and the home's articulate floor plan, must again conclude with this fact of interest, the persons responsible for this child's death had to be more than familiar with the home's layout, especially when John Ramsey had no problem finding JonBenet's body the second time around. A stranger in the home would have to be just as familiar with the home's floor plan just as the Ramseys themselves are. And, it is a proven fact of intent, only the children and the service people were that familiar with the home. The children and the service personnel have been legally ruled out from having anything to do with JonBenet's death.

For Mr. Ramsey, the deceased child's father, the final concourse of forensic investigation finds the father guilty as charge as under the umbrella of suspicion. The voices of public opinion, in conjunction with the latest forensic autopsy report and in association with new compiled evidence, has found the father guilty as is charged; the evidence now compiled against him is factual and valid. In lieu of the fact that no one else, other than his deceased wife could have been responsible for this hideous crime against the travesty of innocence, you are hereby sentenced to death by hanging, and or, life in prison for the crime of assisted murder in the first degree; "as related to the premeditated killing of your six-year old daughter, JonBenet Ramsey!"

John Ramsey Should Be Indicted For Murder In the First Degree. Since the Boulder Colorado Police Department feels that it is inappropriate to indict the Ramseys, John and Patsy Ramsey that is, then the Federal Bureau of Investigation should indict them on conspiracy to commit murder, and for the premeditated senseless murder of JonBenet Ramsey, their former six-year-old beauty queen. Even without forensic evidence, the Ramseys stand clearly accused of the unfortunate death of little JonBenet Ramsey, if for no other reason, then let it be for the false evidence contained and compiled in the ransom note, a false state of a kidnapping, that did not take place, and a false intruder theory that also never took place. All this and other evidence clearly shows that the Ramsey home was never violated in any sense of the word by anyone outside of the home, other than John and Patsy Ramsey themselves.

There is simply not enough evidence to prove undeniably that the Ramsey home was in any remote degree intruded upon, "on or before the night of the heinous murder and the unwarranted death of JonBenet Ramsey!" The case against those who stand guilty of the death of innocence is so resonantly and audibly clear, an indictment against John Ramsey and his deceased wife, should not be in any way now, hard to attain or discern and bring to pass.

The proof of their mischievousness via the death of their daughter should be so clear/plausible, so much so until they should have been arrested and tried for the murder of JBR long before this time. Even now the newly compiled facts speak for themselves, and for anyone to over look them, in their hearts, do sanction the death of innocence.

Her Daddy Is Guilty As Charged: John Ramsey having been duly tried in an ad hoc court of public opinion, the verdict is in, and he has been found guilty of the conspiratorial death of JonBenet Ramsey. Because of the nature of the crime against him, the only safe place for John Ramsey is in a jail cell for the rest of his natural born life, or some place in a six by eight foot plot making flowers. Fortunately, fate has dealt with Patsy Ramsey, and not a moment to soon for her hand in the travesty of innocence. But unfortunately, the court must deal with the fate of her husband for the role he played in the death of his beautiful little daughter.

It is for this reason, the author truly believes that death becomes him. Not only for the role he played in the death of innocence, but also death becomes him for trying to hide his guilt, hoping that the system would fine someone else to blame for the killing of innocence. Not to mention his pedophile nature and the fact that this child was having regular sexual encounters with her dad, and the author feels as though this is the reason her vagina was ruptured in such a way as to try and hide the guilt and the fact that he was sexually involved with his daughter.

John Ramsey Has Two Options Set Before Him, Peradventure There Be Three He Will have to Contend With: The author would hope that there would be a third option for Mr. Ramsey and the crime of murder inflicted upon his daughter by him and his deceased wife, but as fate would have it, nothing at this moment comes to mind in the way of a third option. Which to the author says very little about the fate of this child's father. With only two options to rationale with, ultimately the fate of John Ramsey rests in his own hands. He can speak life to his body, upon a guilty confession, and go to jail for the rest of his life without the possibility of parole. Or he can speak death to his body via a guilty conviction upon a federal indictment of murder for the death of his daughter, little JonBenet Ramsey.

Option #1. A Guilty Confession Life in Prison: An admission of his guilty role in the travesty of innocence would have him to spend the rest of his natural life behind bars, with no remote chance of ever gaining his freedom for as long as he shall live. Which also means no pardon and no parole if he should live to be a hundred years old, and beyond.

He would have to make a statement of confession regarding his role in the death of innocence for all the world to see and hear. His confession must not be coerced nor by any means forced upon him, his decision to confess his role in the death of a princess must be of his own volition and born of a contrite spirit. Then and only then shall he receive a proper and just reward for assisting his wife in the death of a child prodigy.

John Ramsey, by confessing to the murder of JonBenet, may avoid the embarrassment of a lengthy trial, the embarrassing press coverage which will more than likely exploit his name in such a way his own surviving children will be so embarrassed by their father's guilt, they all will at some point in time disown, or disavow the cowardly deed of their father and the now proven fact that he molested time and time again their little sister.

And, to further insult the family, their mother and their father plotted and planned JonBenet's untimely death. The family name would become a hissing and a bad sound wherever they go and wherever they shall live. It is highly likely the family of John Ramsey would go to prison with him-non physically, which may sometimes be just as bad in the mental sense of things.

Option #2. No Confession-the Death Penalty: In a lawful court of law, before anyone can be prosecuted for a crime or an unlawful offense, there must first be an indictment for an unlawful act relative to the commission of a crime that goes against the established law. In the death of innocence, the persons so accused or thought to be the killers of JonBenet must first be indicted for the death of this little child.

Without an official indictment in a legal court of law, the person or persons accused of a felony such as the murder of innocence, the accused must first be indicted for the crime of murder, no matter what the degree. First an indictment, then the trial, and then comes the final verdict of guilty in the first degree for the premeditated murder of young innocence. After the compilation of the new evidence against John Ramsey and his deceased wife, a guilty verdict should be at this point in time, simple and easy. And, upon a guilty verdict, along with his proven guilt, apart from a confession, John Ramsey should receive the death penalty for his role in the bludgeoning death of little JonBenet Ramsey.

When one considers the way in which this young child met up with death, (sexually molested, sexually bruised and tortured, a cracked skull, choked to death with a rope,) this little child did not stand a chance having been attacked by two full grown adults. Add to these accusations, the now proven facts that no one other than the immediate family was present in the home the night of JonBenet's death, which also speaks to the fallacy of the ransom note, the intruder theory, and a false kidnaping. None of these incidents ever took place within the Ramsey home with any credibility of truth. Therefore, the court and the prosecution can prove without a doubt, the Ramseys and the Ramseys alone are responsible for the death of their daughter.

Option #3. No Indictment: There is a third option left for John Ramsey and the courts to consider, and that third option is a refusal to indict him at all again. A non-indictment charge would mean that he would remain a free man, even when the overwhelming evidence points to the fact that he stands accused for the crime of murder and the sexual assault against a minor. In light of this new evidence against him and his deceased wife, the courts can still fail to indict them and him on charges of murder in the first degree, which in turn would be a travesty of justice in anybody's rule book.

The author believes that the only way John Ramsey can escape an indictment this time, is that the entire court favors him and his deceased wife and their guilt, to be innocent. Should the ladder be the case and point, the death of this little child will forever go unsolved. Why? The reason stands to be in the proof positive, there is no one willing to forsake injustice and take a stand for justice in the death of JonBenet Ramsey. So then, John Ramsey there is a way to escape your guilt and the role you played in the travesty of innocence/in the death of innocence, which is for the court to refuse to indict you again for the assisted murder and the sexual assault on your own little daughter.

This author would also have to say, justice, compassion, in conjunction with sympathy and the truth have taken a long hiatus to the other side of injustice. Again, the author hopes those who are guilty of refusing to indict John Ramsey can live with the guilt and their conscious. Now it is believed that there is no excuse whatsoever for the court to not come to a guilty verdict against John and the deceased Patsy Ramsey for the unlawful/heinous killing of this child beauty queen.

This author believes that should the court disallow an indictment against John Ramsey the second time for the murder of his daughter, then one day, justice will come his way, if it has to wait for John Ramsey at the grave. And the court shall be guilty of letting a killer go free, and also in time, those who after seeing the evidence compiled against him, who freely choose to overlook that evidence, they too will one day meet up with the same fate that shall come upon John Ramsey. They must stand before the great throne seat of a universal God, of which there is no escaping.

Concluding Argument and Closing Remarks: Given the complexity of the matter involving the murder of JonBenet Ramsey and the travesty of innocence, her death should now be far from speculation and doubt. The facts of the matter speaks for itself, the young child was killed and brutally murdered by her mother as a result of many dysfunctional innuendoes, and child molestation and incestuous behavior. Jealousy and hate, given to the ill nature of JBR's mother, are the primary elements that prompted the death of innocence.

The ovarian cancer (an unexpected terminal situation) cannot be ruled out as a principal culprit of Patsy Ramsey's mischievous way of getting even with death. She had made up in her mind the simple thought that she was not going to die alone. She would take her little daughter, JonBenet, with her, and the fact of the matter is in the pudding, both of them are dead. Soon her husband, John Ramsey, will join up with them in death, when he is indicted and charged as a co-conspirator in the death of the six-year old.

And as much as it has been proven without the shadow of a doubt that lies and false statements existed relative to the ransom note, intruders in the home of the Ramseys, and the writer of the ransom note, the author feels the Ramseys owe to the public, and all concerned citizens, a more valid response, proving that these incidents indeed did occur. All indications of proof now proves and sanctions the fact that no one other than the Ramseys were in the home the night of JonBenet's death.

And it further pleases the author, and perhaps the public also, that unproven allegations that persons other than the Ramsey family occupied the home on the night and the morning JonBenet Ramsey was so brutally murdered, should be a constant endeavor on the part of the Ramseys to come up with more evidence proving that there were indeed intruders in the home on the night their daughter was killed. But instead of doing more to find the so-called killer (s) of JonBenet, they chose to move out of the house claiming never to return again........Why? Was it because they knew in their hearts that no other persons and no other factions were involved in this murder incident saving they-themselves.

And by moving out of the house, they would secure compassionate response from those who felt they were innocent. Or, was it because they did not want to live up to their guilt? Guilt would cause them to move out of the home, innocence would cause them to stay and find the real culprits of their daughter's murder, if in fact the real culprits did exist other than the Ramseys themselves.

The Ransom Note: Question, if the ransom said, *at this time, we have your daughter in our possession;* Why would anyone begin a search of the Ramseys home, if in fact the ransom specifically said, *we have your daughter in our possession.* Would not searching the house seem ludicrous? Surely the abductors, given to shortness of brains, would not hold the child captive in her own home? So why, then, would the Ramseys orchestrate a search of their home on two separate occasions? If you search the home the first time and find nothing, why would you go back the second time, when the ransom note again, specifically said, *at this time we have your daughter in our possession?* If the bogus ransom note made such a statement, the average person would think the child was not in the home. But here again the Ramseys insisted on searching the home even a second time...Why?

The reason why the Ramseys insisted on searching the house the second time for all intensive purposes, and disregarding the message contained in the ransom note, was because they knew JonBenet was dead, her body was in the basement, in the manner she had been killed and placed there. And, they wanted a person other themselves to witness finding the body of JonBenet. The second time around would also hide any criminal allegations and the fact that the young child had been killed by them for which the death of JBR was indeed an incriminating offense. The search of the basement the second time was also evident that John Ramsey or his wife had carefully placed her body in the basement in that darkened room to make it seem like intruders entered their home and murdered JBR.

They knew the ransom note was phony because they wrote it, and they knew that there had not been intruders in the home because they had been up all night, which was evidenced by the same clothes they had on the previous day.

The whole scenario at this point is given to a carefully planned alibi to protect them from criminal prosecution and the fact that they killed their daughter out of hate and jealousy. And, most of the hatred and jealousy can now be attributed to Patsy Ramsey and the fact that her ovarian cancer had been found to be terminal. The thought of death had become an unwelcomed guest in the Ramsey home, and the sad part of the entire situation is this, there was nothing in the world they could do about it. Death was coming whether they wanted it or not.

John Ramsey's Guilt: His participation in the murder scheme was solely to hide his failure as a father to his daughter and his incestuous behavior which was unbecoming of a parent. He knew if he was exposed in such a way, his shame and his guilt would follow him the rest of his entire life. John Ramsey did not want anyone to know that he was engaging in sexual intercourse with his six year old daughter. His reputation would have been tarnished so bad, he would probably have to pitch camp in some remote part of the world to hide his shame and guilt. He became a pond in his own game, and his wife would see that every move he made was carefully scrutinized. He has now become a pond in her game, and fair play is out of the question. It appears to be her idea of killing two birds with one stone; JonBenet is dead, and her father has become a prisoner of his own making with his wife holding the trump card.

The Ramsey's Are Guilty Based On At Least Three Reasons: Indictments should be handed down to the Ramseys for the murder of their daughter, JonBenet Ramsey. The murder indictments should be based on three criteria relative to felonious lies and felonious accusations, and the proof that proved without a doubt that the Ramseys did in fact kill and murder JonBenet Ramsey in cold blood. But then of course, no one in the community and elsewhere wanted to believe that the Ramseys were remotely capable of committing such an heinous act or remotely associated with the death of JonBenet. Because of the people's care and concern for the Ramseys in conjunction with their wealth, they were allowed to escape prosecutorial indictment. No court in the land wanted to see them convicted because of who they were.

(1) No Home Invaders, No Intruders, No Kidnapers: None of these things occurred at all or in part the night that JonBenet Ramsey was so brutally murdered in her home. The Ramseys cannot produce any proof that anyone other than the Ramsey family was in the home that particular night. The police department cannot prove that there were any of the above violators in the Ramsey home that particular night. And no other element or entity has come forth to prove that any of the above violators entered into the Ramsey home that particular night, the night that little JonBenet Ramsey's life was so brutally taken away from her.

The only resolve left to these false meaningless innuendoes is that none of the above occurred at all or at any time during the night when this child was murdered in her own bedroom and more than likely in her sleep. She never knew what happened, but there is one thing for sure, she is peacefully resting in the arms of God. But the bottom line point of inference remains the same, the Ramsey home at no time that particular night was not in anyway compromised by an outside show of force.

(2) The Fictitious Ransom Note: Fact; from the time the ransom note was discovered to the time the police were summoned to the scene of the crime, and the fact that the ransom note vividly stated, we have your daughter, associated with the fact that no one in the house at the time the ransom note was discovered except the immediate family; and, it is also a known fact that the Ramseys discovered no intruders in the house upon finding the ransom note, because they searched the house.

And, the fact that the ransom note alludes to at least three people associated with the alleged so called kidnapping, (the writer of the ransom note being the first person, and the two men who have your daughter being the second and third persons) obviously somewhere outside of the home, had to here again, perform an impossible feat. Kill the child, bring her dead body back into the home in broad daylight without anyone seeing them, is simply unimaginable by any standards of reality.

"We have your daughter, she is safe, according to the speech of the ransom note, we (the conspirators/kidnappers) would have to be outside of the Ramsey home, to make any kind of legible sense. No such incident occurred. Which again means that the ransom note was not worth the paper it was written on by any stretch of the imagination. The ransom note was nothing but lies on top of lies, and what is so bad about it, the simple minded believed the phony report contained in the note. Those who were given to gullibility of the first magnitude, bit the bait, hook, line, and sinker, "talking about being gullible!"

Hypothetically speaking: For the kidnapers to return to the scene of the kidnapping, the home with the dead child's body....between the time the note was discovered and the time police and other authorities were summoned to the home, for the kidnapers to discreetly place the child's body in a remote area in the basement is not probable if not impossible without exposing themselves in some form or fashion, according to the time the ransom note was discovered by Patsy Ramsey.

If the intruders/kidnapers killed the child before they returned the dead child to her home between the time the note was discovered and the time authorities were summoned- to place her body in the basement poses a huge question of inquisition; how did they manage to escape in broad day light without detection? The answer is no such occurrence ever came to pass in the first place.

The ransom note was only a reality given to the paper it was written on; everything else is just heresy, unproved and unsubstantiated lies. The ransom note and the intruder theory only existed in the mind of those who perpetrated it as an excuse to hide their own guilt. Which further proves to the author that this child's death was a well planned, premeditated act on her life, long before her precious little life was so brutally taken. And, "this is certainly the truth, the whole truth and nothing but the truth, so help us God."

Some Facts In The Case: Therefore, if the ransom note is given to be fictitious and bogus; the *fact* remains that the note itself was found in the home of the Ramseys; the *fact* remains and still unproven and unsubstantiated that there were indeed intruders in the Ramsey home; and the fact still remains that there were only four people in the house, JonBenet, Burke, John and Patsy Ramsey; and since little JonBenet is the victim, and young Burke is sound asleep, and it has not been proven beyond reasonable suspicion that there was anyone else in the home other than the Ramseys.

The truth of the whole matter speaks for itself. These statements of *fact*, leaves no other alternative recourse but to say that John and Patsy Ramsey killed their little daughter by choking and bludgeoning her to death. Since the young child was also sexually assaulted and molested, again, the truth of the matter can only point to her father, John Ramsey, who in the eyes of most people remains under the umbrella of suspicion, appears to be the only one capable of the sexual violation and the only living person capable of this child's death.

Since, Patsy Ramsey, the mother of the dead child, is now deceased, John Ramsey, the only surviving culprit associated with JonBenet's death, will have to take the whole rap for his daughters untimely demise. Which also means John Ramsey could face the death penalty for his part in the death and the travesty of innocence.

Fact: The bottom line scenario to the intruder theory, the ransom note and the phony kidnapping is this: again, it has not been proven beyond reasonable suspicion and doubt that the Ramsey home was indeed compromised by intruders the night JonBenet was murdered. There is simply no concrete evidence given to the intruder theory, not one iota, not even a remote chance alluding to the same has surfaced anywhere, unless the Ramsey home was possessed by ghosts and spirit beings, which is highly unlikely.

All the investigative reports have been by those persons who were on the Ramsey's payroll. It is highly unlikely that someone on the Ramsey's payroll was going to come up with evidence that would put them further under the umbrella of suspicion. It's not going to happen. If the author were an investigative detective, and was hired by the Ramseys, it would be impossible for the author to bite the hands that feed him. When it comes to sense and sensibility, a dog has better sense not to bite the hand that feeds it.

It would also be next to impossible to be impartial in compiling evidence, should most of the evidence put the family dead center of involvement, or the primary culprits related to the death of JBR. Talking about easy money! Those detectives involved in the investigation, at the conclusion of their report, walked away grinning to themselves from ear to ear. Five thousand dollars or more, for a couple of hours work, would make anyone grin from ear to ear, and tell a lie to boot, in light of the authors report denying the fact that an intruder had compromised the Ramsey home the night "sweet innocence was so brutally murdered!"

Finding out the truth would not be the real purpose of the investigation, the real purpose and the truth of the investigation would be to find someone other than the Ramseys to be the culprits of JonBenet's death. Here is the proof of what the author is eluding to, each hired investigative reporter/detective concluded that an intruder was responsible for the death of this little beauty queen. Get enough responsible persons to say that an intruder compromised the Ramsey home, soon or later, people will began to believe a lie to be the truth Judge Carnes!

To say the least (intruders in the home, if the case and point were so) would remove them from under the culpable umbrella and any, perhaps, all suspicion that John and Patsy Ramsey had anything to do with JBR's death. Again, if the Ramseys could prove beyond reasonable suspicion that their home was intruded upon by an outside source, then the umbrella of suspicion and the fact that they had nothing to do with the death of their precious little princess, no accusation of such could be held against them. They would be free of the umbrella of suspicion, plain and as simple as that. So, in the long run, a few thousand dollars here and a few thousand dollars there, and lying detectives, would be well worth the investment and the possible escape from under the umbrella of suspicion.

The ransom note in and of itself is nothing more than a joke with more holes in it than the night Liberty Valance got shot! For crying out loud, we all may be somewhat gullible, and suffering from lack of sense and sensibility, but the Ramseys need to be told that all of us are not stupid. The ransom note is nothing but fool's bait, good enough only for the fool who chooses to believe it!

In plain simple English, the bogus so-called fictitious ransom note does not make any sense whatsoever. Especially when it makes mention of at least three persons who could have been possible but bogus invaders of the Ramsey home. *The two gentlemen watching over your daughter do not particularly like you so I advise you not to provoke them, two men plus the person writing the ransom note equals three individuals who never existed.* But what it does say in expression, Patsy Ramsey's personality traits, speech, and voice recognition is all over it. ***Don't try to grow a brain John. You are not the only fat cat around so don't think that killing will be difficult. Don't under estimate us John.*** *Use that good southern common sense of yours.* ***It is up to you now John!*** Man, for crying out loud, please give us a break! Anybody that close to John Ramsey is got to be his wife, Patsy Ramsey the primary killer of innocence.

Fact: It is just as much the burden of proof on the part of the Ramseys to prove beyond reasonable doubt and suspicion to the public, intruders did violate their home the night JonBenet was so brutally murdered as it is the burden of proof on the part of the District Attorney's Office to prove to the negative or to the positive aspect any remote violation of the sanctity of the Ramsey home.

So far, the Boulder District Attorney's office has not come up with any concrete incriminating evidence to suggest beyond reasonable suspicion/doubt that intruders were in the house. It is more than easy for a judge to say intruders were in the home, because it avoids the tedious efforts of proving the opposite truth.

(3) The Writer of the Ransom Note: Patsy Ramsey's Ransom Note Computer Analyzed: The writing of the ransom note has long since been a mystery, for it is a known fact that the writer of the ransom is to blame for the death of this innocent little child. Computer analogy of the ransom note will prove that Patsy Ramsey wrote it. What the computer will do first is: Analyze her

voice, match it with her speech. And then, analyze her speech personality, match it with her handwriting. The computer then matches speech samples (written samples) with voice recognition or voice recordings given to personality traits, and if the hand-writing matches the person's voice personality through speech recognition, the computer will either accept or reject the writer of the ransom note and its author. And the other side of the coin is this, the end results will prove without the slightest of doubt that she wrote and composed the ransom note.

By just looking at and reading the ransom note, and having some degree of familiarity with the personality of Patsy Ramsey, the letter is a proof positive reflection of her individuality captured in the entire composition of the ransom note. If one knew Patsy Ramsey, and has some idea of her personality, one would imme-diately say that the author of the ransom note is Patricia Ramsey, the mother and the murderer of JonBenet. The writer of the ransom note is indeed the killer of the child in every sense of the word, and her mother alone wrote the ransom note, and is the sole apprentice of its authorship.

Supposition: Throw away the ransom note, and cast the intruder theory to the wind, destroy any concept of a kidnaping; ques-tion: who would there be to blame to accuse for the killing of in-nocence; who would stand accused? Answer: The Ramseys are the sole benefactors of senseless murder and death.

From the onset of this murder mystery, the author made a point of inference relating to the invalidness of the intruder theory, the kidnap theory, and the ransom note. The killers of this young child would have to come from within the home itself. And now, there is no doubt whatsoever as to those who are responsible for the death of innocence. The author feels well within the accusa-tions of reason, John and Patsy Ramsey and no one else to any degree of circumstance are responsible for the bludgeoning death of JonBenet Ramsey; the brutal mutilation of her body, and the sexual molestation of the same.

If therefore none of these innuendos/suppositions are true, (the ransom note, intruder theory, the fictitious kidnaping) and they are not, the bottom line point of inquisition is this, the Ramseys premeditatedly planned, orchestrated and killed their young daughter with malice of intent. And now the time has come to pay to the piper! The Ramseys, John and Patsy, should be indicted for the murder of their daughter, JonBenet Ramsey, to the full extent of the law.

About the Author

A native of Winston-Salem, N.C.; and a divorced father of one child, and three adult step children, one of which is deceased. The author was born in Roanoke, Virginia on August 8, 1946, is now presently living in Los Angeles, California. The author is also presently writing and working together in the gospel ministry promoting, preaching and teaching the blessed gospel of Jesus Christ. Called to the gospel ministry in 1977, the author is also licensed and ordained by the Independent Prelate Council of the United Progressive Baptist Church in the city, by the late Rev. Dr. Quincy Austin Caldwell.

The author is the former associate minister and assistant to the Rev. Dr. J. Ray Butler, now deceased, who was also the former Pastor of the Shiloh Baptist Church of the city. Before his death, he became the Pastor of the Greater Cornerstone Baptist Church of Winston-Salem, N.C. Dr. Butler played a pivotal role in the author's admission to the pastoral studies in ministry at the Shaw University School of Divinity in Raleigh, N.C.

Education: The author has attended and completed grade schools (Atkins High School, Skyland Intermediate School, and Brown Elementary Schools) in Winston-Salem, N.C. Received technical training in the field of automotive and diesel mechanics at the Forsyth Technical Institute of Winston-Salem, N.C. Graduated from the Atlanta School For Truck Driving in 1973, retired from truck driving in 1979 to accept calling into gospel ministry. The author is also a future graduate student of the Bachelor of Theology Degree Program at the Shaw University School of Divinity in Raleigh, N.C.

Brief Military Career: The author served two and a half years on active duty, from July 1966, to January 1969; serving twelve months of those active years in the Vietnam War via the United States Navy. And, was honorably discharged also in January of 1969. The author also served four years in the inactive Reserves of the U.S. Navy.

Passion for Writing: Writing became a passion many years ago and is an outward expression of the writer's innermost desire to contribute to society through this widely accepted medium of written communication. The art of written communication conveys in words those things not so easily spoken in the verbal sense. Thoughts expressed in written words, the author feels appears to have more of a conscious effect on readers who are interested in the written materials contained herein as opposed to other forms of media awareness. And, it is for this reason, the author is greatly influenced to convey his thoughts on different subject matters, through the medium of written correspondence. Though, the author has yet to master the true skills of writing, writing does offer an immediate outlet to the monotony of daily routines.

Passion to Know the Truth: Curiosity of intent and the truth have always been a fascination to the author, not only from a spiritual perspective but also from a moral point of view. The author believes that the truth from any perspective of life, no matter what the situation entails, getting at the truth should be its ultimate outcome. As such is the JonBenet murder mystery, the truth helps one to understand why a certain incident or a certain happenstance occurred in the first place. And, to also find those who are guilty and to bring the law to bare on that guilt.

The child JonBenet Ramsey was so brutally murdered in her own home on Dec. 26, 1966, has left the nation and the world in shear utter disbelief that those responsible for her death have not been brought to justice. This is a travesty of humongous proportion. And, the author has prayed earnestly to God for an answer and the truth as to who the real culprits are. And, by the grace of God, the author has been able to prove beyond reasonable doubt, evidenced primarily in the ransom note, those who were responsible and perpetrated the death of little JonBenet. The author believes with all his heart and soul that the death of this little child will be avenged to the fullest well within the next year, "beginning right here and right now!"

Society may be able to rationalize (try to make sense in some instances-out of nonsense) with the varying subject matters relative to finding out the truth or the apparent cause of wrongful infractions; but society cannot rationalize with the truth itself given to fact and not rationalization, and suppositions, once the truth has been exposed for every one to see and that beyond reasonable suspicion and doubt; the author believes that when the truth of any issue of life is fully exposed and brought to bare on reality, it (the truth) is impossible to change.

And, there is a strange awe of awareness when the truth of a matter/issue is brought to pass, the truth has the uncanny ability to convict the consciousness of the mind on which it is made aware. Which is to simply say, when people hear the truth, they very seldom have difficulty or trouble in accepting it.

Future Expectations: The author's future expectations are to expand his writing abilities to intervene or coincide with all facets of life relative to the fulfillment of the truth both morally and spiritually. The author has begun several other works on Biblical and Doctrinal Truths, politics, and the moral and immoral implications of human behavior, physics, the advanced study of matter, motion, and energy, in the superlative degree, subject matter never before discussed in the human element, which proves how and why all things in the material sense came to exist as it is presently known.

The Existence of God and the Origin of Creation, and the three elements of Divine Ultimate Universal Godism: primarily denoting who God is, his molecular existence, and where God Himself came from. Other subject matters such as the End of Time as it shall be, the four kingdoms of the Universe so given to awareness situated in the Book of Genesis in the second element. And, finally to come within ten years of the ultimate last and latter days of humanity and mankind in the earth; situated in the Apocalyptic War of Armageddon, the last great battle between good and evil; significant to the divine revelation and the divine interpretation of what some call the Omega Code.

The Beginning

ENDNOTES

i. Getting Away With Murder, The Observer Magazine, Sunday June 25, 2006. Http://observer.guardian.co.uk/magazine/story/0,,1803742,00.html

ii. **The Autopsy The Murder of JonBenét Ramsey** by J. J. Maloney & J. Patrick O'Connor
Related Story: Solving the JonBenet Case by Ryan Ross.
(04/14/03)
http://www.crimemagazine.com/jonbenet.htm

iii. **Getting away with murder**. It was the savage killing that gripped America .... Both John and **Patsy Ramsey** told police that Burke was not awake when they ....observer.guardian.co.uk/magazine/story/0,,1803742,00.html - 73k

iv. Http://www.universalquest.com/jonbenet.htm The Astrology of JonBenet Ramsey

v. **Child Beauty Pageants Foster Sexual Abuse, New York Times, Friday, October 19, 2007** RITA N. BROCK St. Paul, Jan. 21, 1997

vi. *Copyright 2006 The Associated Press., All rights reserved. This material may not be published, broadcast, rewritten or redistributed.* **Nation Knew JonBenet Ramsey Only In Death Updated 8/17/2006 6:57 AM ET:**

vii. The study was funded by a National Cancer Institute R01 grants and NCI grants to the Gynecologic Oncology Group and the Gynecologic Oncology Group Statistical Off © 2007 The University of Texas M. D. Anderson Cancer Center 1515 Holcombe Blvd, Houston, TX 77030 1-800-392-1611 (USA) / 1-713-792-6161 (5)

viii. **Pathologist: Ex-cop's third wife was killed Copyright 2007 The Associated Press. All rights reserved.**
This material may not be published, broadcast, rewritten, or redistributed.
http//www.cnn.com/2007/us/law/11/17/cop.wife.ap/index.ht

ix. **It's Time for the FBI to Take Over the JonBenet Case Tuesday, December 26, 2006 By Jeffrey Scott Shapiro**